BLACKLISTED!

Memoirs Out of Africa

Charles Shannon Mallory

BALBOA.
PRESS

A DIVISION OF HAY HOUSE

Balboa Press books may be ordered through booksellers or by contacting:

Balboa Press
A Division of Hay House
1663 Liberty Drive
Bloomington, IN 47403
www.balboapress.com
1 (877) 407-4847

Because of the dynamic nature of the Internet, any web addresses or links contained in this book may have changed since publication and may no longer be valid. The views expressed in this work are solely those of the author and do not necessarily reflect the views of the publisher, and the publisher hereby disclaims any responsibility for them.

The author of this book does not dispense medical advice or prescribe the use of any technique as a form of treatment for physical, emotional, or medical problems without the advice of a physician, either directly or indirectly. The intent of the author is only to offer information of a general nature to help you in your quest for emotional and spiritual well-being. In the event you use any of the information in this book for yourself, which is your constitutional right, the author and the publisher assume no responsibility for your actions.

Graphics and photos by David Fast.

Print information available on the last page.

ISBN: 978-1-5043-5853-8 (sc)
ISBN: 978-1-5043-5852-1 (hc)
ISBN: 978-1-5043-5854-5 (e)

Library of Congress Control Number: 2016908234

Balboa Press rev. date: 10/07/2016

Contents

Preface

Everyone has a story to tell. You hold in your hands a part of mine that has a habit of going out on limbs that don't ever break, but they do get badly bent with misadventures and near-death experiences. It's a story that includes moving to New York City, living there for three thrilling years, and then on to four countries in Africa and returning to the U.S. 18 years later. Two of those countries were too dangerous for human life. One of them was South Africa, under the racist policy of *apartheid*, the other was Uganda under the bloody hand of Idi Amin. We lived in both of those pot-boilers for more than half the time.

Kurt Vonnegut once wrote that strange travel suggestions are dancing lessons from God. He might have written that for me! Our travel plans during those18 years could not have been more strange and unlikely. The dance class lasted a long time and at times I heard God laughing as I stumbled over my feet learning new steps. In the process I'm sure I stepped on many toes, but hopefully no bones were broken.

I soon learned that three years in seminary was just a graduate kindergarten, but had I spent twice that long I wouldn't have been ready for my dance classes in Africa. My dean was against the idea of Africa. I loved him and cherished his wisdom but believed this was something I had to do before I lost the inspiration or the courage. "Sweet hardheadedness" is how one friend has described my determination. He got the second part of it correct, and I wouldn't know how sweet it has been for those who have had to put up with it.

The years of this story are a never-ending stream of freshly minted situations without a book to tell me how or a map to show me where. That's when the dance steps were the hardest. Some of those situations included exorcising a home, learning an African language without a book, dealing with marauding elephants, building with trees and mud, digging wells, collecting thatching grass, driving through flood plains, getting kicked out of a country, surviving armed roadblocks with boy soldiers itching to kill, starting a new diocese, and building a cathedral. I stumbled and tripped a lot.

This is my story. It does not include my children or the mother of our five children, for such a volume would be many times greater. They have their own stories which are equally rich and need to be told.

The socio-political context as well as historical backgrounds of my story are important to me; hence, many such diversions are included in what you are about to read.

Chapter One

Decision Time!

In 1956, the largest continent on earth was having convulsions. Some of it was caused by colonialists who had stayed too long, some by Africa pushing them out, and all of it was messy. It was the most unlikely a place I would someday call home, but for now I was busy being a student with a pre-med major. I was pretty sure what my future would look like. The day I walked into the Powell Library at UCLA, the French delegation walked out of the United Nations. What was happening in Africa had half the world worried; the other half couldn't have cared less. I was among the latter half, but soon those events would change my life forever.

The French were worried over increasing restlessness in one of their colonies, a fear things might come apart. Their fear was justified. The whole of Africa was about to come apart, not just the French colony of Algeria. Most whites glibly figured the trouble was born largely of black insubordination and had to be stopped. Africans felt otherwise. They called the growing unrest *uhuru,* which meant independence and freedom from decades of oppressive colonialism. Africa had started to rumble and it was a movement that could not be stopped

So on that balmy day in autumn, as I walked into my study carrel in the library, the French walked away from Algeria's desire for independence. It was symptomatic of white attitudes, but such intransigence couldn't stop the chain of events that would follow for all colonial powers. Within four years, 21 former colonial countries would be independent; within six, Algeria would follow. Africa was on a roll that could not be supplicated or stopped. It was the beginning of a wave of independence, and the winds of change would sweep the continent and change the map forever. Colonial colors and names would disappear as new nations were being born.

I knew of no winds of change blowing my way, just the gentle breeze from the Pacific Ocean that graced the campus where I was at the time. Earlier that day, I had been fussing over a parking permit. Unknown to me, nine thousand miles away a young African named Jacob had his own troubles. He had to walk to school through the African bush, dreaming of the day when he might have a bicycle to make it easier. He lived on the other side of the world and the other side of my reality. He lived in a forgotten territory known then as South West Africa. In the years to come, our lives would parallel. Within four years, our paths would cross and we would meet in the most unlikely of circumstances.

As Jacob was trying to borrow a pair of old shoes to make the long walk to his new school hundreds of miles away, I was worrying about where to park my car. Surrounded by the comforts of a modern American university, little did I know my preoccupation with parking my car was petty by comparison. As I was finding a parking garage and lecture hall with all the modern coms, Jacob was preoccupied with finding a seat in his new class where chairs were few and arriving late meant sitting on the ground. I fussed because a light rain made things unpleasant; where Jacob lived, crops were failing and people were dying because of a prolonged drought. I was annoyed my textbooks cost almost twenty dollars each; Jacob was happy to find a friend who would share his only dog-eared book, the one with many pages missing as he was struggling to get used to the big mission school. For three years, he had gone to a bush school in his village where he learned the alphabet and enough about reading to follow simple stories in his native tongue. He had learned how numbers fit together to do simple addition and subtraction. That classroom had been under a tree. There he had also learned about classroom manners, when to stand, when to sit, how to greet the teacher and be respectful. Tribal life had taught him how to respect everyone else.

Leaving his village and moving to the big mission school had been an ordeal for Jacob. St. Mary's Mission was weeks away by foot. He had to travel that distance alone, carrying a knapsack of clothes along with a few valued symbols of his learning. Those consisted of a broken pencil, a few pieces of used writing paper and a dog-eared copy of the Church Catechism missing most of the important pages. He had nothing as fine as toiletries, shoes, bed roll or a clean change of clothes. Jacob's family, like all his friends, was dirt poor but happy. With knapsack over his shoulder, a sling shot and knobkerrie for protection, he began the two-week trek to St. Mary's Anglican Mission School. Wild berries and roots were his food along the way, and if he were lucky he would bag a small animal with his sling shot.

Thus young Jacob set off on his journey to a foreign land. The first day went well enough because he knew most of the country west of his homeland. As the shadows lengthened and the sun was setting in the west, he looked for a place to bed down, high on a bank overlooking the Okavango River. He had heard stories of this old river, how it came charging down out of Angola to flood his homeland only to disappear into a huge delta in the neighboring country of Botswana. In his studies at the big Mission School he would learn the Okavango was the only river in Africa that doesn't flow to the sea, but rather inland to supply one of the world's largest inland deltas. That river brought back a terrible memory when he and his friends were swimming in it and one of them got pulled under by a crocodile, never to be seen again. In time, he would learn that hundreds of people and animals go the same way every year. He shuddered as he moved a little higher up the bank.

He awoke the next morning to find crocodiles on the river bank, feasting on the remains of a kudu. Desperately hungry, he hoped for a small piece of the action but didn't risk trying. There was no way a human, especially a small boy, could intimidate crocodiles into moving away from a kill. That day, as he made his way westward, the many footpaths in the sandy forest would be his greatest challenge. Constantly having to decide which one and which way, he usually chose the one most used because they all led somewhere, none for idle adventure. Often he ended up at a neighboring *kraal* and had to ask for directions. Lucky for him, all the country spoke a similar dialect and the people were invariably helpful.

Failing to snag a piece of the kudu, he took to the trees for his food. Birds were an easy target for a herdboy—he'd been doing that since the age of seven when his father had sent him to look after the cattle. He bagged a fat crow with ease and made that his supper, garnished with wild berries from the forest.

That night he had complications. About midnight, out of the tree high above him, a heavy load suddenly dropped on him. Terrified, he rolled out of his blanket to find six feet of snake on top of him. Historically Africans have been terrified of snakes, and Jacob was no exception; normally, they would beat them to a pulp, even the harmless ones. This one on Jacob wasn't harmless; it was a tree snake with deadly fangs, but they were at the back of the mouth which made it unlikely to get a fatal bite. Normally green in color to blend in with vegetation, *boomslangs* stay well above ground unless in search of food on the ground. Jacob slipped out of his blanket and ran to the fire still smoldering, pulled out a log with a glowing ember, and made quick work of the snake. Badly shaken by the whole affair, he slept no more that night. The only good to come out of his night's adventure was that parts of the snake would be his food supply for the next several days.

The next day was long and hard. The sand in the forest was deep, and he plodded less than a mile an hour. A couple of times he got lost and had to ask local farmers which path to take. Days were long and boring, but thinking about being in the big Mission School usually cheered him up. Invariably, he had unexpected excitement on his journey. Once he managed to snag a *dik dik* only to have a hyena descend upon his catch. An awful fight ensued, and Jacob barely managed to get a piece of the quarry without having the beast turn on him. Hyenas are known for their viciousness and in packs have been known to bring down lion. Jacob was lucky it didn't come for him.

And so it went, day after long day, making his way to a new school where he could learn how to read and write and speak English.

St. Mary's Mission School was located in the far north of the country only a few hundred yards from the Angolan border. That border made no sense to the Kwanyama Tribe because it was created by the white man in the late nineteenth century. Like many other borders in Africa, it was established without regard for the people who lived there. This one cut right through the great Kwanyama Tribe, Jacob's people, but they carried on their lives on both sides of the divide like it wasn't there. In years to come it would be harder to do that, with the border fenced and patrolled. Sooner than he knew, it would be a critical crossing for him.

The Mission was located at a place named Odibo ("o-dee-bow"). That was the name of the local headman's area; it meant 'knobkerrie' but no one ever figured out why. Knobkerries were useful things to have when herding cattle, a good club if attacked by wild animals, and Jacob always had one in his belt. Sometimes they were long and made good walking sticks. Jacob carved his out of a straight branch with a knob on one end. Abraham, the local headman of the knobkerrie district, was a kindly man and a good neighbor of the Mission School. It was he who did the naming of many children born in his area. In time, he would give names for three of ours, still years away from their birth.

Being able to speak English was for an African like knowing a little bit of the Queen of England, only more helpful. English was introduced into Ovamboland in 1923 by Major Hahn, who was the Native Affairs Commissioner at the time. Hahn had asked the Anglican Bishop of the country if he could send a missionary into his area to teach the people English. The bishop obliged, and the following year a priest named George Tobias set out for the far north. With an Ovambo assistant, it took him six months in an ox cart to make the journey of some five hundred miles. When he arrived at Major Hahn's outpost on the border, he was assigned the district of Odibo under an existing agreement that kept denominations from squabbling by assigning them different tribal areas. In those days, competition for black souls only involved Finnish Lutheran and Roman Catholic missionaries, neither of them speaking or teaching English in their schools.

English-speaking countries take their language for granted. Not so where it isn't spoken. Teaching English was one of the most important things the Anglican Church did for the African people, but it was never a joy ride. There was constant resistance from the South African government which did not like English spoken, especially by Africans. Dating from the Anglo-Boer War in the late nineteenth century, the Boers had an abiding hatred for the British and their language, and in part for good reason. After 1948, when the National Party came into power and instituted the strict policy of *apartheid,* teaching English in the 'native areas' became an issue because it gave Africans the means of communicating with the rest of the world. This was not something the *apartheid* government wanted. For this reason alone, the Anglican Church in general and St. Mary's Mission School in particular would be in hot water much of the time. The government couldn't actually forbid the teaching of English as long as an attempt was being made to teach Afrikaans as well. The English missionaries, not noted for their linguistic skills, made a half-hearted effort to oblige, but in time the English language would become a major obstacle for the government.

The big primary (elementary) school at St. Mary's consisted of one long, low building with massive mud walls and a corrugated iron roof supported by trusses made from huge trees. Without ceilings but with earthen floors, it made for hot heads and cool feet in the summer heat, a vast improvement over the open-air bush school Jacob had known. At the big school, most classrooms had a blackboard, but chalk was a constant problem. Books were always in short supply, and in living memory there had never been enough books for each student to have their own. Sometimes three or four would have to share a book. But that was also a vast improvement over Jacob's bush school, where books didn't exist unless the teacher happened to have one. And so it went at St. Mary's Mission School. It was a new world, and students were hungry to learn whatever was being taught, especially English.

Living conditions for the boys were appalling, far worse than living at home. They had no hostel building or even huts, and some of the boys stayed in local *kraals* with friends or neighbors. Most were not that lucky, and for them life was miserable. Their physical hardships became a testament to their determination to learn. With nothing to protect them from the beating rains of summer or the biting cold of winter, they improvised with wretchedly flimsy things like cardboard supported on branches, or cloth tents that provided only a modest degree of shelter and privacy. The homeless in most American cities fared better.

Jacob's first week at the big school was one he would never forget. He was placed in the fourth grade along with about forty others, ranging in age from 12 to 50. In the bush school, he had learned to stand when the teacher came in, to stand when spoken to, and to speak politely in reply — but he hadn't learned how to reply in English. That now caused embarrassing silences as he struggled to understand what the teacher was saying, and he wasn't very good at guessing. Other students seemed to get the gist of it and tried to help him, but that didn't work very well either. Learning English was one of the main reasons he had come to St. Mary's, but he hadn't expected to get thrown in head first. So each day was a linguistic trial, each night a replay, with coaching by his friends. He saved every scrap of paper he could find that had English on it and tried to pronounce words that were meaningless to him, as if by doing so he could figure out their meaning. That never worked. He was surrounded by older boys who spoke pretty good English and loved to practice with silly expressions that often didn't make much sense. Sometimes what they came up with was comical. Riding in the back of a truck, they would shout something like, "Apply the brakes urgently!" or "Tate ("tah-tay" meaning "sir" or "Father")), the wild beasts have extreme proximity to the vehicle, make haste speedily!" or "Observe the danger!" "Look out!" was far too simple. Sometimes, in response to a simple greeting, they would come up with something like, "I am magnificently doing well," or on a rainy day, "It looks like precipitation shall fall from the heavens." And their unceremonial command at a certain stop on the road — "Get out!" — was a regular source of amusement, as these polite young people were learning how one day they would speak truth to power.

My first day at UCLA went better than Jacob's. I got all the classes I wanted, met and liked all of my professors, all PhDs in their respective fields, and was able to get all my textbooks at the College Bookstore. Most of my classes would be in grand halls of learning like Royce Hall, Haines Hall or the Powell Library. I took them for granted—air conditioned, handsomely equipped with desks, lighting, illuminated blackboards, and sound systems. I was proud to know that those hallowed walls had produced leaders in every field of American life. There was no way Jacob could know that his humble school would, in time, produce founding fathers for a nation yet unborn.

Jacob would learn a lot of other things at the Mission School; some of them would eventually lead him into conflict and set the course for the rest of his life. St. Mary's School was steeped in an Anglican tradition that sought to question things in the pursuit of meaning and truth. That meant asking questions that could lead into troubling issues of relevance for an African. It was thus wise that students often waded into such dangerous issues as why *apartheid* was morally and ethically wrong and whether violence is ever justified in changing a government. For the first time in their lives, they began to question totalitarian forms of government and what real democracy might look like in their African culture. And so they were confronted with great ethical questions: "If you were going to change your culture, what would you change?" "Can one be a Christian and justify war, killing and violence?" "When is war justified?" "Is killing always wrong?" "Is telling a lie always wrong?" These were seminal questions that would soon demand answers—a few by negotiation but alas, many by violent confrontation.

Imagine never having seen the sea or a city, never having flown in an airplane or seen a distant land or a modern society, or hearing a radio or seeing a movie for the first time. Such were the shocks for Jacob and the other young students at St. Mary's as they began learning about the rest of the world. Every night they would listen to "Voice of America" with its talk of freedom and a better way of life, though the South African government went to great lengths to jam reception. Desperately fearful of the humane freedoms of the liberal West, not only did South Africa ban V.O.A. but the Peace Corps as well, for fear they would encourage the disenfranchised to want self-determination and that would upset the *apartheid* way of life. After all, white South Africans believed they knew best what the African should and shouldn't have. But they couldn't entirely keep the "Voice of America" out, much as they tried. Eventually, over radio and through the grapevine, young students learned there were free African nations, African political organizations, the United Nations, and refugees searching for a better life. A new world suddenly opened, with new possibilities. Most of all, they learned they were not alone in their struggle.

Years later, I would take pride in what St. Mary's stirred in those young students. Their schooling fed into a growing unrest and helped them develop the ability to speak truth to power. But alas, that would come with a price, sometimes the price of life itself. Asking questions of the authorities predictably would bring swift punishment that ranged from a beating to imprisonment and sometimes death. Africans were not allowed to question the powers-that-be or what gave them that power. Countless lives would be sacrificed in what would become known in South West Africa as 'The Struggle." The Struggle embodied the independence movement which eventually engulfed the country and its people for over thirty years, finally giving birth to the new nation of Namibia in 1991.

The Mission School was constantly hounded by the Department of Education; the government's overall assessment was that our school caused trouble for their regime. Which was true. But little did we know at the time, we were also producing future leaders of an independent Republic of Namibia, still decades away. Those young boys and girls would travel a difficult and lonely road, enduring isolation, loneliness, hardships of every kind, betrayals, violence, even assassination. They would be people without a country, political refugees wandering the world, seeking a home and acceptance of their cause. The free world's response would at times be discouraging.

The school was perfectly situated for a quick exit out of the country, only a quarter of a mile from the Angolan border. That made our position even more watched by the South African Defense Force (SADF). In time, I would begin noticing boys missing from the school. Their roommates would routinely come up with lame excuses that often stretched the imagination, but it was impossible to verify such claims and we didn't try. What I learned in later years was that the boys (and a few girls) deliberately kept me from knowing about their nightly escapes because they didn't want to implicate me and risk getting the school closed down. That way, I could honestly claim ignorance if interrogated by the SADF, which did happen from time to time. The young peoples' decision to leave the country was bold and courageous because it meant they could not come back. All political organizations were banned to Africans, so the South West African Peoples' Organization (SWAPO) had established its main Africa office in Lusaka, Zambia, hundreds of miles away. Refugee camps and training camps were scattered throughout southern Angola and parts of Zambia, and it was to these the boys and girls would usually head.

The Caprivi Strip was one major way of escape and probably the most dangerous. This was a tiny slice of land in the far northeast quadrant of the country which had great political and military importance in those days because it was a direct corridor from South West Africa to the free Republic of Zambia. Remarkably, the Caprivi Strip is the only place in Africa where five countries meet: Namibia, Botswana, Angola, Zambia, and Zimbabwe. [1]

Life continued quietly and predictably for me. In my junior year at UCLA, I went through a metamorphosis almost without knowing it. I had met Jim, a young Episcopal priest, the first I had ever known. He was interesting, single and somewhat laid back, and we soon became good drinking buddies. My wife and I had a comfortable pad in Sherman Oaks, and he had enough boredom on his hands to come our way several nights a week. It made it hard to get homework done but it was fun. I frequently wondered what made him tick.

Our new friend never spoke about the priesthood, and it would have fallen on deaf ears if he had. Nothing could have been further from my mind. "The Ministry" had always seemed a strange thing to me, and in my limited experience of it I had met no impressive examples. Until I met Jim. I began wondering why a cool guy like this would choose such

---

[1] The Caprivi Strip was named after German Chancellor Leo van Caprivi, who negotiated a land exchange with Great Britain in 1890 to annex this strip of and to what was then German South West Africa, and thus provide access to the Zambezi River and ultimately Africa's east coast. The venture never worked out, but the territory did become a part of South West Africa. The Caprivi was officially renamed in 2013, now known as the "Zambezi Region."

a profession, but my curiosity never found its way into conversation. Maybe he was a good example of the priesthood, but it wasn't my bag; my future was well mapped out, and I spent no time thinking about it until late in my junior year. It was then I started having an interest in what made other people tick: their attitudes, their beliefs, their behavior, their politics. In time, I would learn that these issues were some of the stuff some people call "spirituality." The religious side of Jim didn't appeal to me, but this other stuff did. In time, I also came to realize the deeper issues of human behavior were a big part of what was drawing me in a different direction. During that academic year, I became more interested in the ethical decisions people make than I was in healing their ailments. I was awakening to a passion for social justice and the things that make for a just social order. In a few years I would come across four questions that would fascinate me for the rest of my life. They were, "Who am I?" "Who are you?" "What are we here for?" and "Where are we going?" Those would become for me the fundamental questions that religion and spirituality ought to be about — and all else is commentary, as a wise rabbi once said of Mishnah. I was just a few years ahead of the decade of the sixties when questions like those would rattle America and change the world forever.

Deciding in my senior year to go to seminary instead of medical school felt like I was taking Robert Frost's road less traveled. Joseph Campbell says somewhere that we must be willing to let go of the life we planned in order to have the life that is waiting for us. I didn't know the truth of those words then, but in time I would feel they were written for me. I was exchanging a lucrative future in a prosperous part of California for an uncertain one in a troubled part of Africa. But it would be a decision I would never regret.

As I was pondering my decision, events were forcing Jacob to make his. It started one day when he was home for summer vacation. That day, he went to visit his grandmother who lived many miles away. Walking the dusty path his ancestors had walked for hundreds of years, as he got closer to Granny's place he gazed over the happy hills of the valley he had known all his life, secure with the sight of the village his tribesmen had built generations ago. Lazy puffs of smoke from the stovepipes sticking through thatched roofs told him the women were preparing the evening meal. It was a scene he took for granted most days, but not today. For some reason, today something made him think hard about that humble place he called Granny's place. Maybe it was the story he had heard in class about what happened thousands of years ago when a man named Abraham was directed by God to leave his home and go in search of a new home. The story made him sad. Why would God ask such a thing? The thought made him especially thankful for his home and his village which he would never leave. He remembered in the Bible his name, Jacob, meant "he who struggled with God," and he didn't want any more of that.

Suddenly, he was shocked out of his reverie. As he came down the dusty path and Granny's village came into view, what he saw nearly collapsed him. Granny's village was being destroyed. Huge bulldozers driven by white men were pushing huts and houses into a mountain of debris and crushing it with their massive machines. Nearby, people were wailing and screaming for them to stop. But they didn't. They just kept coming, scraping the earth where Jacob and his friends had played all their lives, and their fathers and grandfathers before them. On the road, trucks were piled high with the few belongings people had managed to rescue from the pillage.

As Jacob approached, the dusty devastation filled his nose with the musty smell of bedrooms and kitchens. Dust was all that remained of Granny's home. No one could explain what was happening because no one knew. Some had heard a loudspeaker telling them to collect their belongings and leave, but the order had been in Afrikaans and it didn't say where they were to go. Others heard only the bulldozers and screams. Everyone was in shock. It was the worst nightmare of a lifetime — a nightmare, but not a mistake. The devastation was the beginning of a hideous new law that was called the Group Areas Act, and orders to level and destroy Granny's village and move the people off their land had come from Pretoria, the highest authority in the land and the place where most bad news came from.

The Group Areas Act forcibly removed non-whites from their land and assigned them to areas known as "locations," not that different from the Indian Reservations in America. By this legislation, the majority of the population were given areas smaller to live in than the white minority who now owned most of the country. The Act was first promulgated on July 7, 1950, repealed, and then re-enacted in a consolidated form in 1957. After that, it was amended *thirteen times* between 1957 and 1984 as the fearful white minority increased control of the country and the lives of the non-white population. It was a striking example of how *apartheid* spread its evil tentacles, eventually to engulf and strangle all of life in South Africa. (Ironically, America joined the international chorus condemning South Africa for its action, but did nothing to reverse past misdeeds done to Native Americans.)

The Group Areas Act would now tell Granny and her family and friends where they could live. She would be separated from lifelong friends. Bessie, her best friend who was a "Colored" and lived next door, would be sent to a different place. No longer could people choose their friends or live together as they had always done. They would be sent to new areas that would be called *bantustans*. The law racially segregated all non-whites according to their ethnic grouping and divided the country into urban and rural areas. Urban areas were towns almost entirely white, and blacks would need passes to be in them. Never again would blacks be permitted to live freely in those urban areas they had once called home.

Of all the laws of the *apartheid* government, the Group Areas Act was one of the most egregious because it uprooted kith and kin and sent them to areas that were alien to their history, their culture, and way of life. Second-rate, 'unused' land was typically designated for the *bantustans*. This policy of forced removal was aggressively pursued in the 1960's, 70's, and 80's, during which time millions of people were forced to relocate. The government gave a variety of explanations for the removals: slum clearance, black labor tenants on white-owned farms, 'black spots' adjacent to white farms, etc. But they were all excuses to explain away the radically inhumane policy. One of the notorious examples of the Group Areas Act was that of Sophiatown, in Johannesburg. There, in February 1955, bulldozers destroyed what had been home for generations to over 50,000 blacks. A white suburb was built in its place, ironically named Triomf ("triumph"), as if to rub salt in the wounds. Forced removals were not limited just to people of African descent; those of Indian, Colored and Chinese descent were likewise moved. Ultimately, in the Transvaal alone, nearly 600,000 Colored, Indian and Chinese people were moved; nationwide, millions of lives would be uprooted by this law.

It was all reminiscent of the forced removals in American history, little known and not popularly taught in our schools. In the nineteenth century, the American government did essentially the same thing when untold numbers of Native Americans were forceably uprooted from their homes in Florida and sent on a forced march from the East Coast to far-distant Oklahoma Territory. That would be the dumping ground for the five noble and civilized tribes of the Cherokee, Chickasaw, Choctaw, Creek and Seminole people. The most famous of these marches was the Cherokee "Trail of Tears,"in 1838, when President van Buren, building on the work of his predecessor, President Andrew Jackson, enacted a treaty, *forced, not negotiated*, to exchange cultivated Cherokee property for wild land out west. It would become one of the most painful events in Native American history. Americans called the new homes for the indigenous people "reservations." South Africans called them *bantustans* and *homelands*. They were not home to anyone.

And why Granny's village? Because that village and those surrounding it were known for their fertile soil and abundant water from the river. Their only offense was that this land was good land that had been in Jacob's family for generations. Now, with the stroke of a pen, it had become white farmland. For generations, the natural resources of the area had fed and sustained Jacob's family and thousands of others; now it would become the white man's by the law of the land. That same law would provide a new home for the displaced villagers, but it would never be home, it would never be a village of lifelong friends and relatives, and it would never have fertile resources. The new *bantustans* would be farther from towns and cities, on land that was often rocky and unsuitable for cultivation and predictably far from natural streams or rivers. Granny's world had collapsed, and Jacob was beginning to feel like a stranger in his own land.

Six months later came Jacob's Christmas holiday visit to Granny's new home in what was now known as the Police Zone. Her little shack was now in a rural area hundreds of miles from where she had grown up, where Africans and whites had lived together happily for as long as she could remember. Africans now had a two-hour walk to get to work in the white area unless they had enough to pay the bus fare. Most of them didn't.

Jacob's excitement grew as his bus neared Granny's place in the new township called Katatura. The Africans named it that—it meant "No Place to Go." He sat nervously wondering how he would recognize her house or her street or even her neighborhood. He still didn't understand why she had been moved. The bus rounded the corner and pulled to a stop in front of what looked like a concrete shack with a number painted in the upper corner of the house. It matched the address he had been given. His heart sank at the sight.

Granny no longer had a friendly house with plants and flowers and vines covering it. All she had now was a concrete shack with dirt and rocks in front and not much else except a few broken things lying about the place. A water spigot stood in a muddy drainage ditch in front of Granny's house; he learned that was the water supply for the whole block of about twenty five people.

She greeted him with her usual pinch of the cheek, a hug that took his breath away, and the traditional African greeting which necessarily involved many questions that he never tired of hearing. "How is this one, and that one, and the other one?" "And how are the cattle and crops?" "And is everyone well in your village?" "And how have you been?" "And your brother?" "Your sister?" "Your cousins?" On and on it went. Sometimes the ritual would double back and repeat the same questions. Europeans thought African greetings a complete waste of time, infuriating if in a hurry, otherwise just amusing or annoying. But this thoughtful ancient custom was careful of every family member and took as long as necessary to honor each relationship. Then came a tour of the house that took less than a minute. There were four rooms of equal size: a sitting room, a kitchen, and two bedrooms. Granny's cold concrete shack was simply divided into four when it was built, and people used the divisions as they wished. She had decided two bedrooms were needed for the eight family members who would be coming to live with her. Jacob would fit in somewhere.

Behind Granny's house was a collection of buckets and large basins. Devoid of privacy, it served as a bathroom when she could collect enough water for a cold bath. The house had no electricity, although that had been promised before they moved in. Granny tried to make the most of it, but she missed her thatched roofs and mud brick walls that kept her house cool in the summer and warm in winter. All she had now was a corrugated iron roof with no ceiling, so it was very hot in the summer and very cold in winter. The hardest part, she said, was not knowing any of her neighbors. They had come from many different tribal groups and areas, and everyone was a stranger. They didn't even speak the same languages. Gone were the local friendly food shops; now people had to go into the white man's town to buy. That night, Jacob cried himself to sleep thinking how his Granny was living like a gypsy slave in her own land and there was nothing anybody could do about it.

Around midnight he woke to see a candle flickering in Granny's room. Inside she was moaning and rocking to and fro. He hurried in to find her crying with pain in her abdomen. He was so scared to find his Granny sick that he started to cry, but she whispered for him to go and get her daughter to come quickly. Rachel lived in another township on the other side of the white village, about four miles away. If he ran, he could be there in an hour, going straight through the white village. That seemed like a good idea until he was half way through the white area and was stopped by police. Four of them, big ones, shouted at him, *"Waarna gaan je, kaffir?"* (Where are you going, kaffir?). *"Waar is jou dom pas?"* (Where is your pass?). Terrified by the sudden interrogation which he didn't fully understand, he replied, *"Sir, I don't understand what you're saying."* That's when they hit him with a *jaambok* because he didn't address them as *baas* and because he spoke to them in English and not Afrikaans. *Baas* meant master, and clearly they figured this uppity African needed a lesson or two. *"Pas oop, kaffir, jy is in groot moelikheid!"* they replied (Be careful, kaffir you're in big trouble!). Jacob wished he had paid more attention to the little Afrikaans he had been taught at St. Mary's School, but it probably wouldn't have helped now anyway.

Failing the interrogation, Jacob was hauled off to the local jail, where he found company if not sympathy. It was filled with over forty offenders just like him who had been picked up for Pass Law offenses. There were children and old men and everything in between, all picked up and booked for not carrying a piece of paper that gave them permission to be in the white man's village. To get the magical paper, they had to go to the magistrate's office, but to get there they had to walk through the white area—without a pass. That was the Catch-22, and it was too bad if you were caught on the way. Jacob knew none of this, since the Pass Law had come into effect since his last visit to Granny.

Pass Laws were designed to segregate the population and limit the movement of the non-white population, one of the dominant features of the country's *apartheid* system. The black population was required to carry pass books (a *dom pass*, which meant literally a 'dumb pass') when outside their homelands or designated areas, and failure to produce it often resulted in arrest and imprisonment. To make matters more humiliating, even a white child could ask an African adult to produce his or her pass, although that seldom happened. The Nationalist government enforced the Pass Law ruthlessly but in fact was not responsible for creating the system in the first place. The first such laws had been introduced by British settlers as far back as 1797 in an attempt to exclude blacks from what was then the Cape Colony; in 1923, passes were again introduced to regulate black movement in white urban areas throughout the country. The *apartheid* government in power simply built on old British foundations but now carved them in stone. It was a system the Nationalist government intended to last for all time.

The cell Jacob was shoved into was filled with the stench of dozens of sweating bodies, urinating and defecating wherever there was space. It was the first time he had been with people of his own color who didn't speak his language, and that was a little frightening. Some of them had been through this many times before and knew what would happen to them in the morning, most of them did not. They were all victims of a system not of their making nor their understanding.

The next morning, Jacob and some of the others were hauled before a magistrate who read something in Afrikaans which Jacob didn't understand. It was the Pass Law which said Africans were never supposed to walk about anywhere in the Police Zone without an official Pass, which only his office could issue. In Afrikaans, he lectured then that this was not their country or town and they didn't belong there except by permission of the white man. Then the magistrate got very angry and shouted at them that he never wanted to see them in his courtroom again or their punishment would be much worse — but because this was their first offense, they would each receive only twenty-five strokes of the cane. Then he shouted at them, *"Voetsek!"* which is a command usually snapped at dogs meaning *"Beat it!"* But the worst was yet to come.

Jacob and the others were marched into a bare courtyard with high walls and barbed wire around the top, and one by one they were brought before a huge white man with a cane in his hand and hatred in his eye. Bearing his behind, Jacob was beaten with twenty-five blows that broke the skin and made a bloody mess of his back. The pain was excruciating, but he was determined not to cry. It was over not a minute too soon, for he almost passed out from the pain. They were chased out of the jail yard and told one more time to *"Voetsek!"* By this time, Jacob had almost forgotten why he was there and that Granny was sick and he was supposed to fetch his cousin. All he wanted to do was go home and cry, but he pulled his shirt over his bloodied back and headed for Rachel's house.

He arrived as she was about to leave for work in the white town. When he told her Granny needed her, it created a dilemma. She didn't own a telephone, so she couldn't tell her employer she would be late to work, but not letting them know would risk her losing her job. But Granny was sick, and family always came first, so she and Jacob headed to Dr. Motsepe's little clinic two streets away. He had been their doctor as long as she could remember, and he would know how to fix Granny. Fortunately, the clinic was empty when they got there, so the kindly old doctor set off with them to Granny's house, he on his bicycle as they ran along behind. Billows of dust choked them as fast cars and trucks from the white village passed them on the dirt road. An empty ambulance zoomed past them, but that was only for white people.

As Jacob related this story to me, his eyes welled with tears and his voice choked up with the part about Granny's death. They got to her house too late and she was already dead, lying across her bed with the Bible beside her. He said the hardest part was that she died in a strange land without her family with her. And so it went for countless millions of African people who suddenly found they no longer had a place to call home. They all lived in one big Katatura, the place named "No Place to Go". He was now a stranger in his own native land.

Jacob's decision was far greater than mine: it was time for him to leave home, school and country and become a freedom fighter. He had experienced the tragedy of the Group Areas Act inflicted on his grandmother's village. He had experienced the cruelty of the Pass Laws and heard stories of workers who returned from the mines in South Africa and how they were exploited by white overlords. And he had experienced the wrath of government officials who called him a "smart kaffir" just because he asked questions. Inwardly, he seethed with rage, but he dared not let it show. He knew in his heart it was time to leave kith and kin to follow the many who had gone before. Years later, he would return to Granny's Katatura to organize a boycott of the white municipal bus system, cinema and beer halls. For that, he would be forced to flee the country one more time.

Nine thousand miles away, the only pass I needed was to the University Library which I got when I paid my tuition. That consisted of nineteen dollars per unit. One semester at UCLA cost a total of three hundred and four dollars, plus books. The pass was free. I knew nothing about places with Pass Laws that could cost as much as a human life. My world was flourishing: I had just married my high school sweetheart, and we were moving into our charming two-bedroom honeymoon cottage, surrounded by ivy, trees and flowers, in a tony suburb of the San Fernando Valley. Out of our second floor window I could see the elegant sign of a local car dealer that flashed "Casa de Cadillac." I imagined it was a sign of things to come. My wife had a good job in Los Angeles and we were content and wanted for nothing, looking forward to a rosy, affluent future.

Jacob and I were the same age, separated by a world of contrasts. My decision to become a priest involved no risk or hardship, just a move to New York City. Jacob's decision involved life-threatening risks at almost every turn. It would take him to many strange countries in search of people who would listen to a refugee with a story to tell. Few would be interested in listening, and his message would fall on many deaf ears. For both of us, New York City would become our second home.

Exchanging medical school for seminary didn't sound sexy to anyone, including me. Guided by our new friend in Holy Orders, I applied to Episcopal seminaries all across the country and ended up with a choice of New York City, New Haven, Chicago (Evanston) or Berkeley. It wasn't a difficult decision. The Big Apple won hands down because of its location and all that was going on there. For my wife and me, getting there would be our first experience in an airplane, our first experience outside of California, and our first experience of a major international metropolis that had dozens of languages, newspapers, cultures, and cuisines. It would be a culture shock of thrilling proportions.

Our first year in Manhattan, we lived on the top floor of a five-story walkup on Twenty Third Street, one of the main streets that crossed the island. Twenty Third was busy around the clock, with commuters rushing to and from subways, buses heaving with passengers, taxis with horns loud enough to wake the founding fathers, and pedestrians everywhere. The street was home to hawkers, pushers, pimps, prostitutes, and drunks. Then there were the beggars, the street people whose luck had run out, if they ever had any. These were the ones who taught me some early lessons about how to be a Christian. The lesson was simple enough: it was about how to love your neighbor wherever and however you found him or her. The lesson was simple but I usually managed to make it more complicated. I hadn't yet discovered the simplicity in the passage where Jesus says he was sick or in prison and we visited him, a stranger and took him in, hungry and fed him, naked and clothed him. He stopped short of saying he was a beggar and we helped him. But he was.

I didn't know it then, but Jesus was all over the streets of Manhattan; it took me a while to realize that. In time, that passage from Matthew became one of my favorite passages as it dawned on me that the story doesn't say how he came to be in prison or naked or hungry...or a beggar. I think Jesus was implying no questions need to be asked, just be kind to the outcast and as generous as possible, for if you begin asking questions you may prevaricate and never help. I hadn't yet digested that passage enough to let it haunt me as I stepped over the bums and beggars on Twenty Third Street. At first, I dealt with them by not dealing with them. I just stepped over them. Advice from the street-smart old timers said just to ignore them and never make eye contact. I tried doing that most of the first year, giving wide berth 'round a beggar as I made my way to or from class. Some days I felt like I was running a gauntlet and God was watching it all, laughing. I was usually relieved to reach the safety of Chelsea Square and the hallowed halls of The General Theological Seminary, where I could bury myself in studies on how to be a professional Christian and forget the harsh world outside.

The General Theological Seminary was the earliest institution of theological education in America for the Episcopal Church, dating back to the early nineteenth century when Chelsea Square was an orchard and the Hudson River flowed beside it with idyllic meadows for riverside picnics. After an exhausting but exciting flight that took all night, my wife and I arrived at Idyllwild International Airport, soon to be renamed after a president about to be assassinated, John Fitzgerald Kennedy. It was a hot, sticky August day and from there on the south side of Long Island we didn't even know where Manhattan was. Fortunately, the taxi driver did, as he maneuvered us to 475 Ninth Avenue and dropped us and our bags on the sidewalk. I had the address and nothing more— not where to report, to whom or when. The Seminary looked like something out of the world of Charles Dickens: towering brick walls covered with generations of soot and coal dust, formidable black bars on windows and doors, we couldn't even find the front door. Wandering like lost orphans dragging their bags, we circled the entire city block, knocking here and there and hoping to find a friendly front door, to no avail. We were almost in despair, melting from the humidity and heat and discouraged beyond our limit, when a kindly face stepped out of a doorway and asked if he could help. It was the Dean of the Seminary, the top dog himself. He was walking up to the Twenty Third Street drugstore for lunch and asked us to come along. It was a welcome sign. Over the next three years, that kindly Dean would become my friend and mentor and the namesake of our youngest son.

The Seminary was an entire city block, walled in on every side, and stood like a lone fortress of gentility and moral rectitude in a neighborhood that lacked both. In those days, the front door was unlocked but a friendly doorman sat just inside. Today, we would call him a security guard, and he would be armed and the door would be locked and scanned with cameras. In those days, the friendly doorman was there to make sure everyone coming through that portal were students or faculty. The bums seemed to know they weren't welcome. That bothered me whenever I thought about it, which wasn't all that often, because there was so much else to think about. But why didn't the Church welcome these people into its protected square, into that bastion of peace and love that taught us a Gospel that was essentially about love and fair play? Why couldn't we have found a place to take in the stranger and the homeless? Thus Chelsea Square stood like an island apart in the midst of a hurting world, walled off in a protected environment where we could learn about Jesus the Good Shepherd, and programs about how to treat that hurting world and all its poor beggars. Looking back, I think one of the greatest ironies of all was that the Seminary Chapel, the spiritual center of the place, was named the Chapel of the Good Shepherd. Good Shepherd...hm. What would the Good Shepherd do amidst the hurt of that city? That Chapel would be the workbench for my spiritual life over the next three years, along with the dark streets of the City. But in more tangible ways, the streets of Manhattan would teach my heart how to love and serve.

One cold morning in late autumn, we opened our apartment door to find two bums asleep on the doorstep. After the shock of that came the obvious questions: Who were they, how did they get in, and why on our doorstep? It didn't take long to figure some of it out. It was warmer on the fifth floor than the first, and definitely warmer than the street; it was easy to get into the building by following anyone who was buzzed in at the front; and the building superintendent (the "super") lived in the basement and had given up chasing the bums out. They were, after all, a harmless lot, just cold and homeless. When the bitter cold came, they followed the warmer air to the top of the stairwell, where they bedded down for the night. Our door step was claimed by whoever got there first or had seniority. We learned to share our landing, stepping over them when leaving so as not to disturb them.

Jesus said somewhere that the poor would be always with us. He must have had New York City in mind. They became a silent but constant reminder of the other side of life. Good people try different ways to cope with the problem: Ignoring it, avoiding it, moving out of the neighborhood, even trickle down theories of pouring money into wealthy systems believing some of it filters down to the bottom, which it never does. Some give generously and others try to make society more just and equitable. Such thoughts and theories for helping the poor would become extra-curricular conversation during the next three years. For me, they would become issues that would disturb me for the rest of my life.

The subways were a favorite hangout for beggars, probably because the underground was usually dry and had dark corners for protection and sleep. Unfortunately, it also brought stench and filth to the subways. Every morning for three years, my wife maneuvered her way through it all to catch the subway to Greenwich Village. She did that daily without incident. In our years living in Manhattan, not once did the bums or beggars become a threat to us. But their impact was great: it raised for me the never-ending question of what to do with the truly poor. It's one of the Gospel issues Jesus seems to talk about incessantly. In his day, some tried to prevaricate with the question of who the neighbor was. We still do that. We like to assume our neighbor is the person next door with similar economic and social standing as ourselves, easy to get along with. But if the neighbor is someone from the other side of the tracks whom we don't know, we may not be willing to claim this one as a neighbor. And so we also prevaricate with the truth. We tell ourselves the truth we want to hear. We all face questions like these, and how we answer them in a way determines the shape of our souls and the size of our hearts. There is one answer for everyone and that is the answer of love, but that will be defined in many different ways. I learned that I need to be generous and give what I can and not worry about what that beggar does with it.

In recent years, Judaism has taught me much on the subject. If *tekun olam* (repair of the world) is the solemn duty of every good Jew, they say that begins with how we treat the poorest beggar. Not only should we look the beggar in the eye not in judgment, so their teaching goes, we should also say "God bless you!" For when we look one in the eye, we shall see not a beggar but a human being. Jewish teaching quotes the famous Maimonides, twelfth century philosopher and rabbinic scholar, who said "whoever gives charity to a poor man ill-manneredly (like flipping a coin) has lost all the merit of his action even though he gives a thousand gold pieces. He should give with good grace and with joy should sympathize with him in his plight…he should speak to him words of consolation and sympathy" (Mishnah Torah, "Laws of Gifts to the Poor"). And I should add, "there but for the grace of God go I."

One great scheme to help the poor came to our neighborhood during my senior year. The city planners called it Urban Renewal, otherwise known as slum clearance. It encompassed a vast area of Manhattan, from Hell's Kitchen just north of Chelsea, once the center of working class Irish Americans, down to Fourteenth Street. It was a well-intentioned scheme designed by government and local housing authorities to help the poor who lived there by giving them new apartments in high-rise buildings. The best thinking of social and city planners, it included cleaning up neighborhoods, tearing down failing shacks and buildings, and providing neighborhood parks and playgrounds.

And so it got started, knocking down buildings and clearing miles of city streets of the life and traditions people had known for generations. It was heart-wrenching to think that countless families would be uprooted and dispossessed by the scheme, but well-meaning city planners had determined something needed to be done and this was the best they could come up with. Unfortunately, their solution would eventually produce a social nightmare. The result of this massive renewal program brought an upheaval in the lives of thousands of families from which most never fully recovered. Gone were the neighborhood shops and merchants, the friendships and memories that spanned lifetimes, the family connections that bound neighborhoods together. In their place came high-rise apartments with burglar bars, strangers for neighbors, and an increase in crime. Families that had known their neighbors for generations now lived next door to strangers, isolated from one another behind bars and steel doors. It was a Western version of what I would later experience in Africa, the phenomenon of urbanization that drew people off the land and into cities, where they would live as strangers to their neighbors, thrown together by the forces of development…a strange way to develop.

A mere dozen years later, by the late sixties, having already built dozens of high-rise apartments for low-cost housing, the City of New York was having second thoughts about the whole idea. The 1969 edition of *The Plan for New York* reported that "*development pressures related <u>to the same area</u> were driving people of modest means from the area, and today the area has become 'gentrified'.*" The ironic euphemisms in that statement are '*developmental pressures*' and '*gentrified*,' a polite way of saying they were getting rid of the poor in the very area they had made great plans to help the poor! This debacle of urban planning on a massive scale taught me lessons Africa and all the developing world would reinforce. One was the lesson of how we need to approach other societies, cultures and economies with the humility to know we do not always have the answers to their needs. We may, in fact, ultimately have no answers that are helpful.

Africa would teach me one of the hardest lessons for Americans to learn, that the United States does not always have the answer to the problems of the rest of the world. Although Americans make the common assumption that money and technology will solve every problem, in fact money and technology are seldom the primary answer for other cultures and traditions. Yet we continue to think that money *is* the answer, that our brand of material development *is* what the world really needs, and that technology *is* the answer to everything.

The Peace Corps and a few international development organizations like World Neighbors were among the first idealistic do-gooders to think differently and realize the need to tread softly around the world as we seek to serve developing nations. To do this effectively demands a humility that is frequently foreign to Americans, to sit and listen to the wisdom of other cultures and look for solutions *within* that context, by probing the history and traditions of the indigenous people. Years later, having made my own mistakes of this kind in Africa, I chose as a guiding talisman the thought that as we approach another culture or religion or tradition, we need to take off our shoes before we step forth because the ground before us is holy — and always to remember that God was there long before we arrived.

The beggars of New York City taught me lessons that have served me for a lifetime. They taught me what Jesus really meant when he said he was hungry or thirsty or sick or naked or a stranger or in prison. The beggars taught me that I am responsible for my behavior alone and not the other guy's. They taught me that to analyze the motives of the poor usually only complicates a situation that God alone knows and I don't need to know. They taught me that the Church often has an unwelcoming look on its face when it speaks to the poor, and when it locks its doors for security it is also locking the poor out; that what it may need is a friendly doorman and not a security guard. They taught me that the Church often speaks with a voice of judgment instead of listening with an attitude of love; that it often speaks with impatience instead of compassion and has a habit of presiding instead of providing, gathering instead of giving out. For many years, a huge cartoon hung in our home in Africa that greeted everyone who entered. It displayed a frightened Saint Peter holding the Church in his arms, staggering and struggling to protect it from a crowd of needy beggars. But both hands were so occupied with shielding and protecting the Church that he had nothing to give them, neither a kindly word nor a friendly smile. He had only fright and terror on his face that seemed to say "Get lost, you filthy people!"

More lessons came in the hot summer of my Middler Year. They came unexpectedly, as some of the best lessons do, at a venerable old institution of New York City known as Bellevue Hospital. Founded in 1736 as the first public hospital in the United States, Bellevue stood for almost a century in a wilderness overlooking the East River, long before there was a Manhattan Island or a United States. Today, its meandering structure covers several city blocks of the Kips Bay neighborhood. Older than the nation by forty years, Bellevue is the county hospital for Manhattan with a history like no other. It is the grandparent of famous hospitals like Massachusetts General, Johns Hopkins, Cook County in Chicago, and every major county hospital in the country.

When I was first introduced to this stately old dame, she still had original high ceilings with no air conditioning, huge casement windows, walls painted sick-room green, and linoleum down corridors as wide as a city street. Beds and patients were everywhere, especially during the extreme times of summer and winter. Physicians would routinely send elderly patients there to avoid heat stroke in summer or freezing in winter. Anecdotes about Bellevue were legion and I would hear many of them during my hot summer there.

And this is how that came to be. In their second year, all seminarians were required to take a summer course known as "Clinical Pastoral Education." More fortunate seminarians could return to their home diocese for this training. With a working wife and being unable to get out of the city for the summer, this meant my training would have to be in Manhattan, which would involve an intensive twelve weeks at Bellevue under the watchful eye of an ordained chaplain who knew his subject — and Bellevue — like the back of his hand. There were eight in my group, which met in seminar each morning and visited patients in the afternoon. The mornings were rich and challenging, the afternoons usually stressful because I was uncomfortable with sick people. Especially those I didn't know. My discomfort was made worse because we had to wear white coats and ties and official badges that announced us as "Chaplain Interns." I didn't much care for the chaplain title and "intern" suggested I didn't know much about what I didn't like. That was true, but I didn't like announcing it.

The Sixth Floor was a challenge we all dreaded. It was the mental ward. If mingling with the sick made us uncomfortable, having to visit the mentally deranged was almost a step too far. Visits to the Sixth Floor were like shadow boxing: I was never sure who I was talking to or who was talking to me, still less about what was being said. I tried, usually in vain, to take the high road and remember the experience was less about the patient than about me, but I was never quite sure what I was supposed to be learning. Looking back, I can appreciate some of the comedy as we reported on those visits.

One day, a guy named Gregory Blessing appeared on my list. Mercifully, he wasn't on the Sixth Floor, 'though he might as well have been for the stress it brought me. The assignment sheet said simply, "Fourth Floor, Ward Five, white male, 44 years of age." I remember being impressed with how physically robust, well-built and tanned he looked. He didn't look like he belonged in a hospital, but we were not privy to bed charts or medical information and so I didn't know why he was there. Little did I know my many visits with Gregory would be the beginning of my coming of age. He was gay, in those days very judgmentally called "queer." That information wasn't on my assignment sheet, but I quickly learned Gregory was different. He seemed to have known instinctively that I was a naive young man who didn't have a clue about his world.

In my naiveté, I figured maybe his major problem was that he needed healing from homosexuality and that was why he was there. I remember thinking maybe I could just talk him out of it...*surely this is just a bad choice he's made.* I dutifully carried all my anxious concerns to the seminar, hoping the others would know what to do, but that didn't work. As I recall, there was a lot of conversation but none on how to cure homosexuality. I later suspected I was probably the only stranger in town; what I didn't know until weeks later was that the Hospital Chaplain in charge of our training group was also gay. He kept that discretely concealed and never ventured to explain that gays are born, not made or chosen. That would have been helpful, although I'm not sure I would have believed it. These were still the terrible days when gay people had to deny who they were to be accepted by society. The

Chaplain didn't bother explaining any of that to us, probably because he didn't dare expose himself to recriminations and probable dismissal.

In my misguided approach, I kept searching for ways to get through to Gregory. I tried misusing religion to explain that his lifestyle was wrong and that he should clean it up; but of course he had heard that nonsense all his life. Gregory would listen politely and then with a smile simply change the subject. For him my sincerity was more entertaining than convincing. I then tried to relate his being gay to why he was in the hospital with a feeble suggestion that if he stopped his behavior he probably wouldn't be in the hospital. That argument was patently false when he explained to me that his condition was a lung infection. All I had left was to pray for him and I didn't much know how even to do that. I simply concluded how depraved the world of homosexuality must be, but how little did I know. That was the beginning of a lesson that was to be continued in the coming years. I began counting the days until it would all end. To my relief, Gregory Blessing was discharged and disappeared into the anonymity of the Big Apple.

I heaved a sigh of relief when the course ended in late summer. Shortly after that, the Chaplain invited me to his apartment for dinner, making it clear in some manner that he expected me alone, without my wife. That seemed okay to both of us, so along I went, a brisk four-block crosstown walk. The evening started off nicely, with drinks and a few hors d'oeuvres, as we engaged in small talk about Bellevue experiences and such like. After dinner, my host invited me to come sit on the sofa with a cheerful, 'Here, sit right here beside me." That should have raised a flag, but it didn't; after all, this was my mentor and a priest of the church. Sitting side by side on the sofa, I felt a little odd, quickly turning to revulsion when he made a move on me. I was like a babe in the woods, stunned and stammering; all I could think was to get out of his apartment, which I did. Other than my encounter with Gregory Blessing, I had never been introduced to the world of homosexuality except in its condemnation; to be personally assaulted was emotionally overwhelming for this naive kid. The walk home helped clear my mind, but I was still in shock when I reached our apartment and related the evening's events to my wife. I couldn't make sense out of what happened or what to do with the experience. I realized then how severely handicapped I was by having had no experience of the gay world during college years because I was married most of that time. I knew virtually nothing about homosexuality except that it was condemned by the church and most of society, and that would become my knee-jerk position for the next twenty years. I gave the evening no more thought, but I didn't forget it.

Africa has historically had a strained relationship with the gay world in its midst. All tribes and ethnic groups have members who are gay, but they are forced to live in a state of quasi-denial. Traditionally, homosexuality has never been criminalized, as it is today in parts of Africa, but it has been generally regarded as an aberration. Those who are gay generally go quietly into their closets and everyone else simply ignores them. Modern Africa is still sadly conflicted on this issue, and much harm is being done in some countries by Church and State in criminalizing gay behavior. Evangelical churches in North America have played a part in this, misinterpreting Scripture to teach that homosexuality is a sin and exporting this teaching to evangelical churches in Africa. Most of East Africa and all of Nigeria has come under this narrow influence, which, sadly, is spreading to other parts of the continent. South Africa and a few other countries are the refreshing exceptions. During my years in Africa, for a variety of reasons, I didn't have to deal directly with the issue of homosexuality, and this terrible legislation had not come into being.

It was only upon return to America, many years later, that my learning would resume, and on a very public stage. As a newly elected Episcopal bishop in California, I was in the spotlight on a number of liberal issues, but the pressure became even greater when I learned I had a number of gay priests in my diocese. The time had come for me to learn personally about homosexuality and the plight of gay people. It would be a steep learning curve with a fast ascent. Initially, it was for me an issue of justice and fair play, and condemning gay people was certainly an injustice, so I could speak against their persecution. It was easy to have compassion for gay people without much understanding. But as I met and mingled with gay individuals, I began to discover very tender, caring, sensitive qualities and heard heart-rending stories of painful upbringings, of gay children being disowned by their parents and societal persecution of unbelievable proportions, of having to live closeted lives of self-hatred, often driven to drink and sometimes to suicide. It was obvious this lifestyle was not one of choice, as homophobes and some conservatives are inclined to think. It was becoming clear to me that homosexuality is a part of the creation, that people are born gay, that homosexuality couldn't be "caught" by association or taught by influence. It came as a comforting thought for me to know people are simply born gay. It broadened the creation!

Shortly thereafter, I had a great personal experience to drive it all home. The Presiding Bishop had urged all bishops to get involved in the work of HIV/AIDS. That resonated with where I was in my journey. I learned of a weekend training program in Monterey, California, conveniently only a few miles from home. The first weekend of training was mainly informational. The next weekend involved getting to know individuals with AIDS. At the end of the training program we were assigned an AIDS buddy and off we went.

My buddy was Lee, a gentle, pleasant young man in his mid-thirties who lived with his parents in a farming community of the Salinas Valley. His partner had died of AIDS a few years before, and Lee didn't look the picture of health when we met. He had AIDS but was outwardly cavalier about it. He was still full of life and energy and wanted to live his remaining days as fully as he could. We became good friends almost immediately. I learned of the anguish my new friend had endured, even from his own family, and I would learn of the tender, loving sensitivity of a different kind of man. He was the incarnation of a world I had condemned; I made this strange new world a friend, and I would never be the same. I think that's what the incarnation of Jesus was all about: to make the strangeness of God not so strange. Gay people would become human to me in a wholly new way. I had a gay friend to love and care for. Many times since, I have recalled Gregory's last name and smiled. It was all a blessing and God has a delightful sense of humor.

Lee and I got together as frequently as we could. We took drives down the coast, one of his favorite places. Lee told me how the church he had grown up in condemned gay people and how he was driven out and banned from attending church. Strangely, his parents were still regular members, with a judgmental attitude towards gay people. They were kind to Lee, but he knew they disapproved of his lifestyle — and now he had this dreaded disease, probably as a judgment upon him—all of which made their relationship more awkward than ever.

I was determined to show Lee a more compassionate side to Christianity, hopefully a face of the church that was accepting and understanding. Being a bishop probably didn't advance the cause as I would have liked, and I recoiled from any thought of dragging him to a church service to try to convince him. Leaving all that aside, we chose just to be friends. We hung out together. We did simple things like going for a drive or coming to my house for a meal, or I would take him a little gift to let him know I loved him. And then he died.

I was in Singapore when I learned of his death, en route home from a business trip to Southeast Asia. To my surprise, I wept like a kid who had just lost his younger brother. I didn't get back in time for his funeral or any chance to say goodbye to him with his family and friends. And then his family faded out of sight as if trying to erase a lifetime that had gone awry. But the short time I had had with Lee changed me forever.

Over the years since, I have performed more same-sex weddings than I can recount, including my own daughter's, and those moments have been some of the happiest of my ministry. I believe those moments have pleased God too. I've heard it said that God can be a spendthrift when teaching us lessons, and if so, it's a good thing because some lessons may take a very long time.

With the rich but rattling experience of Bellevue behind me I would soon go off to Africa, leaving the lessons of the big city behind, or so I thought. What I would discover is that the human condition is about the same the world over: we are all faced with the pains of life, be they physical, mental, emotional or social. I would spend the rest of my life trying to deal with some of them.

Jacob's odyssey began with his escape from South West Africa, the first of many life-threatening events that would populate the rest of his life. The country wasn't called a Police Zone for nothing, and the last thing the white ruling government wanted was for an African to be roaming freely around the world, telling what was happening to them back home. The once-benign border that separated two countries and split an ancient African tribe was no longer benign. It enclosed a war zone with barbed wire and armed troops but tried to keep it quiet. Now heavily guarded by the South African Defense Force, Saracen tanks and armored vehicles patrolled the border, with young soldiers often itching for a skirmish to give excitement to their otherwise dull patrol. With few exceptions, those soldiers were young white boys from South Africa who knew nothing about South West Africa or its people except what they had been told when they were conscripted. They had been indoctrinated to believe that blacks were potential enemies and that the Ovamboes were probably the most dangerous of all because they were beginning to push back. Within Ovamboland, there was historically a sense of brotherhood and solidarity among the people, which to young white soldiers might have seemed like everyone was an active member of a banned political party. In fact, very few people belonged to SWAPO, the political party originally conceived by an Anglican priest. The time would come when any sense of brotherhood and solidarity that held the Ovambo people together would be shattered in unforgettable ways. That would happen when the South African Defense Force would introduce the practice of "paid betrayal": informers. That clandestine way of obtaining information was so totally foreign to the African way of life that it ripped at the very fabric of what it meant to belong to family. Informers would set brother against brother, children against parents, families against themselves.

Leaving St. Mary's School and his country was gut-wrenching for Jacob, but it was the logical next step for him. He could no longer live under the oppression that pervaded every aspect of life. St. Mary's had been the cradle of his education, where he had really grown up and begun to question injustice and speak for truth — and to do it in English. In the next few years, he would become one of SWAPO's most effective speakers. St. Mary's had been the place where that questioning spirit had begun to stir within him, a questioning spirit that had opened his mind to radically new possibilities. At St. Mary's he had learned that other countries did not live under *apartheid* and that democracy and freedom existed elsewhere in the world. Like others before him who had pursued a dream of freedom, he wondered why it couldn't exist in his country, and he was determined to help make that happen. Jacob's questioning spirit would become his driving force and eventually his nemesis.

He had no papers and no passport, since the government did not issue such things to an African. And he had almost no money. So, like a poor gypsy, he would begin a trek to freedom that would touch a dozen countries on three continents and mean six months of hunger, exhaustion and danger. He would become a refugee without a home for the rest of his life.

A moonless night was the obvious time to make his escape: due north one quarter of a mile and quickly through the barbed wire fence into Angola as countless others had done. But once in Angola, it wasn't so easy. There were no paved roads, few vehicles, and a colonial government that was almost a joke. Whereas the Germans had seized and colonized South West Africa with an iron rod, they had also developed its farming and mining resources and generally built up the country they had dominated. The Portuguese, on the other hand, had done little in Angola. During their centuries of colonial squatting, they were famous for having a *laissez-faire* policy of *assimilado,* which meant letting the indigenous people assimilate the Portuguese culture as and how they wanted. While it sounded like a benevolent policy, it wasn't, and Angola and Mozambique became two glaring examples of colonial neglect. Hence, at the time of independence in 1975 and for years following, Angola was little more than a tribal warring territory. With the prodding of the United Nations, one helpful thing they did do was to designate areas for refugee camps as safe havens for those fleeing surrounding countries. Jacob's goal was to reach one of those camps.

He headed for Cassinga, an abandoned mining town located in southern Angola several hundred miles beyond the border. SWAPO had chosen Cassinga as a regional camp because of its isolation and the availability of water. It would become a major encampment and, in time, a strategic training ground for freedom fighters.[2] At Cassinga, Jacob found many others on their way to Lusaka or elsewhere, some to be trained to fight but many more to receive higher education. Whatever their aspirations or status, they were all categorized as political refugees by the Angolan government and the United Nations, which meant they came under the aegis of the United Nations High Commissioner for Refugees. The UNHCR, as it became known, meant little to Jacob at the time, but it would come to have major significance for him within a few years.

Lusaka was the capitol of the new Republic of Zambia and the African headquarters of SWAPO. There, strategic planning was under way for the ensuing insurgency within South West Africa as well as for nation building. What it would take to form a new government and run a country must have been mind-boggling for these young zealots! It is to SWAPO's credit that they realized early on that there would be a need for educated leaders in many fields to lead a new nation— once independence was achieved. This would involve finding countries and institutions willing to accept and sponser Ovamboes for further education, and SWAPO representatives spent countless hours traveling the world over, searching on both sides of the Iron Curtain. Ironically, the Soviet Union, Cuba, and China were among the more generous in accepting refugees for advanced education. [3] Great Britain took a more cautious line, as did the United States. Both countries were still doing major business with South Africa, which meant quietly turning a blind eye to the whole issue of how blacks were treated. Western boycotts of South Africa had not yet become a major force for change, and few had yet heard of Mandela and the African National Congress (ANC) leaders who were already serving life sentences on Robbin Island for trying to

---

[2] Refugee camps often made permanent gypsies of those who became dependent on their aid, often living under miserable physical and social conditions.

[3] I have often wondered if communist bloc countries were not in fact deliberately pursuing their old 'popular front' strategy in welcoming the underdogs from Africa. In any case, their welcome had the desired effect, for many communist countries ended up befriending and preparing hundreds of political refugees for future governments in Africa.

change things. Britain's Margaret Thatcher and her Tory party quietly accepted South Africa's explanation of why *apartheid* was necessary and figured Mandela and his followers were getting what they deserved. Thatcher's friend "Ronnie" (Reagan) concurred. Because African political parties were banned in South Africa as being anti-government and generally troublesome, similar attitudes were held by conservative governments in the West for anyone involved with SWAPO. Likewise in South West Africa. Even Christians in Great Britain and America were duped into thinking Scripture dictated obedience to Caesar's authority even if Caesar was a despot. All 'political' Africans were regarded as insurgents and probably terrorists. Thus, when a few wayward refugees from South West Africa came knocking on Britain's door, there was a skeptical response and not a few were turned away. The United States was equally leery.

Within the next few years, both major political parties (the ANC in South Africa and SWAPO in South West Africa) would turn to violence. It is important to mention, however, that both parties came to this decision only after they concluded that every other non-violent avenue had been tried.

Jacob reached Lusaka four weeks later, bedraggled and exhausted. He had survived the dense bush of Angola and jungle of Zambia. Already away from home for over six months, he was homesick, hungry and tired from his barefoot journey of over a thousand miles. With little food and no companionship, the tough, lonely life of a political refugee was just beginning for him at the tender age of nineteen. Although he knew many of those he met in Lusaka, his welcome was less than he had hoped for. Everyone had a story as difficult as his, or worse. All had suffered in similar ways, some much more than he had; many had lost their health along the way, some had lost loved ones on the journey. All were weary and homesick. All were fed up and angry with a life they hadn't counted on or deserved. And all were fearful of what lay ahead: an uncertain future with no guarantee they would ever see home or loved ones again, no guarantee they would find justice or a life without persecution, and no guarantee they would even come out of their ordeal alive. During his first few weeks In Lusaka, Jacob quietly adjusted to the reality of his situation as best he could. It was a lot to take in for a young man who had just left country and kin, perhaps forever; but never did he waiver in his conviction this was what he must do. It was like a divine calling for him.

Meanwhile, my divine calling was proceeding without a wrinkle, or so I thought. I was midway through my graduate studies, the world was busy with change and Manhattan seemed to be the center of it. The United Nations was only a few years old, which, for me, added to the excitement. My daily walk down Ninth Avenue to get to class was like "Around the World in Eighty Days" at ground level: the smells of a dozen foreign kitchens with as many languages shouted out of brownstone windows or across the avenue, strange new profiles and skin colors from the Middle East and beyond, dark eyes that darted this way and that with expressions that seemed to signal more than words. It was a world with more cultures and human variety than I knew existed, all crammed into a city that never slept and now I knew why. It was my first year to vote in a presidential election, and I was revved up for John F. Kennedy. In his inaugural address, he spoke the now famous words: *"ask not what your country can do for you, ask what you can do for your country."* Along with many of my generation, I found that idea inspiring, but maybe I heard it a little differently: I expanded his words to include the world…*"ask what you can do for the world."* Kennedy's words helped persuade me to think seriously about the world for the first time, especially the Third World, which until then I hadn't known existed. In fact, I had never heard the term and wondered if there was a Second World I had missed. Not generally referred to by that name, that was the Communist bloc of countries in Eastern Europe which was about to come to an end within a generation.

About that time, there was another famous speech that had a lasting effect on me, one that would become prophetic. It was even unlikely I should have heard it, although in time much of the world and all of Africa would hear it. It was delivered on a distant shore to an audience that was probably yawning or irritated and barely listening. The British Prime Minister, Harold Macmillan, was in Cape Town in the House of Parliament, speaking to the Members of Parliament of the Union of South Africa. There he said, "…the winds of change are blowing across Africa, from Cape Town to Cairo…and change is coming fast to Africa…"[4] Sadly, it would be decades before any constructive change would blow into South Africa.

Those winds of change were also blowing diplomats into New York City. African statesmen were coming to attend the United Nations, either to celebrate their independence or to plead for it. They came in increasing numbers as independence began sweeping their continent. What a decade the sixties would be: Africa was on a roll; I voted in my first presidential election; the man in the moon would soon be visited by men on the moon; Elvis, the Beatles; the Peace Corps; the civil rights movement and the murder of three leaders who were helping bring about much of the change, John F. Kennedy, Robert Kennedy and M.L.King, Jr.. Some of the foreign visitors to the seminary suggested Americans could actually go to other parts of the developing world and be of help. I thought that a novel idea, if only for the adventure of it. As I toyed and fantasized with the idea, it seemed to have my name written on it, and so did a new government program that made it possible for many like me; it was called the Peace Corps, inspired by President Kennedy's brother-in-law, Sargent Shriver.

But there was another reality closer at hand: I was about to enter my senior year, and I had my own winds of change to deal with. One of them came in the form of a wandering priest from Kansas, named Bob Mize, who came through Chelsea Square telling us he had just been appointed bishop to a country known as South West Africa. He had a good line: long before the American military coined the phrase, he said he was looking for a few good men to help him. Fat chance, thought I. Why would any of us leave the spoiling comfort of a secure future in the Episcopal Church for an uncertain future in an unknown country on the backside of the earth? Preposterous as the idea sounded, that was probably what eventually caught my imagination. It certainly wasn't the logic of it because it didn't make much sense.

---

4 Speech delivered February 3, 1960

Logically, I had too many other things on my mind—my last year of study was filled with term papers, dissertations, finals and some tough canonical exams to pass. To make matters worse, I had no idea what I would be doing upon graduation. My future was less secure than that of the wandering bishop from Africa! Los Angeles was on the other side of the country, and the bishop there barely knew who I was. I chose to be at such a distance because General Seminary was the oldest and best of eleven choices and it was located in New York City. But that did separate me from my home diocese and bishop and made me a stranger to both.

More change came with the birth of Karin, our first child, in the summer I was at Bellevue. That was a good wind, and she was a dream child, but she brought new demands. Life was now complicated with babysitting, fatherhood, and more serious thoughts about the future. I had a great wife and a wonderful child, but no certain future. Nights were short and days were full. Life had its own routine, rich with variety. I enjoyed seminary life: chapel; lectures; library time; tutorials; evening study; relaxing with a few choice friends and discovering the wellspring of all Southern comfort, Jack Daniels. Family life was simple and consisted of incessant reading, tending the baby, fixing meals, and the things a happy couple does together. Mondi, my wife, worked in Greenwich Village and commuted by subway, as did most of Manhattan. We found living in Chelsea Square and being in New York City exciting. And then I started reading a new quarterly called "Foreign Affairs" and became fascinated with that Third World I knew nothing about.

Out of my senior class of fifty two students, one-quarter became interested in serving overseas. Such a rash of interest in foreign places was unprecedented for General Seminary, which was not noted historically for sending graduates into what was then called the foreign mission field—until the Class of '61. A full twenty-five percent of the Class signed on for foreign service. Thirteen of us chose to go off to foreign lands: two to Alaska, one to Japan, eight to Latin America, and two to Africa, both of the latter eventually to become bishops in Africa. My interest in Africa had been stimulated by the wandering priest from Kansas but also by an organization known as "Episcopal Churchmen for Southern Africa" (ECUSA). Run by an enthusiastic guy named William Johnston, ECUSA sought to spread information and raise funds to assist those fighting *apartheid*. Johnston managed to find visitors and speakers almost on a weekly basis. Thus, the Seminary was routinely visited by Africans, and *apartheid* was generally the focal point of interest, largely because civil rights was coming into the cross-hairs of the American public and would become a defining issue for the sixties.

The heat was turning up on South Africa over *apartheid,* which was slowly becoming known globally as the harsh racist policy that it was. The South African government made it all but impossible for Africans to attend the United Nations, but there was one lone figure who steadily and faithfully carried the torch for them. His name was Michael Scott, an Anglican priest, officially called a 'troublemaker' by Great Britain from whence he came, by the Diocese of Johannesburg where he was licensed as a priest, and by the United States which he visited regularly to petition the UN on behalf of the indigenous people of South West Africa. Father Scott was a remarkable if enigmatic man who spent his entire life championing the underdog and otherwise lost causes. The case of the ancient Herero people of German South Africa first brought him to South West Africa and from there to the UN. While in New York, he never missed an opportunity to speak passionately and forcefully against *apartheid.* In those early years, the UN had so many pressing causes coming before this new world body that the issue of *apartheid* seemed not to be taken seriously. Moreover, South Africa's justification of *apartheid,* presented to the General Assembly by white diplomats, usually calmed things down at least among the western nations. White men were still attempting to speak for much of Africa, even as the baton of independence was being grasped by the African people. But a new day was about to dawn. Africans from South West Africa were beginning to make their way to New York to tell *their* story before the world body.

In August of 1960, Johnston told us of the arrival of one of them and suggested we invite him to our apartment for an evening discussion. We planned it as an evening of information with questions and answers about the situation in his homeland. A handful of colleagues and spouses showed up, and I was proud to welcome and introduce the first African visitor to our home. Contrary to what we might have expected of a political refugee, this stranger was smartly dressed in a dark suit, starched shirt and tie, slim of figure, and spoke quietly but passionately. He was very articulate and we were impressed by his demeanor and speech. We learned he was an Ovambo of the Kwanyama tribe, in a region known as Ovamboland, in the little-known country of South West Africa. His birthplace had the strangest name of all: Onamunama.

That evening, we received an education about Africa. The stranger told us that since World War I, South Africa had illegally occupied and forced its rule upon his country. Then followed a vivid description of his long journey through Africa and onward to America. *To get here, I had to pass through twelve countries which were all strange to me, but wherever I went I found kind people to help me — even though they were total strangers who did not know my name or the purpose of my journey, they took great risks to help me. First, there was the man from my home village. He walked with me through eighty-six miles of jungle, pushing the bicycle that had my few possessions tied to it. Neither of us had a weapon. At night, we built a small fire, and while one slept the other watched and listened. When we reached a dangerous border, my friend climbed the high barbed wire fence and helped me and the bicycle over. Most of the time, no one spoke my language, but I made gestures that said I was hungry or thirsty or tired and my need would be answered. Most important were the Africans in the big cities. They passed me on from one city to another, usually with a note introducing me. They taught me enough of their native language to make my way. They told me which buses were safe to ride without identification papers and which streets to avoid. They lied for me. More than once, I sat up in bed holding my breath as some new friend answered a midnight knock at the door. 'We're looking for a stranger, is he in here?' 'No sir, no one here,' they replied. Oh God, it was terrible! They lied for me in spite of the danger, and they never asked me to explain my purpose or destination…they just knew.*

Then he talked about the bitter suffering of his people under the laws of *apartheid*. He told us about racially mixed marriages that were forced to separate; stories of forced removals of entire villages and communities which his family had endured; gripping tales of how South Africa's pass laws led to the arrest and imprisonment of thousands of Africans every day. He spoke about the education laws that forced Africans to learn Afrikaans and denied them English, about living conditions in the 'homelands' that were beyond description. Sitting in the comfort of our apartment and surrounded by the security of a privileged lifestyle, some of us began to feel uncomfortable at how much we had and how little these people had. He may have sensed our discomfort; that's when he said the rest of the world didn't seem to know or care about the plight of the millions who were suffering under the heavy hand of *apartheid*. And then, perhaps for a little comic relief, he commented on his first airplane ride from Dar es Salaam to Addis Ababa. *Oh Tatekulu, at take-off I was more terrified than I had been by guns and police and jungle!*

He ended his speech with a passage from the Bible to reinforce everything he had said, as if that were necessary. Quoting words from Saint Paul which I have never forgotten, he said, "for just as the body is one but has many members and all the members are one body, so it is with Christ...and if one member suffers, all suffer together," slowly repeating the final words, "...**if one member suffers, all suffer together.**" (I Cor. 12:12-26). It was true, the average American didn't know or care where Africa was, let alone South West Africa, but I was troubled by what I heard. Having already spoken at the United Nations and to many in Washington, he knew there was little interest in his cause because his country was of no strategic or economic value to America. Maybe it was up to us.

That stranger's name was Jacob, the schoolboy from St. Mary's Mission School. Jacob Kuhangwa would become a leading figure in the ensuing struggle for South West Africa's independence. I would never see him again, but that cameo appearance in our apartment of the stranger named Jacob changed the course of my life.

South West Africa, where the wandering bishop named Bob would find his forlorn diocese, was a troubled land with a difficult history. Previously known as German South West Africa, it lived with the memory of a bitter genocidal war in 1904 between the German settlers and the stately Herero people. That war, basically over land but decidedly about race as well, decimated the Herero Tribe to the point where they never really recovered.[5]

A bit of history is needed to understand the complexities that subsequently developed. Following the defeat of Germany in World War II, German South West Africa was given to the League of Nations to administer as a temporary arrangement until a more permanent one could be found. Known as "mandates," a number of similar orphan territories around the world were placed under the League of Nations at the same time. When the League was superseded by the United Nations in 1945, all of those territories became United Nations Trust Territories *with the sole exception of South West Africa*. That was undoubtedly due to the hovering presence of the Union of South Africa. Jan Smuts, as Prime Minister of South Africa in 1946, tried one last time to incorporate South West Africa into South Africa as a fifth province, a move he defended at the UN "acting in the name of and on behalf of the people of South West Africa." ("Namibia under South African Rule", p. 26) Thus, at the opening session of the United Nations General Assembly, as Michael Scott was making his plea for the Herero people, South Africa was making its own to be guardians of the entire country, their interest anything but humanitarian. Father Scott's words fell on deaf ears, but South Africa's did not. South West Africa was of no strategic or economic value to any country other than the Union of South Africa, so no other country came to its rescue. What appeared to be an unending wasteland of sand and bush had a lot to offer South Africa: virtually unlimited black labor to work their gold and diamond mines, an extremely rich copper mine in the north, raw diamonds on the sandy shore at Oranjemund, later to be developed by DeBeers into an exceedingly rich open pit mine, and uranium on the coast near

---

[5] It was later discovered that Germans researchers had actually taken the heads of four Herero females and sixteen males to Germany to try to prove the racial superiority of white Europeans. Nothing was ever proven, and in 2011 the skulls were finally returned to Namibia with an apology from the university involved. The German government has yet to apologize for that action or for the colonial period.

Swakopmund, in time to become the world's largest open pit uranium mine. South Africa made its case and was awarded oversight of the country for an unspecified length of time. That would spell trouble and suffering for the indigenous people for the next forty years. The lonely figure of Michael Scott would continue to visit the General Assembly each year to plead in vain for a forgotten people. He and the stately Herero people would drift quietly into history and be forgotten.

I learned later that most of Jacob Kuhangwa's time in New York City was spent on behalf of SWAPO, trying to gain support from diplomats at the United Nations when he wasn't flying around the world to speak with foreign governments, seeking the same thing. In many instances, it was a hard sell. Political refugees from Africa, even very articulate ones like Jacob, were something of a new phenomenon, as was the whole idea of African independence. Simultaneously, with all that activity he furthered his passion for learning by enrolling in Lincoln University in Pennsylvania. He had a keen interest in trying to understand what made people do the things they do and how social and ethnic groups interacted. I came into possession of his dog-eared copy of "Social Psychology" by Leonard W. Doob, which was as close as he ever got to Yale University where Doob was tenured. But he devoured Doob's textbook. I could get an idea of how his mind was tracking from his marginal notes and underlining throughout the text. Jacob had already learned more than most about human nature, and he must have yawned to read that "one must go beyond superficial social contact to study the origins and past of a people in order to truly understand them." He knew this from experience: in his home country, whites were routinely guilty of a superficial understanding of Africans, claiming to know them as they would know a child. Most whites in Africa spoke habitually of their paternalistic care for their African servants as they would for children. While self-serving, the assumption was that Africans were of limited intellectual ability, likely to be wild and unruly without white domination. Jacob pounced on passages to the contrary, citing historians who maintained that "unless the genesis of ethnic groups and their institutions are studied, only the fruits and not the roots of that culture can be understood."

Ah, but now he was in the land of the free and the home of the brave, that bastion of democracy that beamed the Voice of America to a world still in chains. How would things appear to him now? He would find out soon enough in the global petri dish of New York City just how other races were treated, particularly the black race. His reading also gave him a harsh dose of what Americans thought of black people. *"Recurring through all aboriginal people is the attitude of humility and respect toward reality, nature and society.* Doob continued…(yet) *I cannot find an adequate English term to apply to a habit of thought so* <u>*alien*</u> *to our American culture. We are aggressive toward reality and our attitude is colored by a desire to control and exploit."* (Doob, 104-105). Jacob expected that in South Africa; it must have come as a shock to learn that Americans were cut from the same cloth as the whites he had known in South Africa.

Doob's text studied religious and ethical issues and probably confirmed things Jacob and his black countrymen had already learned the hard way. *"Ethnic out-groups (read 'blacks') are usually considered inferior on the basis of biological criteria so the in-group (read 'white') feel more justified to exploit a group they consider inferior in intelligence, emotionality and responsibility…this argument combined with a religious one gave imperialists the thought they were carrying out the manifest destiny of their civilization."* (Doob, pp 331-333). Such was the general attitude of Christian explorers and missionaries for colonizing powers. But among the earliest settlers in South Africa there was a distinct difference: their patron saint, John Calvin, and the theology he brought to the sixteenth century Reformation, later to be known as Calvinism. It was the sternest of all the Reformation creeds and held a rigid belief in heaven and hell, the last judgment, and the omnipresence of evil in the world. It insisted on the literal truth of the Bible and absolute submission to that Word *as interpreted by Calvin.* Those who submitted to these beliefs were assured a place among the Elect (in heaven), and those who didn't were condemned. Calvinist theology taught that God intended whites to be masters over blacks, and *apartheid* was based on belief in this divine order. Such beliefs became the dominant foundation of the Dutch Reformed Church in South Africa.

Another passage in Doob's book made a strong impression on Jacob, if his marginal notes are any indication. It was comments made by Gunnar Myrdal, a Swedish socialist, about the white man's rank order of discrimination towards Negroes in the United States. Myrdal concluded the following order is "held nearly unanimously" in the South and to some extent in the North:

1. *The bar against intermarriage and sexual intercourse involving white women.*
2. *The several etiquettes and discriminations which concern behavior in personal relations.*
3. *The segregations and discriminations in the use of public facilities.*
4. *Political disenfranchisement.*
5. *Discrimination in law courts by police and other public servants.*
6. *Discriminations in securing land, credit, jobs, or other means of earning a living.*
(Doob, p. 329)

Jacob was sure to have observed these things during visits to the United States, and it must have been profoundly discouraging to him. Little had changed in basic racial attitudes, going from his own benighted country to the "land of the free." At least, he must have thought, America doesn't have *apartheid*. Interestingly, no mention was made during his evening visit with us of the racial discrimination he had experienced in America. All of this happened in the years before the Civil Rights Movement, which would reverse many of the things Myrdal had observed.

Chapter Two

"You're Thinking of *Africa?*"

While Jacob was reading social psychology, I was reading volumes of history, Old and New Testament, Greek, theology, liturgics, etc. and learning, outside the assigned reading, that God was dead. That astonishing revelation was published in 1960 in a book entitled "Honest to God" by Bishop John Robinson, an English bishop and New Testament scholar. *Aha, dead is he?* Robinson was seeking to address the traditional perceptions and roles that have been assigned to God, but I found his book more exciting than the assigned reading. Bishop Robinson hit a chord with me. I was beginning to think *religion* was dead, for so frequently it seemed not to address some of the deeper values of life, like spirituality and the stuff that should join the human race together. I was growing cynical that religion seemed more of a stumbling block of division than a unifying factor in the lives of people. Clerics have never been at the top of my Best Friends List, which doesn't mean some of my best friends aren't among the clergy. It's just that there is so much in this line of work for us to overcome before we can become the kind person I like to hang out with. Such things as conducting pious services without doing a solitary thing to help make the world a better place; or parading around in ecclesiastical finery while our neighbor goes shirtless; or feeding our own coffers while over half the world goes hungry. Did I really want to become a salesman for an organized religion with shadows like those? I wasn't at all sure.

By the middle of my last year in seminary, with no offers from the Diocese of Los Angeles, I began thinking more seriously about Africa. My interest was probably more fantasy than reality until two things happened to advance the cause: Mondi indicated a cautious willingness to consider going to Africa, and the National Episcopal Church indicated its willingness to take us on. They would pay our passage to Africa and provide the princely salary of $5,200 a year. No medical coverage and no perks, but they would guarantee our travel home at the end of three years. *What a deal!* And then, out of the blue, a counter-offer three times more generous came in a letter from the rector of St. Edmund's Episcopal Church in affluent San Marino, California. It was a solid offer to be on the clergy staff as an assistant (curate). I knew nothing about St. Edmund's or San Marino. This seemed like a God thing, but nonetheless a complicating one. Suddenly, in a matter of weeks, I had gone from no options to two real possibilities that were total opposites. One promised security in the comfort of a wealthy suburb of Los Angeles, the other suggested turbulence and no security and would involve living 9,000 miles from home with health risks, political risks, and financial risks. If we chose Africa, we wouldn't know where we would live or what language we would speak, what food we would eat or who our neighbors would be. *Who in their right mind would choose that over wealthy San Marino?* It's possible I wasn't in my right mind, but I chose Africa.

As long as I can remember, I've had wanderlust. As a kid, I would venture to the end of our block in the San Fernando Valley, look down a long boulevard of tall cypress trees that stretched on both sides as far as my little eye could see, and wonder what was at the end of them. I imagined all sorts of magical destinations. I have childhood memories of riding my bicycle to the end of a road or dirt path and wanting to go further, or watching freight trains disappear into the distance and wondering what the distance looked like. During World War II, there was an air base for P-38's near our house, and I remember watching those planes take off by the hour. I would imagine them flying to faraway places with strange sounding names like Karachi or Morocco, New Delhi or Rangoon, and wanting to go with them. Truth is, they were only flying maneuvers around the San Fernando Valley, but that didn't matter—they were flying someplace beyond, over the rainbow...

Now at the age of discretion, with a wife and child, I had all but made the decision for Africa but it didn't help that the wandering bishop from Africa was so insistent we get on with it. He kept writing and asking when we were coming, and Church Headquarters was getting more serious about supporting the adventure. It was pressuring us, but it was a pressure I liked and I was beginning to ask why not, but I still had one intellectual stumbling block to the whole idea. I had always shied away from the term "missionary" and did not want to be associated too much with it. For me, it conjured up images of zealous evangelicals going forth to convert the world, or passionate Bible thumpers out to save it, or arrogant do-gooders who had all the answers on how to live and prosper. I suspected most of the Third World had already suffered from religious abuse by missionaries from the West and didn't want to be a part of that. Nor did the abuse stop with the passing of colonialism, it just took on a new form. In countries where they are still permitted, many evangelical missionaries continue to drag around as much foreign religion and thinking as they can. But while my wife and I could never be regarded as evangelicals, either by temperament or training, the Episcopal Church had no other name for us, and we would be called "missionaries," at least for a time. Eventually, the terminology was updated and we became "Mission Appointees." That helped a little... but I continued to wonder why they had to call us anything at all.

We made the final decision to go to Africa without much fanfare, in fact none at all that I can remember. My seminary Dean didn't think much of the idea, nor did my parents or in-laws. I have since learned I often have more passion for an idea than common sense to go with it. A friend told me years later I was heavily endowed with "a sweet hard-headedness." My wife didn't much share much of my passion and put one condition on our going to Africa: it would be for three years only. Choosing three years was probably because overseas appointments were made for three years, which meant we would be returning home in three years in any case. I said nothing but hoped she would forget the agreement or change her mind. She didn't forget, but she did change her mind — but that took a few years to happen.

When it became clear we would be going to South West Africa later that year, we were told we would be going to a mining town in the north of the Police Zone, a town known as Tsumeb (pronounced 'sue-meb'). The Germans founded it in 1905 as a mining town, and there was still a lot of German presence, bakeries, farms, even a German newspaper. The name of the town was derived from a Nama,[6] word but no one seemed to know what it meant. The name of the town might as well have meant "owned by the U.S.A." because that's pretty much the way Tsumeb shaped up. In time, we learned the name actually meant "place with a green hill." That green hill turned out to be a Big Rock Candy Mountain for the mining industry. It contained one of the richest copper deposits in the world, but that was just the beginning. It was also one of the world's most prolific mines, yielding copper, lead, silver, gold, arsenic, zinc, germanium, and dozens of other extractable metals

Our first encounter with the Big Rock Candy Mountain happened before we even set sail for Africa. While still in New York City and finishing up at seminary, out of the blue we received an invitation for lunch at the Rainbow Room, high atop the RCA Building in Midtown Manhattan. It came from one Marcus D. Banghart. I forget how we learned who he was, but this invitation came as a command performance. Marcus D. Banghart was the Chairman and CEO of American Metals Climax, which owned the Tsumeb mine and virtually everything in the town. We would learn that Tsumeb Corporation Limited, or simply T.C.L., was stamped, painted or imprinted on everything there. People included. The lunch meeting was for Banghart to put his stamp on

---

[6] The Namas, descendants of the Khoikhoi, are an ancient tribe once called Hottentots. Today they number about 60,000 and have much in common with the ancient San people (Bushmen).

us — ownership if he could, but approval at the least, or we probably wouldn't have been allowed in.

And my God, what a lunch it was. The initial conversation went something like this: "Howdy, I'm Marcus Banghart. Why don't you folks sit right there" — in the two chairs opposite him. He chose to sit on the side with the fiftieth floor view in case the conversation got boring. "Thanks, let me introduce my wife…" "Yes, I know," he replied, before I could speak her name. I wanted to ask how he knew but didn't. It was obvious we were in the presence of The Chairman, who was used to knowing everything and doing all the talking. I don't remember anything about the meal, but it quickly became apparent this meeting wasn't about eating. It was to introduce us to the party line, the rules of engagement, so to speak, for anyone going to Tsumeb, South West Africa. "I hear you kids are planning to go to Tsumeb, is that right?" "Right," I wanted to say, but I still wasn't all that sure it was right, and my wife was far from sure. I wanted to protest we were not kids and ask him how he knew so much about us, but chickened out. Intimidated by his size and buffoonery, I settled for a polite reply, 'Yes sir, that's our plan in a few months' time." We were not yet aware he possessed total control over Tsumeb, but he made that clear in words that followed. In fact, the Chairman didn't waste any time in telling us we needed to fit in with things…*as is.* Marcus D. Banghart wanted to know our views on *apartheid* and this and that. As we spoke, I got the impression he wasn't listening much and didn't really want to know what we thought. He then confirmed my suspicion when he said, "Well, let me give you folks a little advice…" and with that he proceeded to instruct us on how to behave in an *apartheid* society, neatly summed up in three words: **DON'T MAKE TROUBLE.**

There followed the usual gibberish about folks like us coming from the outside and not being able to understand the racist system until they'd lived there awhile. It all reminded me of the guy who wandered into a smoke-drenched pub and blurted out, "My God there's a fug in here!" to which the old timers said, "How the hell would you know, you've only just arrived." Chairman Banghart was the first of many to tell us that people in America just didn't know what they were talking about in criticizing *apartheid*…"we take good care of our boys in the mine" was the mantra at Tsumeb. That was a line we would hear a lot in years to come. Some of those "boys" were as old as Banghart. I was acutely aware we were still outsiders and didn't know how things really were. But we did know what we read, and it wasn't good: how labor was conscripted into the Chairman's fiefdom for up to three years at a time, how laborers were transported without wife or family and told where they would work and for how long, and where they would sleep, get drunk, have sex, and otherwise behave as good slaves — in short, how to be "good boys" of good old T.C.L.

We passed the interview, thanks in large part to my wife's way with people. I think she charmed him out of what seemed like permanent indigestion or a foul mood. But it wasn't easy. For starters, he had a glass eye, probably a souvenir from a mining accident in his youth. The glass eye was unnerving. It has since reminded me of the bank president, who also had one. When he was interviewing an innocent young lady for a loan application, he said jokingly, "I'll give you the loan if you can tell me which eye is the glass one." "It's the left one," she replied, to which he said, "You're right little lady, but how'd you know?" "That's the warm one," she said. Banghart's eye was neither warm nor inviting, it just stayed fixed on you while the other one gave you the third degree.

We got our lecture and sizing up over a splendid lunch that we hardly tasted. I remember thinking how ironic it was to be sitting atop the RCA Building with a magnificent view of the world and talking about such a narrow view of life. But as we would soon learn, such was the world of South Africa, a world that was rapidly growing smaller and more fearful. When it was over, I felt like throwing up.

Perhaps the Chairman's motives were more reasonable than I gave him credit for, but our meeting was nothing more than an interrogation. Somehow, Banghart knew I would be going to Tsumeb as an Episcopal priest and working with the Anglican Church. I often wondered about his sources, but it was openly known the Anglican Church in South Africa had a reputation for being an antagonist in its stand against *apartheid*. More of that in Tsumeb could make things unpleasant for Banghart's kingdom. Rocking the boat over *apartheid* could upset the work force, the living conditions, and everything to do with what made the town work. We didn't know until we got there that not only did the mine depend totally on black labor, but so did the entire town: every home, shop, business, and all town services. Nor did I realize it at the time, but Chairman Banghart had enough power and influence to prevent us from receiving visas to enter the country.

Shortly after we arrived in Tsumeb, we met Banghart's son, Richard, who was a mine boss and a thoroughly likable guy. He hadn't yet lost an eye or his good humor, but mining is a rough business and I was never sure how far from the tree that apple had fallen.

Our hope was to obtain 90-day visas and apply for permanent status once in the country. That was fairly standard procedure. But as we were about to apply, the world was shaken by an event that could have permanently scuttled our visas and left us in the U.S. It took place in an unknown black township known as Sharpeville, not far from Johannesburg. On March 21, 1960 a group of between 5,000 and 7,000 blacks converged on the local police station offering themselves for arrest, Ghandhi style, for not carrying their pass books. The atmosphere was initially peaceful, even festive. At the start of the protest fewer than twenty police officers were on hand in the station. Later that morning, the crowd grew to around 20,000 and the mood turned ugly. About 130 police reinforcements were rushed in, supported by four Saracen armored cars. The police were well armed with firearms and sub-machine guns, the crowd had nothing. Soon Sabre jets and helicopters were flying low over the crowd attempting to intimidate them. The crowd responded not by dispersing but with rocks which was the only thing they had since it was unlawful for Africans to have firearms. There was a scuffle, the crowd advanced, the police panicked and started shooting. The mayhem that ensued didn't end until sixty nine Africans were killed and over 180 wounded. Many had been shot in the back as they turned to flee. In his statement of what happened, the commanding officer stated precisely what white South Africans wanted to hear: "*...the native mentality does not allow them to gather for a peaceful demonstration, for them to gather means violence.*" It was a shameful statement, indeed. The authorities either didn't know or care to learn that for centuries Africans had been gathering peacefully before tribal councils, courts, headmen and kings to conduct their affairs and voice their concerns. Peaceably.

The next day, South Africa's newspapers conjured up a dreadful image of the Afrikaner's vision of 'separate development' that set off a shock wave of black rioting, arson and more killings. To some Afrikaners it suggested that a revolution was at hand. To others it was clear that a police state was in the making to keep what fragile peace remained in the country.

Since South Africa's independence, in memory of those who died at Sharpeville, March 21 has been designated as Human Rights Day in South Africa. UNESCO observes that date annually as International Day for the Elimination of Racial Discrimination.

One other classmate and his wife had applied for visas to enter South Africa at the same time. We waited in trepidation, but quietly figured our chance of getting visas in the wake of Sharpeville was nil. Neither of us had another plan if we were denied entry; our every intention was set on going to Africa. But the massacre at Sharpeville put a heavy pall over it all and our possibilities looked bleak. The incident made international news and became a subject of major discussion at the United Nations. While I wanted the world to know of the slaughter at Sharpeville, with visas pending I also wanted to duck my head and keep quiet. We waited months, with no word from the South African Embassy. Then one day a reply came. Certain our applications had been denied, we opened the registered mail to witness a miracle. We had to re-read it several times to believe it: we had been issued *Permanent Residence Visas* which meant we could remain in the country as long as we wanted. My classmate and his wife received the same. It was astonishing that the events at Sharpeville had not derailed the processing of our visa applications. To this day I believe it was a lucky clerical error that gave us those visas because it made no sense to allow two young clergy of the provocative Anglican variety into the country, certainly not at a time when the eyes of the world were upon the South African government. Those Permanent Residence Visas would be our most valuable possessions for years to come.

Industry in South Africa was basically amoral regarding racial policy and eschewed political involvement entirely. This was understandable but unfortunate because industry wielded so much power. In principle, mining companies were passively for the human rights of their African workers but in practice they did whatever was necessary to get along and make a profit. It was not surprising therefore that living conditions for African labor were generally sub-standard. Eventually the inhumane treatment of South African mine workers was challenged the world over, no less in shareholder meetings in New York and London. That was exactly what the titans of industry like Banghart feared: do-gooder crusaders upsetting annual meetings—although we never did that nor gave it a thought. Companies like American Metals Climax were eventually forced to do more than give lip service to the human rights of workers. They would have to state clearly to their shareholders that they would no longer support the *apartheid* practices of the South African government. Sadly, it took years of international boycotts to make that happen.

In the process, virtually everything produced in South Africa and South West Africa got swept into the fray. On a visit to the States, I remember going to dinner with friends in Cambridge, Massachusetts, and dropping into a local wine store to buy a house gift. I wanted to treat them to a bottle of fine South African wine. You'd have thought I had asked to inspect the owner's circumcision. In a whisper he told me to wait a minute while he went behind a wall. After some time, he came out and asked me where I was from. That settled, he asked me to wait another minute while he made a phone call. Finally, rather secretively, he indicated he could sell me a bottle of Stellenbosch's finest, but only one, and I wasn't to say where I got it. He produced the contraband from a hidden source, handed it to me in a sack without a word, and was happy to see me go. Such was the degree of pressure on South Africa that reverberated virtually around the world. I had a momentary twinge of conscience breaking the boycott with my purchase but probably experienced the conflict many good South Africans of conscience must have had on a daily basis. Our host enjoyed the fine Stellenbosch wine and I never told him how I got it.

As planned, I got ordained in Van Nuys, California, where we had spent the summer. Much of that time was spent packing up what remained of our worldly goods and sending them off to a warehouse in Brooklyn. I figured only the gods of great freighters would know when the stuff would arrive in Africa. The date for our arrival was a little more certain but getting there was not. En route to Brooklyn to catch our ship were unforeseen obstacles. The first came in New Orleans. We had stopped there to visit a classmate and were looking forward to a few days' visit and a great dinner at Brennan's. That's when the trouble started. On our way to Brennan's I began shivering wildly and became delirious. Instead of going to the restaurant, we went to the hospital where I was admitted with a diagnosis of meningitis. Nice way to begin a move to Africa. Spinal taps were ordered for the next morning, the thought of which scared the hell out of me. But by morning the fever had gone and the worst was over. No spinal taps. My condition turned out to be aseptic meningitis, and with antibiotics it cleared up in the next few days. It could have been more serious, even fatal. Looking back, I wondered why it never occurred to us to reconsider our plans but it didn't, and onward we went without giving it a thought.

We arrived in New York in early September. Still a little tender from the medical ordeal in New Orleans, the plan was to spend a week in Manhattan before boarding our Farrell Lines freighter. Four days before sailing, excruciating pain hit again, this time in my lower abdomen. I recalled similar pains a few years before while in seminary. Dr. Perrone, the resident physician, determined it was a troublesome appendix and in time would have to come out. Splendid timing that should be now! The appendix had ruptured and I was rushed to St. Luke's Hospital for emergency surgery. The medical side of things went well enough but the timing didn't: the doctor ordered five days in the hospital following the surgery. Our ship was due to sail in three and the dream of Africa seemed lost forever.

Two things would make memorable the week that followed. One was the sad news the world received of the death of one of its great leaders, Dag Hammerschold. The charismatic Secretary General of the United Nations died in a mysterious plane crash in the Congo while on a peace mission. [7] Hammerschold had been one of my heroes, and I found it strangely upsetting to learn of his death and that sad thought hung over me for days. Years later, I would visit the site of the crash and see the simple memorial erected to honor the Swedish diplomat and man of peace. The other remarkable thing of the week was that the ship's sailing date was postponed by four days! And it came to pass, I was released from the hospital three days later, and we boarded our ship the next day. The thought haunted me for years what would have happened if my appendix had ruptured at sea. Passengers on freighters sign waivers acknowledging they understand no medical services are available at sea. I would simply have been buried at sea—half way to Africa.

Twenty Eight Days at Sea

I never had a fondness for the sea except for its beaches and beauty, in the same way I never cared for the deep end of swimming pools. But there we were at last in Brooklyn Harbor, ready to board a huge ship to take us into a vast watery unknown. Except for some years in the Naval Reserve, I had never been on a real ship that sailed on a real ocean. Having grown up on the sunny Pacific where skies and sea are predictably blue and peaceful, the Atlantic Ocean had always seemed a little on the dark side, at times even menacing, and here we were, about to commit our lives to it for weeks. The ship that would be our maritime home for the next month was big enough to swallow a small city. It was built to carry a lot of freight and not much else, just a sparse crew and twelve passengers. A late moment of truth swept over me when I saw

---

[7] September 18, 1961.

it: *what could I have been thinking to launch us into this vast unknown?* Fortunately the moment passed without causing trouble.

Sailing from Brooklyn Harbor to Walvis Bay took twenty-eight days, twenty-four of them without seeing land. It was a challenge mentally and socially, as most of the passengers could have been our grandparents. We were forty years younger than the next youngest passengers, a pleasant couple in their sixties. Mr. Schwelnus was a mining geologist at a place called Messina, in South Africa's Northern Transvaal. Our fellow travelers gave us more practice than we wanted talking about *apartheid* which was awkward conversation most of the time. His mine depended totally on *apartheid* labor, as did every mine in the country. We discovered that most South Africans were so preoccupied with the racial situation they didn't seem to know how to talk about much else. Our infant daughter gave us an excuse to leave most of those conversations.

Weeks later, I stood at the rail and mused on the fact that we were almost at the middle of the world and about to enter the Southern Hemisphere for the first time in our life. This was day twenty-two and it had a special significance for me for today we would cross the equator. I had been getting ready for this day for almost a week. To bring a little excitement into fairly boring days, I conjured up a science project which required digging around in my mental trash bin of forgotten information. I remembered learning in physics about "Corioli's Force," an obscure piece of information of meaningless application. Corioli was a little-known French scientist of the nineteenth century who observed that the spin of the earth caused water to go down a drain circling to the right in the Northern Hemisphere and to the left in the Southern. It wouldn't be a monumental observation but it was my only chance to witness concrete evidence to what I wondered: would the water stall and go straight down if you were on the equator, since Corioli had said nothing about that. Would I really see my wash water swirl first this way and then no way and then that way down the ship's drain pipe? And other questions arose: how much water was needed? Would it make any difference if it was hot or cold? If it was dirty shaving water or clean? I decided it didn't matter and with a basin full of whisker water pulled the plug. And then, like water had been doing since drains were invented, down it went swirling gently, almost imperceptibly, to the right. A half hour later it went straight down, and in about an hour it swirled to the left. I had it on Corioli's authority we were indeed in the Southern Hemisphere and heading to Africa!

Being at sea for four weeks with nothing to look at but mountains and valleys of water gave a new sense of the world and the vastness of the water that covers most of it. We were a tiny speck on this body of water that was miles deep and thousands wide. Once or twice, I fantasized we were lost and thought of things that could go wrong in the middle of nowhere, such as a ruptured appendix, the sudden death of an elderly passenger, a serious mechanical problem, or running out of fuel. Maybe there's a fine line between faith and foolishness, and I wasn't entirely sure which side of the line I was on in this venture. For the time being, I knew someone was in charge, and he wore a navy blue uniform with four bold stripes on his sleeve to prove it. The captain even took meals with us from time to time, perhaps to reassure us there was someone in charge. Whatever the reason, it was a nice touch.

Then it happened: our first glimpse of land. It was little more than nondescript mounds of sand on the hazy horizon, but it was Africa. That moment was surreal for me, perhaps like it was for Columbus when he spotted the New World. It was relief from the sea and reassurance of land, like approaching treasure at the end of my childhood row of trees. I fantasied those distant mounds were larger than life and had strange names where the big planes flew. In reality, they were probably nothing more than coastal sand dunes in some obscure West African country, still thousands of miles from our destination. I didn't know at the time that Africa is five thousand miles from top to bottom and we were somewhere near the top.

While at sea, I had done a lot of reading about the missionary venture in Africa over the past century. It brought up many provocative thoughts and a little bit of soul-searching. I had always enjoyed helping people, and the bigger the need, the greater the satisfaction. So I grew up being called a people pleaser, never sure if that was a compliment or a criticism. Probably both. It never occurred to me that the unsolicited gift of my enthusiastic help could ever be unwanted, but I learned from my reading that it could. Not too many years later, on the knee of Mother Africa, I would learn the difference between doing and just being present, the difference between saying and doing, between shouting out one's beliefs and just quietly living up to them. Best friends are usually remembered for the latter. I had read of the early years when the do-gooders arrived in Africa and found a continent where their services were needed, welcomed and wanted. Years passed, Africa started doing for herself, and the do-gooders were no longer so welcome. More years passed and they were no longer much wanted either. And the foundations started crumbling for the colonial expatriates who thought they had found a home in Africa with all those black children to look after in perpetuity. The ensuing years of new-colonialism carried the message that the services of foreigners, missionaries or other philanthropists, were neither welcomed nor necessarily wanted, and only occasionally needed. And if the expatriate couldn't live without feeling welcomed or appreciated, then this was not the place to be. Many foreigners left and others became confused as Africa started thinking and acting for itself. It was an exciting time for Africa but a trying one for many expatriates. I would soon learn when to remain silent and when not to offer help. In the middle of the Atlantic, with boundless time to think I was beginning to realize that just up ahead I had a learning curve that was taking shape. It looked like it might be a steep climb at times.

We sailed for many more days without seeing land. For the first time I realized all my geography books projected the Southern Hemisphere from a *northern* perspective, which greatly reduces its relative size. I would never have guessed there is a geopolitical bias even in the projection of maps! Neither I nor the average American knew that Africa is *three and a half times larger* than the United States, and that if it is projected on a map from the northern hemisphere, it looks much smaller. We sailed many more days down the west coast of Africa before seeing the northernmost tip of South West Africa. Then two more days down the Skeleton Coast to reach our destination at Walvis Bay. Emotions shifted dramatically when word came we would be disembarking in Walvis Bay the next morning. None of us had given a thought to sea legs giving way to land after nearly a month without it. After years of dreaming, hours of discussing and not as many praying, we were about to set a wobbly foot on Africa. We were about to stand on the Dark Continent, a hideous name no longer politically, socially or morally acceptable. As the reality of the moment sank in, my excitement bordered on panic. *Would there be anyone there to meet us? What would we do first? Where would we go from there? How would we get our stuff through the necessary channels and shipped up country? And where was the bishop-named-Bob who got us into this?*

We were met without fanfare by the resident priest and his wife, an English couple who had lived in South West Africa for years, Frank and Grace Haythornthwaite. Frank was Rector of St. Matthews, Walvis Bay and all points north. He lived most of the time in the comfort of Walvis Bay and visited his "inland safari," as he called the northern territories, as little as possible. During those visits he spent long days in Tsumeb, feted in the homes of the rich and powerful. His periodic visits were probably the ritual cure for lives of laxity during the long months without him. Frank was a bit of a bore, and more British than the Queen. I came to suspect the ruling Anglicans 'up north' put up with his visits and jokes with a wink and a Scotch whiskey, but probably heaved a sigh of relief when he left. I was to learn that the British were generally uncomfortable with clergy around.

It always amazed me how guys with such thick British accents seemed to revel in hearing themselves talk but wouldn't bend a syllable to accommodate a local language. I never figured out how a name like Haythornthwaite with fifteen letters could be reduced to less than three syllables when mine was half as long and required three. By the time the British finished gargling up the fifteen letters it was barely two syllables, something like 'Haythnthwaite', sliding over the middle syllable so it actually became just two. Neither lips nor chin must move during enunciation and the volume should be kept as inaudible as possible. And I thought, my God, have I got to learn this language too?

Frank and Grace were old enough to be our parents. That made things awkward. Moreover, Frank enjoyed free rein over virtually half the country and was known by all as "Padre Haythornthwaite" or simply "Frank," the Anglican parson who would borrow your spare bed and sip your Scotch at the drop of a dusty suitcase. The good father was addressed as 'Padre' by the whites. The term came out of the World Wars and was a handle for chaplains that was slightly less religious than 'Father' but denoted someone more connected to the Powers-that-be than the rank and file. Padres were regarded as good insurance to have around in wartime. They were known to drink with the boys, tell real jokes and be regular guys. They also made Sundays comfortable for the troops who had no obligation to attend services or tip a coin into the collection bag. Frank scored well on all of that for the local whites. As for tipping the coin in the collection bag, I would learn that the British used a soft velvet bag for that, sometimes extended at the end of a long pole. I figured maybe that was because of the filthy nature of money: on a long pole and held at a safe distance it could be quarantined until counted which then cleaned it up quite nicely. The bag also had the advantage of not embarrassing anyone who had only a Widow's Mite to put in, which was a good thing.

The few times I was addressed as Padre I figured either I had arrived or was well on the way, where, I was never quite sure. The last thing I wanted to do was cozy up to the white establishment in Tsumeb and be called by their pet names. I suspect for the most part, Father Haythornthwaite was a good man but I didn't have time to learn that for myself. Walvis Bay, his permanent comfort stop, was the beginning of the line and hundreds of miles from where we would end up, and we never really got to know each other.

The Padre had a distinct attitude towards Africans which did not endear him to me. Actually, that went for most of the Europeans. As far as I could tell, Frank never provided regular religious services or any other kind for the teeming Africans in the mining towns. Traveling five hundred miles to hold services for the paltry handful of whites who managed the mines, while doing nothing for the masses who kept them running, was truly a chaplaincy mentality. *"Here here! Best the British Empire has to offer and by damn we've got to look after those colonials now, don't we, old chap!"* That colonial stick-together attitude was consistent with the thinking of the Mine Management. It was but another version of the *laager* mentality.[8] Hence, while good people winced at the more egregious parts of the race laws, they nevertheless went along with them. To buck the establishment took more courage than expatriates like us probably realized. Everything would be put in danger to step out of line and say *apartheid* was wrong: home, family, job, reputation, perhaps life itself. Thus people fell quietly in line and lived by the unwritten creed, "my country right or wrong, I'll support my country!" Padre Frank lived comfortably within those limits, assisted by the fact that he didn't relate well to anyone whose first language wasn't English—the Cambridge version.

Frank was not given to too much diligence, so his visits were more likely to be infrequent, like every four to six months. He was a great raconteur and people generally put up with his stories and British mannerisms. We found him a bit dry but harmless and he usually meant well. Having a brash young American horning in on his domain was a major game changer for the peripatetic Padre. I was aware of that dynamic from the beginning and watched for signs of trouble. Basically there were none because we would be stationed six hundred miles away at the far end of his world, but where he was still known and held in some esteem. But alas, the plan was that his visits would continue. After all, young and untried as I was, it was felt some oversight would be needed and it was as likely to be him overseeing me as the

---

[8] An Afrikaans word, the laager was a circling of the wagons to defend against attack.

bishop. I would gladly have done without either and wished I was ten years older than I was. A wisp of gray hair would have been welcome too. As it worked out, the plan didn't go as scheduled and four months after our arrival Frank participated in my priesting and I rarely saw him after that.

The next few days in Walvis Bay were a blur. Everything was new. The English language we thought we knew had been replaced with British accents, words and expressions. And then there was Afrikaans,[9] harsh, guttural and spoken without smile or soft face, like they were barking at you. That was a little frightening and my first instinct was to retreat and say as little as possible. I thought about faking a British accent or at least softening my "r's" and making my lips move as little as possible but knew that wouldn't fly too well either. Afrikaners seemed allergic to English spoken by anybody. They had an inferiority complex about life in general and were suspicious of outsiders, "*buitelanders*" they called us. American English was probably even more offensive to them than South African English—the British thought both had funny accents. From the day we arrived I lowered the volume of my voice, partly not wanting to be noticed in a place where I didn't feel particularly welcome. It had become obvious how loud and boisterous Americans were even in normal conversation, most of the time without knowing it. The bishop was a prime example. His American accent stood out like a Kansas cornfield in summer. For years he struggled in vain to pronounce even basic Afrikaans expressions. I was almost super-sensitive to the fact that we were Americans and everyone knew it. Along with our funny speech we were generally suspected of being political liberals and staunchly opposed to *apartheid*, which we were. That didn't endear us to the port officials either.

Although physically situated in the middle of the coast of South West Africa, Walvis Bay was technically a part of South Africa. By some strange political arrangement from bygone years, the entire city and port were considered South African soil. Padre Frank gave us a brief history

---

[9] Afrikaans is a bastardized derivation from High Dutch and looked upon with some disdain by Hollanders.

of how that all happened which was wasted on me. I had an irrational aversion to the whites I met and had no interest in spending time with them or listening overmuch to what they had to say. I had come to Africa to work with Africans and they just seemed like an interference and probably all supported *apartheid*, or so I thought. Unfortunately, the latter was mainly true. But it was the arrogance of youth and a hasty judgment on my part to assume that all whites supported *apartheid*, for there were many of good will who did not. But most of them still held attitudes of privilege and superiority that kept Africans in servitude. I felt uncomfortable in Walvis Bay and wanted to start moving towards Tsumeb as quickly as possible.

To our great relief, we discovered our worldly goods had come on the same ship and were 'offloaded' with us. A great English term, 'offloaded,' opposite of 'onloaded,' except nothing ever got 'onloaded.' What was offloaded consisted of several crates that could easily fit into a pickup truck, now known as a *'baakie'*. That was the easy moving. The harder would be the paperwork. Nothing was going to move without the paperwork and countless official stamps to say it was so. Watching the paperwork get stamped was entertaining at first. In consisted of taking a hand stamp and with great gusto beating hell out of a stamp pad, and then with consummate authority beating multiple copies of this and that on the counter. Countertops would shake, Africans would quiver, and lowly white clerks would beam with pride as they made the noise that said things were official. I think the sound of the stamp gave them a sense of importance; it was the sound of business being conducted which no one else was allowed to make. The colonial British did such a fine job spreading bureaucracy around the world. Parts of Africa are still awash in the remains.[10]

At last we were ready to head north. Little did we know that the small port town of Walvis Bay was the second largest town in the

---

[10] Years later, when we moved to Uganda, almost a decade after the British had departed, I visited government offices that had piles of dusty paperwork stacked from floor to ceiling the remnants of colonial days They were still afraid to throw any of it away without an order.

country. In a few years we would return on holiday to the city lights of that little port town and it would look like a great big city.

I was fascinated by the train tracks that would take us north. They looked funny, like the tracks of an amusement park train that weren't really serious. I subsequently learned those tracks were very serious and dominated most of Africa. They looked funny because they were narrower than any I had seen before, called narrow gauge or sometimes Cape Gauge. They were three and a half feet apart, fifteen inches narrower than the Standard Gauge found in America. Presumably the wider gauge is safer on curves and can carry heavier loads; so presumably, trains in Africa don't care to speed on curves or carry heavier loads.

Just before sundown, we boarded the train that would take us far into the interior, actually to the end of the line. At first glance, it looked like a friendly train: fine wood paneling and green leather seats that smelled of old leather, folded down at bedtime when porters dimmed the lights and transformed seats into beds complete with crisp, starched sheets. Just like an old movie, the train rocked and rolled along with a clickity clack of the wheels, pulled by a steam engine that belched out smoke and soot that found its way into your cabin. Those were the high points of the friendly train. The low points came later. They consisted of innumerable bumps and stops all through the night and sitting silently on the tracks in the dark African bush for no apparent reason. The stops made the African wild seem darker and the silence more intense. Rarely did we know why we had stopped. Trains just seem to do those things.

Heading off into the dark night in a strange continent, my surreal thoughts returned and I started wondering what we were doing here and where we were going. Any fantasy I may have had that got us here had vanished and reality was beginning to settle in. Now the details were emerging and I wondered if the devil was hiding in them. I was aware I should be bolstering confidence and calm for my little family, but both were now in short supply. It helped a little that the bishop was with us. He had been in the country only a year which hardly made him a veteran of the territory, but at least he had ridden this train once or twice. His enthusiasm was not all that helpful but it propped us up a little. On the one hand I was excited we were finally in Africa; on the other, having an eighteen-month-old baby, a wife, and all our worldly goods on a night train heading into the unknown was a withering thought that required more energy than I presently had. I decided it would do no good to share my anxieties with my wife. She was dealing with her own, which included fixing us all a bite to eat from a picnic basket and balancing it all on her knee.

The bishop talked on as the train rolled into darkness. The night was warm and we were tired and wanted to bed down in our cozy cabin, but the bishop kept handing me note after note and name after name. Mondi was patient and never said what we both needed to hear, that enough was enough for one day. I could barely nod my head through it all to appear somewhat interested, and I wondered why the urgency to convey all this information. I would soon learn why. We didn't know it then but this hurried visit with our new bishop would be our only orientation to Africa. The welcome wagon had arrived and was dumping its load upon us in great piles. There were pages of information, columns of names and an occasional picture, all aimed at briefing me about what I could expect to find at the end of the line. That was a town with a funny name and a mine that required a lot of labor, which was the main reason people traveled to the end of this line. The other was to escape from life or the law. My job would be to start a church and help make it a better place, and I had no idea how that was going to happen.

Mondi was busy trying to get Karin to sleep and I tried to look interested in a growing pile of information that was hardly interesting. I had flashbacks of the bishop's visit to the seminary during my seniorr year. *How did I ever let this guy talk me into coming to Africa?* A group of us with little more than a cerebral interest in Africa, but a lot of passion, had met with him in our apartment. What he had talked about had been engaging stuff, especially the part about the political situation in South West Africa and the suffering of the native people. Like typical senior seminarians, we had all felt burning indignation over the racial injustice. No one had yet heard of Selma, Alabama, and Rosa Parks was just an unknown black lady.

The bishop was now droning with a degree of urgency. I tried to take notes but that didn't work. Finally I just let him talk and tried to stay awake and show as much interest as I could. When it was almost midnight he stood up and said, "Well kids, this is where I get my train back to Windhoek. Good luck and I'll see you in two months' time." I could have died and my wife almost did. *He's getting off this train? Leaving us alone on this Choo Choo to nowhere, charging wildly into the night? In Africa?* All that and more was racing through our minds. We had expected he would accompany us to Tsumeb, introduce us and get us settled into our new life where everything would be new: the place, the people, the language, the food, the sounds and smells, the sights and the scenes. How do you prepare for so much change without at least a trail guide? Our heads were already spinning from culture shock. The pace of new experiences had been killing and tomorrow would bring even more, and we would be facing it *all on our own!* Tomorrow all of life would be new and like it or not, it wouldn't be on our terms.

At midnight our train pulled into a lonely country dorp called Usakos, and the bishop bade us good luck and disappeared into the night to board his train going the other way. Just like that. I remember the quiet of the night as the two trains sat in silence and did whatever trains do. By the light of the moon, I could see shadows of the African wild and hear animal noises and drums in the distance. My pulse quickened. It was one of the unforgettable moments of my young life. My brief reverie was interrupted by the gnawing question, *My God what have I brought upon us and what happens next?* The question had an urgency, and however complicated it had become, the answer was simple: we had to go through with what we had committed ourselves to doing, and maybe three years wouldn't be so long. Years later, I came across words of Zen wisdom out of life's crucible that summed it up nicely: *"The only way out is all the way in, the only way round is through."* I've learned that life has moments like that for all of us. How we handle them usually shapes both us and the outcome. I knew on that night train there was no turning back.

We trundled on into what remained of the night. With bleary eyes, I pondered the fact that we had just said goodbye to the only person we knew in a continent over three times the size of the United States and that we wouldn't see him again for months. Exhausted from that much pondering, we bedded down for what remained of the night, which wasn't much.

Day begins early in Africa. Our Little Engine That Could chugged and belched its way slowly along the narrow gauge track, the clickity clack of the wheels no longer charming. Our first African sunrise in the country was spectacularly beautiful, sufficient to make up for the deficits of the night. I have always loved sunrises. We had slept with our windows open so the freshness of the morning air seemed even more special in the middle of Africa. Morning clouds highlighted a golden sunrise over the savannah, uniform with rugged bush, dotted with thorn trees and anthills that stood like sentinels over the African wild.

The endless bush was actually cattle country, vast ranches which the locals called 'farms', a term that belied their immense size. They were not owned by blacks but by Germans and Afrikaners, or an occasional Brit, usually the rugged Scottish type. We learned later there were wild animals in that bush in great abundance: hyenas, springbok, kudu, wildebeest, all manner of reptile, and the occasional giraffe. These lived more or less as a peaceable kingdom with the domestic livestock. Not so with the occasional lion, leopard or cheetah that were a constant menace to the farmer-ranchers.

It was exciting finally to be in Africa, though we were still a little numb from the thought we were alone on a train heading to a place we didn't know to be met by people we didn't know. *Good morning dear, how did you sleep?* seemed a little out of place, so I didn't say it. As if I didn't know. My wife was a tough one, a real corker the Irish would say, but so far she had had a rough introduction to her future home. I was sensitive to that fact but didn't know what to do about it. *What should*

I say...sorry dear for messing up our young family life and railroading you and the baby into the unknown? Having no control over our situation made me all the more edgy, but in typical form my wife was quietly taking it all in stride, seeming to understand me better than I did. We had been told a nice English-speaking couple, Harold and Dorothy Gibbs, would meet us at the Tsumeb station. It was comforting to know at least we would be met upon arrival.

Hour after long hour, our train chugged northeastward through endless miles of bush with anthills as tall as an elephant's eye and a sky that could match Montana's ten times over. It was hot and humid. October in the Southern Hemisphere meant late spring. Thunderclouds gathering in the east were magnificent, but it was still too early for rain. Heat and humidity were not a part of any October we had known and it was odd to be heading into another summer having just left one back home. We were both too much into our own anxieties to talk about how we were feeling which was a mistake. It was the silly bravado of youth that kept us from talking about our own fears and insecurities— or maybe we were just trying to be strong for each other. But not sharing our deeper thoughts and fears and staying in touch with each other would lead to a serious crisis within our first year in Africa.

The day wore on as best it could on board an old train of the South African Railroad. We figured there were other white passengers, but that was a guess because everyone kept to themselves. Who knows how many of them were running to the end of the line to run away from something. Preposterous thought but could we be doing that? We were learning that white South Africans, whether English or Afrikaners, were not very friendly to strangers, and we wondered what that was all about. Maybe it was some distant memory of the hideous Boer War that made them suspicious of outsiders in general. More likely, it was a collective guilt people had when outsiders came into their country where racial tension was growing because of a mindless race policy. Maybe they knew in their gut something was wrong on a huge scale. We would find all South Africans defensive whenever the subject came up. Some warmed up when they got to know us but most were short on talk and less on greeting. That made it even more apparent how talkative and outgoing Americans generally are, a trait that can be misunderstood in a country where people don't readily talk to strangers.

There were non-white passengers as well, lots of them, but we never saw them. God forbid, along with the laws of *apartheid* that helped him do that. Non-whites were given Fourth Class accommodation, which was as far away from the white passengers as possible, at the rear of the train where the smoke and soot eventually came to rest. Their carriages had only wooden bench seats, filled with passengers beyond any reasonable capacity. In between Fourth Class and ours were the freight cars, in all maybe twenty.

We figured we should arrive in Tsumeb around three in the afternoon. With the gentle rocking of the train and the afternoon heat, somnolence took over and we all dozed off. Little Karin was the first to awaken as the train pulled into the station. Tsumeb? So soon? I bolted up as if caught sleeping on the job. *My God, to be asleep for the arrival my life has been waiting for, how could this have happened?* I thought, as if this were the defining moment of my life. I had thought we were overly ready for that big moment but we weren't. For starters, there was no one there to meet us. No one. *Young priest with wife and infant child, bags without number, and no one to meet them!* The experience probably did more for my humility than seminary had managed in three years. Back in my senior year, had I had enough humility and common sense to listen to the other side of my brain, we would now be meeting the affluent parishioners of San Marino who would be showering us with the creature comforts that parish had to offer. I had chosen Africa, for better or worse. and I wondered which of those was to come first.

Chapter Three

The Big Rock Candy Mountain

The Tsumeb train station looked like it came right out of a Wild West ghost town. The sun baked down on everything and nothing moved, not even the dogs sprawled in the shade. It was dead quiet except for the eerie noises trains make when they're sitting still. I wouldn't have been surprised to see two gunslingers face off on the siding (there was no platform). In the distance was a sign that indicated it was Tsumeb but nothing more. No friendly signs like 'Waiting Room" or "This Way to Town." Not even "Welcome Suckers—it's the End of the Line." Nothing. In the silence, we tried to be brave and hide our despair. Our lives had been pretty predictable up until now; neither of us had ever traveled overseas, so we had nothing to prepare us for a moment like this. I was beginning to realize what a sheltered existence we had had even in New York City which I thought was big stuff at the time. Except for the very poor, Americans are sheltered from the harsh realities the rest of the world faces on a daily basis—most of us don't have a clue what the majority of the world is really like. We didn't either but we were learning fast.

As I recall, we were the only passengers to leave the train and a lot of freight. We stood in the ghostly silence of a Sunday afternoon. Heat and humidity and a few buzzing flies added to our discomfort. It was an experience I would have many times in the years to come. Africa has lots of heat and lots of buzzing. I thought there must be a simple explanation to all of this, and that nice Gibbs couple was probably coming down the road any minute. No such luck. We were miles out of town and didn't know which way to walk if we could. From the train we had noticed huge dust clouds followed anything that moved on the dirt roads, so we watched for that hopeful sign. Only there were no dust clouds coming down the road. The heat was oppressive, the baby was getting agitated, and we were nearer to being undone than ever. *What in God's name do we do now?* God apparently didn't have a lot to do with the situation and basically left us to figure it out for ourselves.

After a wait that probably wasn't as long as it seemed, we saw one lone cloud of dust coming down Station Road. It was our welcoming party, all of one person. Could this be the power of one? Harold Gibbs himself. We were badly in need of some mothering comfort at that point but were happy to settle for a matter-of-fact male rescue. True to his British upbringing and reinforced with training as an accountant, Harold Gibbs met us with stiff English formality. There may have been a smile under that British mustache, but I don't remember. He was the picture of a colonial English gentleman: mustached and dressed in the ubiquitous short pants and knee socks that clothed every South African male. His words were clipped and slightly muttered, with lips that barely moved under the mustache, so you couldn't even lip read what he was saying. Learning what these English speakers were saying was going to be a challenge. He said nothing about being late (we learned later it was we who were late). I got the impression our arrival may have disturbed some time-honored Sunday afternoon tradition. We were driven, not to the Gibbs, but to the van der Merwe home (pronounced 'fun dur Merva'), a typical Tsumeb house owned by Tsumeb Corporation Limited. *Welcome to Banghartsville,* I thought, only 'villes' were now 'dorps.' We were in Banghartsdorp, but no one dared call it that.

Dorothy Gibbs met us at the house, along with Peggy and Vanny van der Merwe. We would learn Vanny lived in the shadows most of the time and never told anyone his real name. Van der Merwe was an Afrikaans name and Vanny was indeed a son of the Voortrekkers, as fiercely patriotic as one could find. Dorothy was a warm English-speaking German and a welcome sight. We felt like falling into her arms but wouldn't have admitted it. We were welcomed with afternoon tea on the verandah, a screened-in porch typical of most houses in Southern Africa. But instead of the traditional afternoon tea we were offered a 'cool drink', an expression we would hear for the remainder of our years in Africa. A cool drink might mean anything liquid but generally a soft drink, with or without bubbles. This time it meant a *shandy*, pronounced 'shan-dee'. And what, pray tell, was a shandy we both wondered? Was this a play on our first names, Shannon and Mondi? Nope. It turned out to be one of the best kept secrets of the British Empire. The shandy is a mix of beer and lemonade or 7-Up, more or less in equal proportions, tasty and wonderfully thirst quenching. With our shandys we were offered homemade biscuits with butter and jam and given our first lesson in pronunciation. The British and everyone in their dwindling Empire spelled the name of these biscuits 'scones' but pronounced it 'scawns'. Americans insisted on pronouncing it like it was spelled and South Africans politely put up with it, but in time it became embarrassing that most Yankees didn't make the slightest effort to pronounce things with a local accent. I came to conclude it was probably because of an innate laziness Americans have in learning foreign languages.

And as the sun set on our first Sunday in Africa, we wondered what the morrow could bring…

It turned out the welcoming party that wasn't had made no arrangements for our accommodation so we ended up staying at the van der Merwe household sort of indefinitely. That had a couple of strange things about it that were not immediately apparent. One was that they were not members of the Anglican Church. Being Afrikaners, their natural affiliation on high holy days would have been the Dutch Reformed Church, but they didn't seem inclined to go that way either. And they were definitely not the welcome wagon type, so we thought it strange they would be offering room and board to the new Anglican priest and his family. Being either too polite or too shy, we never asked why they did that. We just assumed they were good folks with a welcoming heart, but in time we would discover that was not entirely the case. It was strange moving into a house where the first language was not English. The reason we were placed there would be revealed on the eve of our departure, almost two years later.

"Vanny," as he was called by everyone, didn't seem to have another name—he kept it neatly hidden from public view, like a lot of other things in his life. One day he confessed his real name was Johannes Christoph van der Merwe but he said no one knew that. A name like that should have made any Afrikaner proud except for the fact that the van der Merwe name is the butt end of thousands of South African jokes. Van der Merwe plays the dumb guy in all of them. For some reason, this John Christopher wasn't proud enough to be called by his name either in Afrikaans or English. While I have never been entirely happy with the names I was given at birth, I never thought of going without them. That would be sort of like going without clothes. If Vanny was hiding his names, what else might he be hiding? I had early reservations.

Why were there no members of the Anglican Church to offer hospitality to their long-awaited priest and his family? We had the naive assumption that all of Tsumeb would be waiting, if not with bated breath at least with enough breath to say welcome to their new priest and his pretty wife. Nice thought, but it didn't happen. No welcome high tea from the local nabobs. Not even a low one. No welcome luncheon or gathering for the ever-popular sundowner. No one at the first Sunday Service to introduce us. Nothing. It was another of those moments that made me wonder why we were there. I began to wonder if it was only the bishop's idea to have a priest in Tsumeb. For a kid fresh out of seminary, this was a pretty severe hazing.

In the months to come, we struggled with the feeling we had been betrayed by our flock. I've since learned that betrayal is an essential part of growing up, but to have it happen now was not a great way to begin a ministry in Africa or anywhere else. As time went by, I wasn't happy and neither was my wife.

We had been told the white Anglicans in the area had complained they didn't have a resident priest and had put pressure on the bishop to do what he could to get one. This may have been a case of getting what they prayed for and not wanting what they got. Truth is they were probably content to have old Padre Frank happen around now and then to sip scotch whiskey and communion wine with them and they didn't want much more than that. Even one such visit every four or five months was probably a stretch for most of them. Years later, having returned to America, I was taking the Sacrament to an elderly couple who, over the 'phone, described my visit to their daughter in similar fashion: "Oh we're just having a little drink with the bishop." Holy Communion, no less, but I guess you could call it that. For the Tsumeb Anglicans, there may have been little difference. I was never quite sure about that. But an uneasy feeling about the whites we met in South West Africa would grow deeper and lead to a restlessness in the ensuing year. I have never been good at maintaining the status quo, and it would become clear I was not going to make a good chaplain to this tiny group of self-sufficient whites who didn't take the church or themselves very seriously.

In time, several church members acknowledged they had let us down by not being more supportive when we arrived. But they were unsupportive in other ways as well, ways that matter to any church, like attendance and financial support. We had little of either. Butts and bucks are generally one litmus test of a healthy congregation, and we had little of either. In my youthful enthusiasm, I had expected a modest crowd would be anxious to see their new priest. For the first time in their lives they might even sing, perhaps even mutter an audible amen now and then. Wrong. I learned it was almost a taboo for Anglicans in that part of the world to utter either the prayer or the amen. Likewise with hymns. That was why they hired me: to be their surrogate presence in church, both priest and choir. I was learning why Anglicans were called God's frozen chosen. Frozen yes, but chosen highly doubtful. As for financial support, we were met with a wondrous creation of the British Empire known as the Sustentation Fund. This meant you slipped your tiny offering into a velvet collection bag, not to *further* the work of the Church but to *sustain* it, like it was on life support. The oxygen bottle was near to hand for this bunch.

Christmas was the high water mark for attendance, with about fifty people in one form or another, otherwise, attendance was sporadic, seldom more than a dozen. Every known Anglican in the northern Police Zone would not have made a crowd. That wasn't because there was not plenty of them scattered around on farms and in towns but because they didn't want to be known as Anglicans and tended to hide their identity. That was for a couple of reasons. First was public opinion. Living as a small minority in an Afrikaner and German environment, "Anglican Church" translated into Afrikaans became "English Church" or "Church of England," and the Afrikaners had bidden good riddance to the British Empire long ago. Their hated presence included their Church as well. The Anglican name, therefore, created a lot of misunderstanding and discomfort for an English-speaking member trying to fit into a community that was overwhelmingly Afrikaner. Simply put, the brand name wasn't as smooth as Coca Cola and would become a problem all over Africa when translated into local dialects. It invariably amounted to "English Church," the last thing any indigenous African church wanted.

The other reason Anglicans were shy about showing their colors was because some of the Church's prominent leaders were in the forefront of the fight against *apartheid,* and most folks wanted to keep their heads down in that fight. Those at the Anglican helm were leading by example, sometimes with great courage and sacrifice but not always with onward Christian soldiers marching behind them. A succession of bishops and archbishops were strong advocates for racial justice, including my bishop, the priest from the Kansas cornfields. He and others like him would eventually be deported because of it.

We were officially a part of the Diocese of Damaraland, which was another misnomer. "Damaraland" will not be found on any map of the country, new or old, because as a land it doesn't exist. The Damaras are a very old ethnic group in South West Africa, related to the Nama, but have never had a specific area of their own. Moreover, very few of them were Anglicans. "Damaraland" existed therefore in the minds of those who conjured up names of dioceses, in this case someone from the British Empire, many of whose subjects were good at naming things and getting traditional names mixed up. No one knew why the diocese went by that name, and with the coming of independence the name would be changed to the Diocese of Namibia. (Curiously, the Anglican Church has an historical habit of arcane terminology: ordained people are called by the generic term *"clergy"*; but when they convene in a meeting, they become a *clericus* which might include *deacons, deans, priests, presbyters, rectors, vicars, canons, archdeacons* or even the *Ordinary* who is the top dog, the Diocesan Bishop. Church buildings are equally shrouded in mysterious terminology: parts may include a *nave, an apse, a transept, a narthex, a vestibule, a columbarium, a baptistry, a Lady Chapel or Chapel of the BVM, a sanctuary* and a *sacristy*. Both the faithful and the not so faithful get confused).

The bishop of the Diocese of Damaraland was our wandering priest from Kansas, a bachelor and a man with a great heart and a fierce sense of right and wrong. To him there was nothing right about *apartheid*. He was totally color blind when it came to race, which became a source of irritation to the majority of whites in the country who felt one ought not to aggravate the authorities by treating Africans as equals. He would routinely share his house with whoever needed a bed and a meal and thought nothing of it. In time, even those of us who loved and admired him became sensitive to what he was doing. It was this slow drip drip drip of charity that would eventually be his undoing.

One of my heroic models for the priestly life in Southern Africa was the men's religious Community of the Resurrection known as the 'Mirfield Dads' because their home was in Mirfield, England and were "dads" in the religious sense only. They had a sizable presence in Johannesburg, where Fathers Trevor Huddleston and Raymond Raines were regularly in the spotlight for upsetting the apple cart over race relations. A number of Fathers lived and worked in Sophiatown, which was later bulldozed to make way for a white community. The Mirfield Fathers were constantly in the news, in the streets, the jails and courts, defending the defenseless and getting pilloried for it, constantly under surveillance but greatly loved by the non-white underdogs. Most white people, including many Anglicans, wondered why the clergy couldn't just settle down and preach the Gospel and leave out the distressful parts about justice and fair play. I never figured out how to do that and be true to the Gospel. It's been the same the world over. The saintly Archbishop of Recife (Brazil) used to say "when I feed the poor you call me a saint; but when I ask why they are poor you call me a communist." Such is the interplay between the words of the Gospel and the world of politics. Early on I came to realize that politics and religion seem to antagonize people most when matters of truth and justice are involved; that would be especially true where we would live for most of the next ten years. Any question with the word "why" in it was often the spark to light the fire.

Within the first year, the diocese provided us with out own residence, one of the few that wasn't owned by T.C.L. It was an enormous old house, obviously given to fine living and parties in earlier days. On the south side, running the entire length of the house, was a huge party room with a bar at one end. The bishop had his eye on the party room when the diocese bought the place, not because he liked to party, because he didn't. As I would discover, he had a penchant for starting churches, anywhere with anything, just like his penchant for asking total strangers what church they belonged to, an embarrassment for me more than once. In our new residence, he had his eye on the party room for the new church in Tsumeb. I grew up building things but what he had in mind would be a first.

Many a morning I sat in the party room-come-church, trying to concentrate on my morning prayers. People assume prayer and spiritual stuff come easily to clergy, but they never did for me. Even halos painted around our heads didn't make us any closer to the Source than anyone else, 'though medieval artists liked to think so. The closest I came to spirituality was in seminary, with a strict daily Chapel routine. It was a good framework, maybe even a crutch, but I sure wished I had it now, thousands of miles from the comfort of the past. Now I had to do it on my own, with failing degrees of success. Swatting flies made it harder and Africa was filled with them. They had an uncanny knack of buzzing me and out-maneuvering the swat, which frequently turned prayer time into a shambles and I ended up wondering what God had in mind when he created them. I figured he must have been in a foul mood at the time.

With help from the flies, my mind wandered a lot. Actually, there were many distractions that made it seem okay for my mind to wander: the sights, sounds and smells were all new to me. Even the air felt different as I took in the cool spring morning, strangely now in late October. I even wondered about the tilt of the earth that makes that happen, always right on schedule. My vagrant thoughts came to rest on the sound of foot traffic outside, where droves of blacks were walking to their places of work, miles away. I remember thinking they were at least doing something productive even if it was somebody else's idea. All I was doing was sitting in a big barren bar room, fiddling with my Prayer Book, trying to be quiet and say my prayers. Then a preposterous thought came over me: I imagined that everyone in the entire world was producing something but me! I was an abject failure to the workforce, just sitting there while the rest of the world went off to work. Most of the world had concluded what I was doing wasn't worth the bother anyway; but there I was, an activist who loved to get things going, just sitting in a lonely bar room, now part of my house.

Most of the morning traffic by my window was on foot and all of it was African. They were the only ones who walked to work. Laughing, joking, boisterous, sometimes singing as they walked, you'd have thought they didn't have a care in the world. The fact of the matter was, they all had plenty of cares. They had a long walk into town and back at the end of a hard day's work, in fair weather or foul. For the hours they were allowed into the white man's world, they had to suffer the insults of being called "boy" or "girl" or the biggest insult of all, "kaffir." Without 'thank you' in the white man's vocabulary, they would tend his children, cook his meals, clean his house, fix his elevenses (morning tea), do his shopping and polish his cement floors. Polishing floors was of paramount importance to South Africans: years of wax layered onto cement gave a shine only an African knew how to produce.

The amazing thing about the indentured African race was how they seemed to keep their innate joy, rising above their physical travail with singing and rhythm. Now I knew where the inner spirit and vitality of American Negro spirituals came from. That ability to hold the spirit together through great adversity was one of the African's greatest strengths. Most whites probably misunderstood this about their black neighbors when they would laugh and sing as they worked. It might have seemed like the childish banter of an inferior race who laughed their way through life. In truth, that childish banter was the singing of their souls, encouraging and supporting one another in the face of a hurtful, hateful life they could do nothing about. It's one of the tragedies of the world, how badly we misunderstand each other's cultures and traditions. So much of the richness of life is lost that way.

Most of the crowd-on-foot had risen long before daybreak to tend their families which involved scrounging for firewood, fetching water from a public standpipe, fixing the morning meal by candlelight, getting children ready for school, bathing in cold water outside in a makeshift shower, and then making sure they arrived at the white man's place on time. There was little joy in any of it. Yet they would find the resilience to laugh as they walked down that long road to do the white man's bidding. I think the rest of the world is still inclined to think the white man's work is more meaningful, purposeful and productive than any other, technology always valued over the hard work that goes behind it. That has been the white man's mindset from the beginning of his adventure in Africa. The colonial world determined that Africa was underdeveloped and that the way to develop it was to import work that was "productive" and "profitable." I would soon see what development meant in Tsumeb. It meant tearing up vast areas of land to remove rich copper ore and then exploiting its proceeds in others parts of the world, far from Africa. That was called development, but for whom? It didn't develop Africa, it only used it. Only the international mining industry and foreign economies truly profited from that development. That labor force walking down my road would work their whole lives long and never see the profit returned to their own country.

It would be years before I would learn that Africans don't value things like production and work in the way Westerners do. More's the pity that Westerners still don't seem to understand the African mind. Competition, amassing wealth, and materialism are alien ideas to traditional African society. Those questionable pursuits came late to the African world-view with the coming of the white man.[11] Ironically, none of the European intruders came by invitation, but such is the nature of conquest. As my mind wandered with thoughts such as these, it hadn't yet occurred to me that I, too, could be importing more alien baggage.

The room I sat in had known more parties in its time than prayers in mine. When we got the party room shaped into a church, we named it after St. John Mark, who happened to be the bishop's favorite saint, a young lad for whom Jesus had a special affection. I wondered if little St. John Mark's Church would ever seem like a 'real' church, like those churches where so many prayers had washed over them they even smelled holy. Only time would tell, a lot more time than I would have there.

---

[11] With the coming of independence in many countries in Africa, blacks are repeating the lessons they learned about capitalism and the wealth that comes from it; they are reproducing the behavior they saw when whites were in power, and a huge divide is growing between the rich and poor.

The bar at one end of the party room had an alcove that made a perfect sanctuary for the altar. That idea really grabbed me, taking the booze space and making it a holy space—not that I had anything against booze, but it just seemed like an Anglican thing to do. Jesus was great at doing stuff like that. He loved parties and he must have loved wine. He once made so much of it at a wedding in Cana of Galilee, they're still talking about it. The dance floor of the party room became the chapel where I sat idly with a fly and a few fleeting thoughts. As I listened to the real world marching off to industry, I asked myself if this is what I had come half way around the world to do, sit there at prime time and do my holy thing. I didn't think so, but for now it was the only structure I had to face the unstructured life I now faced.

Bishop Bob was an enigma, but I loved and trusted the man. He was the closest thing to a Franciscan I had ever known, saintly in many ways, and utterly impractical in the ways of the world. He was equally infuriating and dense. Over the next eight years, our lives would intertwine, sometimes for weeks at a time, and he would become almost like a father to me. Over those years, his influence on me would grow, as would some very funny stories of his adventures. One of them occurred when he got up early at St. Mary's Mission in the far north and went zooming towards home, 600 miles away, blithely forgetting to check his gas tank—petrol, we called it. Impractical Franciscan, there he was, driving a car that had been given to him, made to be driven only on the few paved city streets in the country. It was an Austin Touring Sedan, a low-slung luxury model and a ready victim for the rough roads and sandy conditions that existed virtually everywhere in the country. Even less suited was this limousine when the fuel level was low and the bishop was oblivious. Sure enough, on the journey homeward he ran out of fuel in the middle of the Etosha Game Park, hundreds of miles from civilization. When he recalled the story, we were incredulous. "Well, bishop, what did you do? everyone chimed. "Oh, I just bowed my head, closed my eyes and said a prayer; and before long down the road came a petrol truck!" Stuff like this was always happening to this guy.

That first year, he did indirectly help break my boredom with the white town of Tsumeb. That's when he was still exploring his vast

Diocese and occasionally he would ask me to come along. One of those adventures was to the far northeast of the country, to a place known as Runtu, on the Okavango River. Nothing could get my enthusiasm going more than a trip like that—into the total unknown, deep in the heart of Africa. Runtu was virtually inaccessible to tourists, hunters and day trippers, as well as anyone with much sense. To get there, a distance of only about two hundred miles, required a heavy four-wheel drive truck and sixteen hours of slogging through bush and sand. There was no semblance of a road, just a trail through sand that at times was as deep as the axle. We hitched a ride on a government lorry and left long before sunrise. Pitched into the behemoth almost as crudely as its load of freight, what followed was a day from hell.

I remember the day only by the heat and fatigue and what happened when we reached Runtu. It was well after nine at night, and all I wanted was a flat surface and sleep. Not Bishop Bob. He wanted to eat. He was always hungry. That's when he would develop a sort of whine that invariably galvanized me into action. "Shan-non, (with a sing song whine) don't we have some canned peaches?" was the usual plea. That's when he thought he was still in America and cans of Del Monte peaches were at the ready. "No Bishop, we do not have *any* food, remember?", trying to break it to him gently. "Then go get something!". "Yes, Bishop." And off I went into the dark night in a strange settlement that didn't have a town or stores and certainly not Del Monte peaches. I got no further than the back door of our lodging, a government building they let us sleep in for the night. Just outside the door the ground was covered with guavas, gifts from a huge guava tree overhead. "Oh Bishop, I've got the next best thing to Del Monte peaches—Runtu guavas!" But by that time he had drifted off to sleep, hungry. Failing that assignment, I returned to the guavas to scarf up in the dark what I could to deal with my own hunger and then bedded down. The next morning it was guava time; I knew the way to food for a hungry Bishop. But not quite. Every guava I collected was teeming with white maggots! I had eaten plenty of 'meat' the night before and got sick just thinking about it.

It was this man who had cast the spell in my senior year in seminary that brought us into the African wild, ordained me priest, then left me alone to be the rector, build a new church and organize everything in it. It was a replay of the farewell at midnight, not long before, sort of like "it's all in your lap now, see ya later!" I was barely twenty five, the youngest priest they had ever seen in Tsumeb, and I was thinking, feeling a little sorry for myself, probably the youngest rector in the history of the world! Why would this new bishop entrust such a major assignment to a newly ordained kid like me? It was because he had no other choice, there simply were no other clergy available. He obviously had more faith in me than I had in myself.

Fortunately, I had other work than swatting flies, fumbling with my prayers in a bar room, and tending the absent white congregation of St. John Mark. I was also responsible for hundreds of African workers in three mines over great distances. I took to that part of my work like a hunting dog to water. Curiously enough, swatting flies wasn't so bad when I was with two hundred sweating African men, crammed shoulder to shoulder into a tin-roofed building designed to hold fifty. That was the only worship facility provided by the Tsumeb Corporation, the largest of the three mines, and we were grateful to have it. Religious activities of the sort we provided never turned a profit and were considered superfluous, sort of like Africans when they weren't working. By the Corporation's logic, these *kaffirs* were lucky to get a small room for their own church. Before my arrival, they hadn't had that much. In my first week I learned the term *kaffir* was one of the most offensive and insulting things to call an African—although it was used all the time, and probably for that reason. In Arabic, it meant 'infidel'. In Afrikaans it was worse, akin to "nigger." In today's free South Africa, the word is never uttered. But in this warped make-believe town, I would hear it spoken many times a day. Calling Africans *kaffirs* had become a way of life and a way of thinking. In a country where ethnic groups were identified by what they were *not,* where anyone without a white skin was officially designated "*non*-white" or "*non*-European", over time such diminished designations of others diminished the minds of those who used them. It produced a pathetically small worldview for an entire nation.

We started seeing this small worldview in our first month. Often, it went with a boast. It would happen like this: we would be invited for tea to an elegant white home and be shown the gorgeous roses the "lady of the house" had grown. *Some gardener, thought I.* At another time it might be the landscaping or the highly polished floors or the beautiful garden. Elsewhere, it might be a bridge, a building, or an entire country. In each instance, we were supposed to be impressed at how well the white man or woman had turned chaos into order. The hard work to do that had been done solely by black labor but nobody ever mentioned that. Africans did the work, whites got the credit. Everyone simply knew the African couldn't build anything without white supervision. But I had learned my first month in Africa that this country and this town had been built by the people marching by my chapel window. If I hadn't sufficiently appreciated the belief that God is always on the side of the poor and the oppressed, I did now. And I would learn that powerlessness has an innate goodness to it.

The sweating masses at the mine services grew beyond two hundred, and then beyond three hundred as they spilled onto the porch of our tiny worship space, crowding outside the only window to hear what was going on inside. African contract laborers at T.C.L. had never been given the chance to gather for Holy Communion in their own space with their own language and their own hymns, and I thought the problem of space was becoming delicious. But it was becoming an annoyance to Management. With the help of Vanny van der Merwe we got our hands on an abandoned house not far from the men's living quarters. I remember the fun of getting it ready. We took out a wall or two and erected an altar in one corner with an altar rail around it. The altar rail may have been a bad idea. The African men had never seen an altar rail and wanted to know why I had put a fence around the altar. They had a good point: altar rails originally were designed to keep the masses from coming too close to the holy hardware. I didn't have a good answer for this strange practice but we kept it anyway. In time the men became quite proud of the fence around their altar.

We named the new church after St. Cyprian, who was an early African martyr. I remember my shock to learn there was not one church in all the country named after an African. But then, why should I have been surprised? Nothing else in their own land was named for them. Those honors were reserved for the great white fathers who "discovered" the continent and "civilized" the place, men like Cecil John Rhodes. He even managed to get two countries named after him. Justice eventually prevailed and those names didn't survive independence. I doubt if many could locate the former Southern or Northern Rhodesia on a map or know the current names of those countries.[12]

My first year in the priesthood brought unimaginable surprises. One was named Cornelius, a man in his fifties who had worked at the mine for years. His home was just east of St. Mary's Mission in Ovamboland and he was known by all as a faithful son of Great St. Mary's Church. That gave him a lot of respect among the workers. He was a catechist, which meant he could teach the Catechism and the basics required for baptism. Even with his limited English he was a godsend. He had a self-effacing manner and by age could have been my father. With a humble reticence, he came to say that now that I was a priest, they were expecting me to "make a service" at the Compound, in three days' time—which happened to be Christmas, so this would be a major service. Not only that, but Cornelius expected me to conduct the Christmas Service in the local language, *chanting* all the usual parts. All this would take place in three days.

The Anglican mine workers were mainly from the Kwanyama Tribe, the largest of eight Ovambo tribes, and their language was Kwanyama. There had been no time to learn any of the language up until this point, nor had I even heard it spoken. It time, I would come to love their language, but not now. Now was a time for the quiet panic I was getting used to. This time I wondered if I would even survive my public trial by fire. It was some comfort to learn there was a Kwanyama Prayer Book and that most of the language was pronounced phonetically. With a dry mouth and a voice about to leave me, I tried to be cool and put the best face on what felt like a calamity-in-the-making. Before he left

---

[12] Northern Rhodesia became Zambia in 1964 and Southern Rhodesia became Zimbabwe in 1980.

Cornelius dropped one more surprise: he explained to me there was the usual practice of listening to Sacramental Confessions the night before a major festival, like Christmas. In this case, that meant hearing between 150 and 200 confessions, each one in Kwanyama. Could it get any worse?

Singing the Mass would be challenge enough but nothing like hearing a couple hundred confessions in a foreign language. The whole thing would have been impossible had not earlier missionaries come up with an ingenious but somewhat mindless system of doing it. At the back of the Kwanyama Prayer Book was a list of transgressions (aka sins), each with a brief interpretation in English. There is surely no end to the creative possibilities of human misbehavior, but the early missionaries trimmed it down to about 225 and gave each misdeed a number. *What an interesting way to deal with sin: confession by number!* The point was, of course, that the priest would have an approximate idea what the penitent was confessing. In time I came to recognize some of the hearty annuals and the top of the list was always Number 68: Adultery. That was no small wonder, given a teeming mass of virile men denied even conjugal visits from their wives for up to thirty six months. Understandably, the local brothels were popular. So was Number 68.

How the list worked was pretty crude. The penitent was supposed to peruse the list, jot down their transgressions by number and hand me the list as they knelt down. More than once it occurred to me the whole exercise could be a farce and I would be none the wiser. These guys could be picking their birth date for all I knew. It was only after sitting for hours in a sweltering room with the heavy smell of sweat and crotch and the mumble of an unintelligible language that my patience would wear thin and I would figure it *was* a farce. I thought the system was dumb, only a step away from confession by machine, if not mail order. But it was meaningful for thousands of Ovambo Anglicans. Who was I to judge what went on in the hearts of those who knelt before God and said they were sorry in the only way they had been taught? Seminary hadn't prepared me for this either. God had been doing a lot of strange things during the previous months, and I just had to believe he was doing something through all this mumbo jumbo. Many years later, the writings of Thomas Merton helped me make sense of it. Someplace he wrote that God honors sincere intentions as much as the deed, even when we don't quite follow through. At least it was a comforting thought. Merton's words spoke to those men and to me.

When I arrived at St. Cyprian's I was moved to see hundreds of men, living almost like slaves, turn that place into a happy church where they would dance and sing and do what Africans do to enjoy life. After a hard day's work, they celebrated that they were still together and life was okay. It was Africa at its best. But how was I to begin relating to these men who were so subservient and brow-beaten in the presence of a white man? How was I to begin working among these strange people to whom I was attracted? I sensed in my bones this was what had brought me to Africa and the language would be the key.

The Compound was where literally thousands of contract laborers lived and spent their time when not working a mile below ground. The Native Compound, as it was called, was disgusting to the African men in every way. Even its name was offensive. By the sixties, the word "native" was a pejorative and some whites used it for that reason. Physically, the Compound was an insult to human dignity. It consisted of dormitories with concrete beds but no mattresses, no interior walls or ceilings, no heating or air conditioning. Other amenities and mod coms included outdoor latrines, cold water showers, crowded living quarters and food that barely resembled a traditional diet. A mine worker's life was miserable for anyone not lucky enough to be born white.

The life was particularly hard because of the contract labor system. All African labor was strictly controlled by a State-owned organization known as South West Africa Native Labor Association (SWANLA) which had sole rights to recruit Africans from their homeland, sign them on for a two or three-year contract, and transport them to their place of work, decided by SWANLA. The mines were the major employers. Labor unions were illegal so living conditions, work hours and wages were never negotiated but fixed by the State in conjunction with industry. Wages were minimal. Sixty hours of labor in a week were rewarded with approximately twenty five dollars. Remarkably, many of the men managed to send a portion of their earnings home to help their families. Since wives and family were not permitted to visit their husbands, the system wreaked havoc on the families and communities left behind.

My first Saturday afternoon and evening was spent listening to unintelligible confessions for four hours. Exhausted, I fell into bed with a foreign Prayer Book and worked into the night trying to get ready for the next morning. The first problem would be pronunciation. The second would be trying to recognize the rubrics that were interspersed within the communion prayer. These are directions for the priest in the course of the Mass, usually printed in a margin or at the top or bottom of a page. In the Kwanyama book they appeared without italics along with the words of the prayer, identified only by parentheses.

With only a few hours of sleep, Christmas Day came much too fast, as did the events that followed. As it turned out, the light in the space we were using for Mass was so poor we had to rely on candles to read; and by the time we got to the communion prayer, my eyes were so clouded with sweat I could barely see the page. I couldn't tell what were rubrical directions from the prayers themselves. And so the consecration prayer sounded something like this: "*…who in the same night that Jesus was betrayed he took the break (and here the priest is to take the paten into his hands) and when he had given thanks he broke it (and here to break the bread)…*" and so on. I cringed realizing how stupid this sounded but could do nothing about it. I was in the Tower of Babel. When the Service was over, the men expressed only joy and gratitude for Christmas Mass, no matter how badly their new priest had mangled it. I was ready to drop, but they stayed and sang their hearts out, not wanting the four-hour ordeal to end.

The following day, Cornelius came around to the house. I was prepared for a discussion on how badly things had gone, but like the men, he was content with the outcome. Cornelius had simply come to hear if Father would be coming the next week "to make a Mess." Vowels in English not being his strong suit, what he meant to say was would I be coming to say Mass. I figured his mispronunciation was right on. "You bet," I replied, "and I promise a better Mess next week!" It did get better and in time I would come to love the language without a mess.

In time, we learned that our host and constant visitor, Vanny van der Merwe, was the Chief of Mine Security. Even knowing what I did about him, I was appalled to learn he was Big Brother looking over our shoulder, had his fingers in every pie, knew most of everybody's business, and saw ghosts of trouble where they didn't exist. We were like babes in the woods, typical Americans in those days who never gave a thought to security. We didn't lock our houses, often left keys in the car, and didn't worry about our kids being kidnapped. The only place I had ever heard the word security was in the name of my father's bank. We soon learned that security was a hot issue for the South African government. That should have come as no surprise.

Vanny flew under the radar of public information most of the time which was why we never knew what he did or when or where he did it. The work of security was for lesser mortals to know as little as possible what was going on. That was especially true in the Police State South West Africa had become, although no one was willing to admit it. Whites were watched over by the South African Police and the Special Branch, the bureau in charge of state security. Vanny worked hand in hand with both agencies and drove around town in a Landrover *bakkie* at all hours of the day and night. His practice of dropping in on us didn't stop when we moved into the house provided by the diocese. He tried to make his visits seem natural and relaxed, frequently bringing vegetables or meat or the occasional bottle of Limousin Brandy, the cheap well stock of most bars. Then he would chatter on and on about anything and everything and always knew a lot about what was going on. That was helpful at times, unsettling at others. I began to wonder how much information he took away from those visits with us and to whom it went. Year later I would find out. Maybe Chairman Banghart had reason to be worried after all. He probably knew Vanny van der Merwe well.

Vanny was always in a hurry, always with a cigarette, nervous about everything. He smoked Peter Stuyvesants. They came in a long flat box, which was the most prominent thing about him: the box was too big for his pocket, so he carried it about like a purse. He was close to a chain smoker, but in those days we didn't think much about that. Everyone was going up in smoke. Years later, I observed a similar pattern of heavy smoking in Israel, probably because that nation's nerves were also constantly on edge from political turmoil. But the nervous twitch in South West Africa, as in South Africa, was self-inflicted by the racial system they had devised. *Apartheid* created fear in everyone. In time, it became a fear of mythic proportions on both side of the color bar: non-whites perceived whites as heartless racist brutes while whites were terrified the non-whites were ready to rape, kill and plunder if given the slightest chance. Smoking relieved the tension for a little while. So did drinking.

I kept myself busy with a congregation that didn't want much attention, so on many afternoons we would sit with the van der Merwes and have sundowners. When I first read Alexandra Fuller's story about growing up in Rhodesia, "Don't Let's Go to the Dogs Tonight," it seemed the perfect title for colonial life in Africa, for so often whites did go to the dogs when the sun hung low and the day got mellow. So many whites seemed to lose their way and just wandered through life, living a comfortable existence made possible because of black help. Drinking always seemed to accentuate whatever there was to celebrate or complain about. Sitting on the verandah, with ice, booze, and ashtrays brought out by 'the boy' and getting bombed was the order of most days. For Vanny and Peggy, it was a nightly routine. It made it difficult for us since we were guests in their home and didn't drink that much or feel free to invade their kitchen to prepare our own dinner. The dinner hour became a dilemma that grew more uncomfortable as time went on.

The laxity of the whites would change dramatically when independence came to South West Africa in 1991. Gone would be the racial system of *apartheid* and people would have to decide what they really believed in. Those who supported the former way of handling race relations would leave and immigrate elsewhere. Those who believed whites and non-whites could live and work together would stay and try to make it work. And then there would be those who were committed to neither side who would wait to see which way the wind would blow. I have often wondered what happened to van der Merwe when the day of reckoning came. I doubt if he remained there long. Vanny wasn't mean-spirited but he was a typical Afrikaner who honestly believed that Africans were inferior to whites and would always need parental supervision. "They are like children" he would say to us over and over with all sincerity. While they wouldn't admit it, whites with attitudes like that had no intention of ever letting those "children" grow up. Africa was better off without them.

Before independence, white immigrants to Southern Africa were an interesting study. Many came from humble origins in Europe or Great Britain and upon arrival found themselves several notches up the social scale. They were suddenly masters simply by virtue of skin color. For a pittance, servants were available to do their bidding in home and garden, shop and office. They might even be able to have a driver. Most of those immigrants could quickly figure out what had improved their standing and dutifully became staunch supporters of the ruling National Party. Others joined the United Party which tacitly supported *apartheid* but didn't say so officially. The United Party was an opposition party that in practice didn't stand for much but believed in going along to get along. But not all immigrants were influenced by either party. One outstanding example were those who came from Holland in the sixties. They came at the invitation of the South African government as part of a scheme to bolster the white population. A generous financial incentive was provided to drum up European immigration. The logic was basically what better place to recruit immigrants than Holland, the historical homeland of the Voortrekkers.[13] So off to Holland they went with their offer.

But a funny thing happened along the way. The Afrikaners were apparently unaware that modern day Hollanders no longer think as their forefathers did and the Netherlands had become a liberal society, noted for their strong opinions and not afraid to say so. Almost upon arrival the Dutch immigrants began speaking out about *apartheid* and the narrow society they found in South Africa. Many became some of the harshest critics of the government. They did not make congenial citizens and the Holland import scheme was quickly dropped. Some years later the entire immigration plan was quietly abandoned. It was a whacky idea in the first place for South African whites to think they could balance the population odds of a black-white ratio of almost twenty-to-one by importing more whites. Even multiplying like rabbits they wouldn't have caught up. But alas, the alternative idea of an equal society living side by side with their black neighbors was simply unthinkable.

Peggy van der Merwe was an enigmatic figure with the makings of a staunch alcoholic. When she was sober, she worked as a bookkeeper in a local office, although we were never sure where that was. She didn't talk about that side of her life, or any side really. She was born Margaret Ann deVilliers and grew up in the Western Cape of South Africa. The deVilliers were originally French Huguenots, a small group of Protestant refugees who had settled in the Western Cape in the seventeenth century. They joined with the Dutch and other European settlers and in time produced the Afrikaner people. Peggy was a nervous little thing who probably smoked and drank herself to an early death. We suspected Vanny made life hard for her when we weren't looking. People try to put on all sorts of airs and good behavior around clergy, and this household was no exception. The minimal church influence Vanny and Peggy had was from their childhood in a strict Dutch Reformed background that forbade things like smoking, drinking, and

---

[13] The Voortrekkers, Afrikaans for 'pioneer', were the earliest Dutch settlers who left the Cape Colony in the 1830s and 1840s to move (trek) into the interior of what is now South Africa.

having a good time. Vanny and Peggy were good at all three, although the third, not so much. I was a *predicant* (Afrikaans for minister), so they never quite knew what to do with me when they were in their cups. When they got smashed, which happened with some regularity, they got into fierce arguments that often ended in physical fights. They were careful never to hang one of those on in our presence but we frequently saw the evidence the next morning.

Out of this stormy union came three kids, Margaret, Conrad and Aiden, all unlikely names for Afrikaner children. They were all under fifteen at the time, shadowy shy little people, uncertain about mother and afraid of father. Like most children who learn to adjust, the van der Merwe kids knew how to adapt to whatever was ailing the family which was invariably too much booze and too little affection. All of this made for too many awkward moments for our happy little family, with few places for escape.

During our time in Tsumeb, more than once I had to deal with situations totally beyond my competence. That's when my Dean's early admonition that I should get some experience before going to Africa came back to haunt me. Everything was new, and almost everything was a challenge. Marge Perreira was one of them. She was mother to a large Portuguese family and a faithful member of the flock. Her husband was a cheerful soul who worked for the mine. The Portuguese were known for being able to grow vegetables and on the side they grew fabulous veggies which were always in great demand. They might also have been a bit prone to superstition. One day Marge Perreira 'phoned me up me in great distress. She reported that pictures and crosses were flying off the walls and cruising about the house, there was mayhem in the household, and the family was scared witless. So was I when she told me. Marge wanted me to come right over and restore order. She said there were also apparitions of ghosts and willowy things that sashayed through the house at all hours of the day and night, could I please get rid of those too? A thousand thoughts went through my mind: *Oh yes mam, I'll be right over. We covered exorcism extensively in my priestly training, and I'm fully competent to deal with this. Surely they didn't expect their brand new priest to deal with this??* But they did. Marge thought the Fathers of the Church could do anything and it didn't matter that seminary preparation never gave the necessary training or that I was still very wet behind the ears. Exorcism was never offered, even in the more exotic elective courses of my senior year, nor ever in the history of the seminary. I was terrified, but my wife was a pillar of strength in calming me down—since she wasn't planning on being there. This was something I knew I had to handle by myself, or at least appear to handle, but exorcism was a subject I knew nothing about and the Church had wisely avoided it for a very long time. Now I knew why.

Marge Perreira would not be put off and wanted me to come right away, making it sound like a matter of life and death. I expected to find the house in shambles, but there was little evidence that things had been flying around or rearranging themselves on the walls. Marge had cleaned things up but swore bad things were happening and insisted I make the place safe for habitation. The Perreiras were not a drinking family or I would have suspected it all came out of a bottle. Marge was so worked up; I was too but but couldn't chicken out now. With a degree of phony bravado, there I was, dressed in black cassock and clutching a big cross, water pot in one hand and cross in the other. I at least knew Holy Water has, for centuries, been used in shady situations so I improvised a few prayers to bless it and hoped God would do the rest. I had neither Prayer Book nor Priest's Manual to instruct me on what to do next, beyond my whimpering beginning. (This was the first but not the last time I would gladly have traded my clerical collar for a medical stethoscope).

With cross and Holy Water we marched from room to room. I had a momentary flashback to a kid's TV program that brought a fleeting moment of humor…*I'm a brave, brave mouse, I go marching through the house and I'm not afraid of anything…"* Like hell I wasn't. I sprinkled each room with Holy Water, and with stiffest upper lip in the name of God ordered the ghosts and goblins to be gone. We concluded with a few prayers and a blessing for the family and I departed, hoping they hadn't noticed my shirt and cassock drenched in sweat. The next day Marge reported things had remained calm and she was ever so grateful. *Deo Gratias!* In years to come I learned that if the intention is good,

God may honor that more than the deed—especially when we don't know what we're doing.

We had a papaya tree in our backyard, known throughout the British Empire as a 'paw paw' tree. Having never tasted the fruit, and after getting over the shock of finding it filled with black seeds, we became quite fond of it. A popular myth circulating at the time was that the fruit of the paw paw could enhance fertility. It was probably a prank for unsuspecting Americans, but in our early years we did eat a lot of it and produced a lot of kids. We figured the one in our backyard was a lazy male because it didn't produce fruit. One day, three-year-old Karin came home from nursery school with the preposterous story that if you kicked a male tree at the base, it would change its sex and bear fruit. It sounded ridiculous, but we thought what could it hurt, and it would make our little girl happy to be taking her tale so seriously. Probably to placate her and out of dumb curiosity, we sheepishly gathered at the errant paw paw tree for the great operation. There was much discussion about where to kick it and how hard and how many times, like this was some kind of backyard science. Following that mindless discussion, our daughter gave it her best three-year-old kick right at the base and looked up, expecting an instant fix. The tree never produced fruit, but it produced a good family story for years to come.

Then there was the tree in our front garden that appeared dead upon our arrival. We had moved in late winter when the garden was pretty dormant, and this tree looked totally dried up and finished. On that basis I took a dislike to it and figured it had to come out but never got around to chopping it down. Good thing, too: when spring came a few months later, this awful looking tree began to flower with masses of orchid-like flowers. Within a few more weeks, it was one of the most beautiful trees I had ever seen. I learned it was a member of the vast Acacia family, *Acacia cuspidifolia* by name, indigenous to Western Australia and commonly known as the 'wait-a-while' tree. That lesson was almost lost on me. Having grown up with trees and orchards, I should have known better than to pronounce judgment on a tree in winter. Now I try not to pronounce judgment at all. Maybe that was the point of the experience—and people are of greater value than trees.

Roofs in rural Africa were generally thatched or corrugated iron. Our house had a huge corrugated iron roof that made a lot of noise when it rained, but it was a perfect watershed. At one corner of the house stood an enormous corrugated iron tank to collect rainwater run-off. Such tanks were common throughout the colonial world, especially in Africa. This one was seven feet high, at least eight feet in diameter, and could hold over a thousand gallons of water. Everyone saved rainwater because the town water from the mine had a foul taste from a heavy lead content. The tank water tasted even worse because it hadn't been cleaned out in the fifteen years it had been there. In fact, all that trickled out of the spigot was rotten leaves and sludge. I had never cleaned a rain tank in my life but figured it was time to try; so squeezing through a small hole at the top, I dropped onto the unknown tank bottom. It was dark and smelly and the heat was extreme. I landed in several inches of muck and swamp that contained lizards, frogs, and a harmless water snake. After straining to shovel most of the muck out the little hole over my head, I realized I had a greater problem than the cleaning: I had no way to get out. The hole in the top was too high to pull myself up and through. Exhausted, beaten and smelling like a swamp, I banged on the side until my wife came with a kitchen stool. It was my first and last time to clean a rain tank.

And then there was the kitchen stove. It sat in one corner of the kitchen like a big blast furnace, looking menacing. It was beige with hospital green trim, not very attractive but apparently the top of the line for its day. We had seen versions of it in the homes we had visited. It had a large vent pipe going straight up and other pipes going in and out to heat water for the kitchen and the rest of the house. It looked like a real Rube Goldberg, a home-on-the-range stove that worked pretty well once it was stoked. Stoking it was a major operation and downdrafts were notorious for blowing smoke in your face. Once the fire was going it was an inferno that puffed and roared and would occasionally get too hot to use. It was amazing it could produce any great cooking at all, but it did—especially pastry.

If things like microwaves had been around they would have seemed like space age gadgets where we were. Most of the time we were a lot closer to the edge of civilization than we realized.

Chapter Four

Further Into the Wild

Before the end of the second year, things in Tsumeb had reached an impasse. My wife wasn't happy, I wasn't happy, and living in a white mining town wasn't why we had come to Africa. The bishop knew all of this; our situation had produced what might now be called the perfect storm. He needed a Mission Director in Ovamboland, hundreds of miles northward, into the bush, and he knew I had found my niche working with the African people. The appointment was made and the date was set; we would leave Tsumeb the end of the year, only months away. We would be moving into the traditional land of the Ovambo people, where the few whites who lived there were missionaries and government officials. Living conditions would be primitive, generally described as living "in the bush."

Our moving looked like something out of Tobacco Road. We had purchased a ton-and-a-half pickup (*bakkie*) and loaded it with the remainder of our worldly goods, rakishly draped with canvas and rope. It looked funny but it was a happy gypsy caravan. Once again, we were heading into the unknown, up a long, rough, dirt trail, several hundred miles into new country. I loved the prospect, and Mondi had to admit a degree of excitement. Getting there involved driving through the Etosha Pan, a huge game reserve that contained every variety of Southern Africa's big game and millions of pink flamingos when there was water in the pan. Onward we drove, through thick dust clouds as other vehicles passed us, further into the African wilderness as vegetation changed from savannah to sparse forests of huge trees and ant hills and African huts and villages.

Moving was cause for much joy. We would be leaving a white-dominated mining town that had its own complexes and problems, to live and work with the African people that had theirs. But to be given the opportunity to head up a huge mission enterprise that extended throughout dozens of villages in Ovamboland was a dream challenge. It felt like the sky was the limit.

We slipped into St. Mary's Mission late in the afternoon with little notice. It was another welcome that didn't really exist and we were getting used to that happening to us. The dwindled missionary staff had suffered one calamity after another, morale was down, and they were apathetic to the arrival of a much-too-young Mission Director who probably left most of them doubting if I could bring new life to the place. I wondered too, but didn't mind trying. I had been given free rein to build up a mission field that was broken in substance and morale. Most of the remaining missionaries were British nurses, had been there for years and had developed a hard crust that comes from surviving in the bush as long as they had. By contrast, we were young, unimpressive, untried Americans who knew nothing of these missionaries' lives of dedicated service. The only ones who were happy to see Americans march in were the Africans who had grown tired and disillusioned of the steady but plodding British. They were ready for change and hoped we would bring it. I was constantly aware we were of a younger generation, young enough to be children to some of the old crusts, to whom my appointment as Director didn't mean much; the only saving grace was that I was a priest of the Church and the British still had high regard for that. But I was acutely aware that even that had a downside: I had been ordained less than two years!

The Mission had a long-established routine that was easy to fit into. It all centered around the Great Church of St. Mary, patron saint of the Mission. I have always loved the early morning and this place gave plenty of it. That was a time to experience this ancient continent waking up: the sounds, smells, and early morning freshness were like no other.

Our big thatched house sat in the middle of the Mission, a stone's throw from both the school and hospital. A little farther away, up beyond old Macdonald's workshop and on a path that led to the Angola border, was Great St. Mary's Church, the spiritual heartbeat of the mission.

The border between South West Africa and Angola didn't exist in the minds of the Africans but it had been proclaimed a border by the white man of earlier generations. In reality, the Kwanyama tribe extended further into Angola than into South West Africa, and hundreds of thousands of friends and family lived across the border. Many borders in Africa, such as this one, are the remains of the colonial "Scramble for Africa' that had taken place in the 1880s and that led to a frenzy of European colonizing. The ensuing borders of over fifty countries have become today's political reality, and it would be virtually impossible to return to traditional boundaries (although efforts to do so continue to be made now and then).[14]

Khaki shorts were the dress of the day for every white male in Southern Africa. I was no exception, but priests covered them with cassocks when "on duty". Thus clad, I made my way to the Great Church every morning, where I wrestled with an hour of silence before services began. In those days, my expectations of a great insight happening during the silence were unrealistically high; when that didn't happen, the long silence was made longer, but at least I didn't hear busy feet outside, marching to work in the white world. Nevertheless, the battle with silence continued. After the silence came the Morning Office, which we called 'Matins' in seminary. Great St. Mary's was of enormous size and could easily hold a thousand on a major feast day. In the dark of early morning it seemed cavernous, almost overwhelming. I was generally the first to arrive unless Seminary got there first. Seminary was the self-appointed verger, so nicknamed because of his habit of hanging around church and seminary. On another shore we called them

---

[14] Eritrea is a current example of a realignment in which it has been recognized as its own country, formerly a part of Ethiopia. The even newer nation of South Sudan is another.

church rats. Alas, even in Africa churches collected people who liked to hang around the holy hardware. It seemed like an awful bore to me.

A bit shy mentally, Seminary was utterly dependable with unnoticed tasks like lighting the candles, preparing the altar, and ringing the bell. Before there was a bell, he beat on an old railway tie. The clang made a god-awful noise, so the bell was a great improvement. It was a simple church bell that sat atop Great St. Mary's, at least sixty feet in the air, put there by a devoted contractor from Missouri who gave several years of his life to work in Africa. He had a passion for helping others but was happiest doing it in the Third World. He also had a passion for finding bells and sending them to missions all over the world. He'd find old locomotives or decommissioned ships and somehow manage to get their bells. Seminary made the bell and the ringing of it larger than life. It became such a symbol of power that even the clergy dared not touch it. Like an annoying rooster, it would announce to the world the sun was rising at six thirty sharp and so should everyone else. Seminary hoped his noise would get people to church but that didn't happen. The hospital and school staff were encouraged to attend Mass but that didn't always happen either. Major feast days were the exception when almost everyone showed up.

Seminary didn't invent the practice of making noise at six-thirty, that practice had been around a long time. It was the basis for keeping time in the wilderness. Whether the sun called forth the bell or the other way 'round, all watches and clocks were reset each day at six-thirty when they heard the bell. That meant the sun was on the horizon. Outside the Mission compound, life went on as it had for centuries, without time pieces and the fuss of keeping them. All of Africa knew time couldn't be kept anyway, it was only the whites who insisted on trying. Africans had devised a much simpler way of doing it: time was indicated by pointing where the sun would be at an appointed time and saying *etango apa* ("the sun will be here"). It was simple and foolproof and never needed winding or resetting. Showing up at *etango apa* was another thing. Many years later, while living in New York City a second time, I was escorting a visiting African around the city. Feeling rather proud of myself for mastering a few of the tricks of the subway, off we went, African guest dragging in tow. Hopping the IND local to another station, we raced to catch the BMT crosstown and then ran for another to get us to Times Square. After three or four races to catch different trains, we finally settled down on the Uptown Express. Out of breath, I muttered something like "whew, we've just saved eight minutes." My African guest thought for a moment and then quietly muttered in return, "and what shall we do with the eight minutes?" He still knew time couldn't be saved.

Europeans in general found the Great Church of St. Mary as uncomfortable as hell is alleged to be. Like the ancient cathedrals, it had no chairs or pews and people sat on the floor, which was a sure test of posture. Africans could sit for hours with legs straight out and backs erect. They could do the same thing on their haunches. Europeans were putty by comparison, caving into wilting postures that needed back rests or recliners. Benches were available in the Side Chapel and a few of those had backs, only slightly more comfortable than the floor. But the benches were few in number and usually reserved for Morning and Evening Prayer in the Chapel. If a bench was available, kneeling was done from behind, leaning over it with head up or down. Up was uncomfortable but would keep you awake, down was comfortable but conducive to sleep. Down was frequently my favorite position.

Old MacDonald and his wife were usually next to make their way to the church. Mac was trained in England as a tool and die maker and could make or fix anything. He maintained all the vehicles and if a part wasn't available he would often make it himself. He was a mainstay to the place. Bowed of legs and with a gait that was recognizable at a hundred yards, his Yorkshire accent sounded like he'd just come off the boat, though he'd been there for years. His wife, who was South African, doubted he had an accent until one day a helper came to her door with the message from Mac that *"Tatekulu wants a boo-kit"*. Hearing an African speak with an unmistakable Yorkshire accent, she realized he was asking for a bucket as only her husband could say it. A man of deep but private piety, Mac knew more stories and anecdotes than anyone else. Another one old enough to be my father, I was perpetually embarrassed that he unfailingly called me "Father." I always tried to get to church before Mac, like he was secretly keeping attendance—which he was not. How I struggled with rules in those days. I knew Mac expected an example from me as the much-too-young Mission Director, but I was never quite sure what the example was supposed to be. Getting to church early was probably on the list. It didn't help that the British had a strange way of going slim with compliments and eschewing praise, especially for Americans. I sometimes wondered if they may have thought it was their bloody empire and Americans were Johnnie-come-lately interlopers. In any case they seemed a hard lot to please and I never knew if I did.

After the Macdonalds arrived, various Mission Staff would drift in…the white nursing staff, mainly British with a South African or two, a few teachers, a couple of priests, one American and one English, some of the Mission workers, and the parish priest. The latter was Father Gabriel, one of only four African priests. He was like a wise old owl around the place, saw a lot and said little. His assistant was far less wise and a little less regular in church, probably owing to a serious drinking problem which eventually killed him.

When the sun was on the horizon, the big bell would ring and Matins would begin, always conducted in English by one of the priests, as if no one else knew how to read or pray. That was another tradition around the place that went back to the days when no one else *did* know how to read or pray.[15] All that changed in later years, when every service was in the vernacular. Mass followed Matins with the ringing of the Angelus. That's when Seminary really got his kicks—a total of twenty-one bells for the Angelus. My wife would usually sneak in at that point and kneel beside me. Those were special moments when we felt connected and grounded in our calling to be there. We were contented in our passion to do good and serve and had a strong sense we were meant to be doing that at St. Mary's Mission. Every day was

---

[15] A favorite tale was told of the first Christian convert when learning how to pray. In the early days he and Mac were crossing the Etosha Pan Game Reserve in an ox wagon and had to pitch camp in lion country. During the night when the growling lions were coming closer he was heard to utter the frantic prayer, "Oh lions, save us from God!"

a new adventure and most of them began on our knees. Our life in Ovamboland would bring treasured memories together, including the birth of three of our children.

Once churched up, one of the great rituals of the morning came next: breakfast at the Mallory table. It was a big table, filled with our large family and often visitors of one sort or another. Breakfast was solely in the hands of Tate (pronounced "Tah-Tay", meaning sir, father or mister) Augustine. Tate had learned to cook in South Africa as a contract worker and breakfast was his specialty. He was in his mid-fifties but seemed older. We often referred to him as Old Tate Augustine because he looked older than his years. With a head of grey, he was stable as a rock and almost as immovable. He was also known to be grumpy on some days, as reported by our kids. They had a knack of getting his goat and always seemed to know where it was tied up. When that happened, we would hear him shout *"to dengua nena!"* That's when they knew to run or the big wooden spoon would come down. I'm not sure he ever used it on them but it was a great deterrent.

Breakfast usually consisted of bacon and eggs, crispy potato pancakes, toast, marmalade and coffee. The kids usually had hot cereal— "porridge" the British called it. We called it oatmeal. Sometimes it was mealie meal, best known to Americans as cream of wheat. Most of our food came from hundreds of miles away on a lumbering behemoth known as the railway bus, operated by the South African Railways. Carrying few passengers and much freight, it was nothing more than a huge truck, prone to break downs because of the impossible and often impassable roads. That's when things got really screwed up. When supplies didn't arrive, kitchens and households went without, which could mean almost anything. My wife managed the ordering of food and supplies, kept inventory and calculated when to order, all the while keeping a gentle eye on Augustine. He in turn kept a keen eye on the big wood burning stove that cooked it all. Sometimes, he would get it so hot it glowed as it sat hidden away in the corner of our mud floored kitchen.

The morning hours were filled with a variety of tasks, no two days alike. Mondi taught our three eldest using The Calvert Series, which was a home-schooling system developed around the turn of the century for missionary families. It included the three R's, Greek mythology, history, and simple lessons of life. Amazingly, my wife also found time to manage the Mission books, supervise the general staff kitchen, and be *Memekulu* ("great mother") to a multitude of people and causes. So much depended on her that her role sometimes seemed larger than life. Without complaint she pulled it off with amazing grace, long before we knew a song by that name. There were memorable exceptions, like the morning Tate Augustine arrived to find an anthill in the middle of the kitchen floor. In one night, ants had built a twenty four inch anthill in the dirt floor. It would have grown a lot taller had we not attacked it. That involved finding the queen's nest which took most of the next day and digging up most of the floor. Unless the queen was found, there would be another anthill. And another and another.

Slightly greater crises came when the kids' nanny didn't show up but those days were rare. Julia was in her late teens and a mainstay of the household. We thought of her as part of the family. One year she went with us on a family holiday to the southern coast of Angola, to a little town known as Mocamedes. It was probably the greatest adventure of her life. She had never been more than a few miles from home and didn't know the sea existed. Coming upon the Atlantic Ocean, she got very quiet, about as overcome as Africans ever are with nature. She was speechless for minutes as she looked at this immense body of water. Finally, she burst her silence when she saw an Angolan Navy cruiser anchored offshore. Overwhelmed and a little embarrassed she said, "Oh Tate, how long are its legs?" Charming as it was, I realized it was a perfectly understandable question. I forgot what I said, but it was a moment when two cultures touched each other, ever so gently.

Mornings usually went in many directions, and I loved the challenge of a lot going on. I'm not sure if my excitement was from an interest in many things or a lack of discipline to focus on one. Old MacDonald, on the other hand, being precisely trained, was meticulous and thorough in his work. That meant he was calculating and slow but his work was always near perfect. I saw the need for less perfection and more speed, so my way of doing things probably annoyed him, but he was too polite to say so. I was happiest when building, teaching, or writing.

Every morning, life stopped abruptly at eleven for a great British tradition that spanned the Empire. It was almost as sacred as the Crown. The British called it elevenses, the rest of us called it morning tea (or coffee). This daily ritual took place in the Single Mess where the single staff gathered for meals, relaxation, and general ventilation. Life-and-death communications took place at elevenses, such as who got mail and who didn't, local gossip, and who was out of sorts with whom. It was a pressure valve for single people living in a remote situation with a lot of work and not much diversion. The only contact with the rest of the world was by shortwave radio once a week and that was intended primarily for the hospital, so the radio was firmly under the epaulets of the hospital matron, who brooked no nonsense over its use.

A few weeks after we arrived, my wife nearly came unhinged at elevenses. It was a Tuesday and someone casually announced there had been a killing at the top end of the Mission near the Church. Was anyone interested in going to see it? *Good God*, she thought, *a killing on the Mission and is anyone interested in seeing it! As casually as that they talk about killing?* She was on her way into shock when it was explained the message meant the local meat market was open for business. If it was Tuesday, there was a killing which meant the local butcher had slaughtered an ox, pig or goat and was selling the meat under a big old tree near the Church. And what a meat market it was: filet mignon sold for ten cents a pound! Augustine would visit the meat market and fill a bucket with fine meat for less than a buck. That was because the locals said the filet mignon cuts were soft meat and not good; a tough chew was considered far superior. They figured they should know about meat: their tribal name, Kwanyama, meant "meat eater."

The day took another abrupt halt at noon with the ringing of the Angelus. Earlier missionaries of the High Church Party had instilled that discipline in everyone, sort of. All activity came to a stop as kids in classrooms and nurses on their rounds parroted the words of the Angelus while the bell tolled. For everyone else, it was just a chance to stop work. In theory, the Angelus was a good thing: rung thrice daily, it framed the day and reminded us why we were there by honoring the Blessed Virgin

Mary for whom the Mission was named. Over time, it became a rote exercise with little meaning. Too much religion can do that.

At sundown, most of the missionary staff and a few locals would make their way back up to Great St. Mary's for Evening Prayer. It was a nice way to end the day. I had learned to appreciate the beauty of Evensong in seminary, where it was sung daily. Occasionally, there had been a hymn, the words of which now took on a deeper meaning than they ever had:

> *"As o'er each continent and island the dawn leads on another day; the voice of prayer is never silent, nor dies the strain of praise away."*

It was hard to imagine America yawning awake as our sun was setting. Sometimes it all seemed terribly romantic…but not usually.

Since there was no electricity, evening brought the unwanted task of lighting gas lanterns. They were unpredictable and temperamental and ran on kerosene, which the British called 'paraffin'. Those lamps had their own demons; the trick was to get the pressure right and the flame settled down without breaking the mantle or the whole thing would go up in flames. Only old Mac seemed to have a way with the lamp gods. Legend had it that a careless missionary once lit a lamp too close to the thatch and destroyed both roof and hut in an instant. True or not, it was enough to scare most of us into immobility when we had trouble with our lamps. We were glad Mac was there.

When day was done, bath time came for the Mallory brood. It was another favorite time of the day because it was something we did together. It involved a little hike down to the tiny bath house which stood alone and left quite a few things to be desired. It was the only bath facility for the staff and consisted of one tub in a space hardly big enough for the tub. Hot water came from a barrel propped up outside and heated over an open fire, forty-four gallons of hot water for fifteen to eighteen people. It usually meant one modest tub of water for our kids which taught us about conserving natural resources long before it was in vogue.

Though conditions were primitive, I always felt we were the lucky ones to be living where we were. The vast population outside the Mission compound had the daily chore of fetching a day's supply of water, sometimes from miles away. Much of the Third World still lives with the harsh reality of spending many hours a day searching for firewood and drinkable water.

Our gang had fond memories of some great family reads at bedtime, like "The Lion, the Witch and the Wardrobe" and the rest of the Narnia Series; "Charlie and the Chocolate Factory" and "James and the Giant Peach". Nightly story time had those magical moments when we could sense bright, young imaginations at work, wonderfully quiet during that hour. Rarely did a little one nod off to sleep. We often marveled at the sheer wonder of raising a family deep in the wilds of Africa and loving almost every moment of it. It was a good life.

As the lamps went out around the Mission, the day ended as silently as it began, but with one difference: we usually heard dancing and singing in the distance. It was either the boys and girls in their boarding school hostels or the drumbeat from a neighboring kraal. Whatever its source, we knew it was the rhythm of a people we had come to love. Some of that rhythm was now within us too, for we had discovered Africa's great Spirit, the One that connects drumbeats and Angelus bells and good night stories. It connects us all, the world over. Sometimes places like Africa understand that best.

Africa grabbed us in powerful ways, but it took a while. Soon after arriving I remember thinking I would never learn all the names and faces. My wife thought everyone looked alike—all were black, all had black woolly hair, noses, with mouths and faces different from what we had known all our lives. In time, each would become as unique to us as Caucasian features. Eventually, this strange new continent made its mark that became indelible. I have often wondered what it was that made a lasting impression that would become a part of us. Undoubtedly some of it was the African mystique, the *'elan vitale'* or life force, anthropologists speak of. Africa has a mysterious life force that cannot be known unless experienced.

Physically, Africa is a vast continent of jungles, rivers, mountains, and deserts with over five thousand ethnic groups (once called 'tribes'), some barely recorded in human history, and almost that many linguistic dialects. Today, with fifty-five countries and capitals, it is sociologically the most complex continent on earth. The shameful parts of the colonial past have, at times, been romanticized to attract tourists, an attraction we also experienced. Closer to our hearts, we found a simplicity and childlikeness in the people that was refreshing and endearing. The young were eager to absorb anything from the West, the elderly a bit more cautious. In those days, if it came from the United States of America it was assumed to be both good and necessary. If only they had known. In time, Africa would make its own determination, not always in our favor. The drive for independence brought its own excitement as the winds of change blew through Africa. The decade of the sixties was a heady time to be in Africa and we felt the energy of nation-building long before 'regime change' became the new colonialism. As we learned of a complex variety of spirit-world beliefs, it made Africa's mystique even richer.

In dealing with the spirituality of Africa, missionaries have probably done their worst and I unwittingly had a part in that. With no real understanding of African Traditional Religion I followed in a long line of Anglican clergy who basically imported an alien approach to the spirit world. It was called Christianity, and our particular franchise was Anglican, known as Episcopalian in the United States. It was 'high church" and it provided a performance Africans seemed to love. Such tradition was rich with colorful vestments, incense, bells and seasonal pageantry that had entertained peasants and royalty for centuries.

But alas, when the tradition arrived, it was totally foreign to African Traditional Religion and hostile to its practice.

By contrast, African Traditional Religion was more a way of life than a religion, not observed by worship or gathering for services, saying prayers or singing hymns. African Traditional Religion was not threatened by the arrival of Christianity, it was the other way 'round. Unfortunately, with no understanding of ancient traditions, the early missionaries were quick to condemn and ban. In time we would discover that it was a ban that didn't work—only the missionaries convinced themselves that it had.

Along with their religion, missionaries brought other imports as well: vestments, clothing, books, household items, diets, eating utensils, and all manner of customs from their home lands. We didn't drag too much of that paraphernalia ourselves, not out of virtue but because we didn't have much to drag. My load consisted of a lot of books. It could seem like missionaries set out to be as different as they possibly could from the local culture. Paul Tillich once posed the question whether it had to be Christ *and* culture or Christ *against* culture. In retrospect, I see no reason why Christianity couldn't have embraced the local culture and had a more gracious attitude than it had with traditional religion, but that bridge of understanding was passed long ago.

When the first missionaries arrived, it was widely assumed the African had a pagan spirituality with little morality. That was a self-serving assumption that was radically changed by the experience of World War II. It happened largely on the battlefields of Europe and North Africa when, for the first time, Africans saw their white masters experience fear and suffer pain just as they did. There they learned that the white man and his religion were no longer invincible. As they saw hideous deeds perpetrated in the name of the missionaries' religion, they learned that bigotry and hatred existed in the countries from whence they came; in short, the African discovered the white man had tribal hatreds and wars just like he had. Following the war, that experience began to change the equation between blacks and whites in Africa. Africans no longer accepted the unquestioned authority they had naively given whites in an earlier day. Young Africans were finding their own dignity and voice. Nelson Mandela was one of those young men in South Africa. In South West Africa it was men like Sam Nujomo and Toivo ja Toivo; Nujomo would eventually become the first President and Toivo would serve in many ministerial positions.

There were monthly visits to the "outstations", dozens of them which consisted of tiny villages to larger settlements, most of them isolated in bush and forest. Those visits served a variety of purposes: to take the meager monthly payroll to catechists, bush teachers and nurses, sometimes to barter for thatching reeds and grass or to check on a local well-digging project, but always to celebrate the Sacrament which they would not otherwise have because no priests were available. One of my favorite stops was an outstation roughly thirty miles east of St. Mary's, a village known as Epinga. I liked it because of the beauty that surrounded it, roughly a half mile from the Angola border, neat, vibrant, with bush school, clinic and church. Stephen, the catechist, looked after the place and in time he would become a priest. His presence in the village was never disputed, always respected. Half of his family and half of the community lived across the border in Angola, so he knew that part of the geography well. One day he brought a young herd boy to me, a tall, lanky, shy lad who told me his name was Johannes Muafangejo. No one could have known it then, but this simple John-the-herd-boy was destined to become a national hero of the art world. As he watched his father's cattle, he spent his time carving things like knives, egg cups, plates, figures, candle sticks, you name it. After they were carved, he would burn designs into them with a the edge of a hot knife. He had an artistic enthusiasm that was more than the average lad sitting by the herd, trading carving for boredom. John seemed different.

John was different: he had a passion for his primitive art, and in time we talked about getting more training for him. But there would be problems for he would have to travel into South Africa for that training. Africans were not allowed to leave the country to study, even in South Africa, but with a degree of naive optimism we looked for art schools in South Africa and found a Lutheran School at a place known as Rorke's Drift, in faraway Natal. Getting all of his traveling papers in order and then praying for a miracle, we were given one. John finally boarded the big bus that came rumbling into the Mission twice a month, and off he went. It amazed me how comfortably he settled into his new environment where there was no common language other than English, which was not John's long suit. But he took to his studies with enthusiasm and became one of their foremost students, excelling in primitive lino-cut prints. What made John's work different was that each piece had a social comment, each one spoke to the political situation of its time, and God knows, there was plenty to speak to. Every one of John's now-famous lino cuts make a powerful socio/political comment. Tragically, he died young at Odibo during the struggle for independence, but his name lives on in Namibia. He is honored in the National Art Gallery and on a Namibian stamp.

Africa began asserting the legitimacy of its traditional religion in the fifties. This began in Ghana and Kenya in historic universities that produced scholars like John Mbiti, who became an early authority on African Traditional Religion. In the years to come, I would meet John when we moved to Uganda and he would become my boss at Makerere University. An Anglican priest, Mbiti's writings on African Traditional Religion have become classics in the field.

My moment of awakening to African spirituality minimally got my attention in the early years when I was busy learning the local language. I had a young man named Andrew helping me. One day I asked Andrew the Kwanyama word for religion. There was an awkward pause in the conversation and I assumed that was probably because there was no word, because there was no religion. I repeated the question, and with the innate humility of Africans when speaking to whites, Andrew replied simply, "Well Tate, we don't have a word for religion because for Africans all of life is holy." *"All of life is holy!"* Fifty years later, I am still struck by the impact of that statement. I had been woefully wrong and so were countless missionaries before me to assume they had no word for religion and didn't know what "holy" was all about!

It was a moment of enlightenment I never forgot but unfortunately didn't pursue for many years. Instead, I blended in with the practice of the "Anglican tradition" for the next eight years, which was the robust practice of Christian sacramental worship and teaching. Years later, while teaching at Makerere, I would learn that Africa had an ancient spirituality that was alive and well long before Christian missionaries came to help. It's rooted in the life of the people and is in fact more naturally attuned to daily life than is Christianity. Serious Christians have, for example, forever struggled to practice the presence of God in daily life; that's what monasteries and convents are all about it—but it comes naturally to the African. *All of life is holy.* Traditional Africa was not caught up in dualistic (either-or) thinking so there was a constant sense of the presence of the Great Spirit. In Ovamboland that Great Spirit was *Kalunga*, the giver and taker of all life.

Western thought has for centuries separated the sacred from the secular, the pious from the profane, and the spirituality of the West has been profoundly influenced by this duality. Thus when missionaries came to Africa and began to divide life into categories of good and not-so-good, acceptable and unacceptable, the same was done with time, like the week. Sunday was set apart and became known to the African in a new way as "the day of the books." Those books consisted of Prayer Books, Catechisms, Bibles and Hymnals. Such printed stuff was dragged, sometimes awkwardly, to a place set apart and known as a church. Time and place suddenly took on a new importance. Becoming a Christian was an academic exercise and matters of the spirit became matters of the head. Prayers and the catechism had to be learned, often memorized by rote, in order to become a Christian. One's birthright was to be born into the world of the Great Spirit, but it could take years to qualify as a Christian. Traditional Africa wondered why these walls and fences were put between people and their God, but were too polite to ask. All were expected to study the Catechism for a year before baptism, another year or more before confirmation. Africans were taught to take their books with them to say prayers, make confession or just sing songs of joy. In the new Christian scheme of things, Sunday was the holy day of the week and presumably the other six days could take care of themselves. Sunday had become a day of obligation—and a lot of mental effort.

So what should the missionaries have done differently? It could probably be summed up in a few words: *a lot of humble listening.* In meeting another culture or religion, the first thing a missionary needed to do was to take off their shoes for the ground on which they were about to step was holy. But instead, missionaries acted as though God was an import and they were the import company. We should have known that no people or culture have ever been without God, but we didn't. Missionaries to Africa had good intentions but we took with us an assumption that our way was the correct way, our religion was the enlightened revelation and our culture was vastly superior. Most of the time, those assumptions were arrogant and rarely were they correct. An astonishing example of this was a statement I came across while working in Uganda, made by the Regius Professor of History at Oxford University. Speaking on the subject of oral tradition, he said that oral history did not constitute real history and that *"history in Africa didn't begin until the white man arrived."* Oxford University, no less…

African Traditional Religion had a lot to teach outsiders, had we listened. African belief in the 'living dead' corresponds nicely with the Christian belief in the Communion of the Saints. Belief in the power of evil spirits is not that different from our understanding of the power of evil thought. Talking to the departed relates to the Christian practice of invoking the saints in our prayers. And so on. Why didn't we take the time to discover these meeting points between our spirituality and theirs? In our failure to do so, we alienated an entire continent at a profound level, and generated mutual misunderstanding. Eventually, this alienation gave rise to an enormous growth of indigenous churches throughout Africa, churches that are made up of an amalgamation of beliefs, some of them Christian, many of them not, but no longer in communication with the Christian missionary movement that gave them rise, and more's the pity.

Witchcraft has long been an aspect of African culture that has tantalized and confused Westerners, like a gator lying just under the surface. Maybe that's because of a suppressed part of us that once spent more time above the surface but is no longer safe to talk about. Westerners now placate our gator with everything from Gatorade to Rolaids to Medicaid for a short term fix. Traditionally, Africa had a more direct way of dealing with the demons that stalked at noonday or midnight. When the spirit world wasn't behaving in a cordial manner, a visit to the local medicine man would usually put things right. The medicine man, or more rarely woman, was like the Native American shaman. They knew things ordinary folks didn't know, everything from how to smooth the ruffled feathers of an annoyed spirit to treating a physical or mental malady. They were the wise nabobs of the village who kept people's lids on when their pot was about to boil.

Outsiders coming to Africa called these shadowy healers witchdoctors, suggesting they were a fraud. That only confused things because they were really practitioners of healing and therefore doctors of a sort, and they did not use witchery to do it. They were traditional doctors without the witch. Clergy spend so much time tending the God-place in people's lives that people sometimes get us confused and think we're closer to the power switch than we really are. In fact, we become a spiritual placebo. The same thing was believed of the medicine man: because he, or she, knew things the average person didn't know, they were believed to have self-charging batteries with divine power.

Dark witchcraft was another matter. This is the kind that was up to no good and practitioners of this satanic trade were definitely not upstanding members of the local medical association. White people called the whole bunch witchdoctors which confused the fragile understanding still further, for there were good "witchdoctors" (shamans), who did good and helped the village and there were rogues who for one reason or another chose to deal on the malevolent side of life.

We once had an experience of the bad sort near the Mission. One night, a stranger moved into the area, believed to have come from Angola. Upon closer inquiry, it was determined he was witchdoctor with bad credentials. That would bring big trouble to the peaceful village of Odibo sooner if not later. Thus far, no one had seen him, and no trouble seemed to be coming out of his kraal, just puffs of smoke. How to deal with an interloper like this was another course not in my seminary training. Fortunately, we had Father Gabriel, who was as wise as an owl and as cunning as a fox. He was the local African priest who saw a lot and said little. In this case, he didn't mince words. He said the stranger-who-came-by-night had to be shifted out as quickly as possible before he set up shop and started messing with the villagers. The wise old owl came up with an ingenious plan of how to do it.

He gathered a sturdy handful of us, draped us in black cassocks, and lined us up to look as frightening as an African version of the Klan—a black one, since mine was the only white face. He put me in the lead with a towering processional cross leading the troupe. I wasn't sure of the battle strategy but Father Gabriel seemed to be a confident field commander. He had us gather at the Church and then make a silent procession to the scene of battle. "Onward Christian Soldiers" might have been an appropriate drum-beat but I wasn't at all sure whether what we were up to was Christian, and we certainly weren't soldiers charging onward. Silently, we approached the intruder's kraal. It still wasn't clear what we would say or do when we got there, but we trusted our priest. He was easily as cagey as the interloper.

It was the easiest battle ever fought. At Gabriel's direction, we walked silently around the kraal, seven times one way seven times the other, and returned to the Church. The exercise was lost on me and I returned to my day's work, clueless as to what we had done. I'm not sure anyone else knew either. The next morning the stranger and all his belongings were gone. He had disappeared in the night as suddenly as he had arrived. It had been a short war of symbols: simply walking silently one way and then the other had some mysterious symbolism that related to the witchdoctor. Maybe it was the cross, maybe the black cassocks and silent procession, but whatever it was it scared the hell out of him.

We never had occasion to use that trick again, but I never forget the strategy.

People think of elephants when they think of Africa. African elephants, known as one of the "Big Five," are considerably larger than those found in India and the sub-continent. Both varieties are the largest land dwelling mammals on earth, remarkable for their emotional sensitivity and gregarious nature. They have tight-knit family groups which usually consist of an older matriarch and several generations of relatives. The African elephant, known as *Laxodonta africana*, stands up to eleven feet tall, weighs as much as seven tons and can live up to seventy years. Most of the time they stayed out of our way, herding in the Etosha Game Park to the south or in Angola to our north. But not always.

In the mid-sixties, there was an outbreak of anthrax in the country and elephants started dying along with the infected cattle. One day, there was great excitement on the Mission: word had gone out that a huge elephant had died not far away and that meant a lot of meat for the taking. People went running towards the border with axes and buckets. The missionaries weren't all that interested in elephant steak because of its uncertain death, but the locals knew how to deal with meat no matter how it had died. They also had stronger stomachs than white people. In cooking meat, their practice was to throw it in the fire, let it get well burned and have a glorious feast, ash and all, that could last for days. Much as they liked meat, they hoarded their own cattle and disliked giving it up unless for a great occasion. They were happiest when wild game was available, like this elephant.

Not long after the border incident, the school boys and I went far into the bush to build a primitive school shelter. On occasions such as this, we would take what was popularly known as "the old lorry", which was an army surplus three-ton monster, the only four-wheel drive that big in all the area. The people had nicknamed it "Onkwanime" (pron. *'onk-kwa-neem-ay'*) because it resembled a lion: short nosed, powerful and making terrible noises. It had another name yet more difficult, "hamukombanyata' (pron. *'ham-comb-ban-yata'*) which meant 'it sweeps up everything in its path,' implying it was big and strong and could do fearful wonders. It was a cumbersome beast and drank petrol like no other vehicle, so we had to carry 44-gallon drums with us.

We arrived at our destination just before sunset, strangers in a strange land. It was an area none of us knew and some of the locals had never even seen a white man. I was their only specimen and must have looked strange, and 'though well-tanned, terribly anemic. The sound and appearance of the old lorry loaded with boys gathered anxious looks all through the day. I was nervous about the strangers, the strangers were nervous about us and the boys were nervous about elephants. It was a nervy beginning. We hadn't spotted elephants all day but the boys had an inner compass that told them where the wild things were, sort of like an American's inner compass for Starbucks.

There we were, surrounded by thick bush, with a few gardens nearby and nothing else. Beyond that was Angola where the elephants were believed to be. Much anxious discussion followed about where we should set up camp. The boys finally chose a spot next to a watermelon patch, ironically only a stone's throw from the border. I could tell they were nervous just being in the neighborhood of the Big Trunks but that problem went with the area. The boys were wise to be scared. Africans grew up knowing to be wary of elephants, *ondjaba* they called them. Normally quiet beasts that keep to themselves, they can become cranky and dangerous if provoked and it wasn't always obvious what provoked them; it could be color or noise or movement. Rogues were males that had been driven from the herd and were generally mad at the world. An elephant's trunk is probably the most ingenious part of their anatomy, also the most dangerous. It consists of more than 40,000 muscles that serve a wide range of purposes which can include picking up large men and hurling them to the ground like rag dolls. That's what worried the boys. As for me, I had such little experience of elephants in the wild that I didn't know what to expect. It all seemed like a great adventure to me.

With no elephants in sight, we eventually calmed our fears and bedded down for the night. Within minutes, noises were heard coming from the watermelon patch. Then appeared huge shadows moving in the moonlight. Sure enough it was a small herd of big elephants. Those boys reacted like they came straight out of New York City. They were sure the worst had befallen us and we were all about to die. Their fear wasn't lessened by the fact that the elephants weren't interested in us at all—they were in the watermelon patch having a good time. By the moonlight we could see them plucking enormous melons and tossing them down their throats like peanuts. One young elephant was a real clown. He figured out how to impale the melons on his tusk, then toss them in the air and catch them in his mouth. He was as funny as the sound of the watermelons landing in his cavernous stomach, the envy of any circus trainer. For a moment the boys forgot their fear and laughed at the sound, but their entertainment didn't last long. Convinced they were next on the menu, they screamed *"Tatekulu, tatekulu, save us from the ondjaba"* dashing wildly, looking for a safe place, as if I knew how to save them. Some climbed into the flatbed of the lorry, some tried to get inside the cab, some even dived under it hoping the monsters couldn't reach that far. Their fear of the wild came as a surprise, but it was probably what had helped them survive for centuries living side by side with dangerous animals. As for the elephants, they hardly gave us a look. They casually finished off the melon patch and ambled off across the border to sleep it off.

We didn't sleep it off. Not surprisingly, it turned out to be a restless night, and I heard anxious chatter all night. Africans love to make fun of each other after moments of great drama, but this time no one was poking fun. By the next day we could laugh a little nervously over what had happened. The sound of watermelons hitting the bottom of the elephants' stomachs was the funniest part of a story they would no doubt embellish when they told their friends. But the first thing they wanted to do the next day was build a lean-to shelter, "protection," they said, from future elephant attacks. It wasn't any safer than the lorry, but the boys thought it was. "Elephants don't attack buildings", they insisted, "only watermelons and young boys."

Many years later and in a neighboring African country, we attended an art exhibit at the National Museum a few blocks from where we lived. I fell in love with a huge oil painting of a rogue elephant but we couldn't afford to buy it. Word got out that I was in love with the painting, and a few weeks later it showed up in our living room, a gift from the Assistant Curator. It was a magnificent thing. We named it "Jumbo" and hung it over the mantle, where it stayed for the remainder of our years in Africa. We learned later it had been painted by the Curator of the Museum, Alex Campbell, who became a good friend of the family.

I can't remember how we met Alex, but I liked this quiet, taciturn Scot from the beginning. He owned a farm about fifteen miles out of town and carried a brown bag lunch into town every day. When we learned of this, we invited him to have lunch with us every Thursday. And thus, every Thursday Alex became a part of the family, along with his painting.

We had a bizarre piece of elephantry that dominated our living room—known as the lounge or sitting room. The bizarre object was an elephant's foot that had been made into a footstool. Such things were popular with the tourist crowd and were probably a taxidermist's dream: the huge nails were well polished, the skin was black and well preserved, even the long bristles stood at attention. To us it was an irritant: we weren't into chopping off elephant feet or pulling out their tusks or messing with wild life in general, but here this foot sat in our lounge as a weird piece of furniture. It had been given with gratitude for my services to the safari folks of the Okavango Delta.

It was our custom after lunch to retire to the sitting room for coffee, where the amputated foot sometimes served as a stool. One Thursday Alex-the-Curator sat at one end of the lounge, contentedly sipping his cup. Then he started muttering to himself, his eyes fixed on the pathetic foot in the middle of the room. "Looks like the left front foot of a young male to me" we heard him say. What was that all about? We proceeded to learn the quiet Scot knew quite a lot about elephants. Years before, while at school in Scotland, he had seen an advertisement for "Bounty Hunters" needed by the Southern Rhodesian Government. They were needed to thin elephant herds that were becoming a problem in Southern Rhodesia[16]. Alex moved to Southern Rhodesia, learned how to hunt elephant and fell in love with Africa. In time, he settled in Botswana and became Curator of the National Museum and an environmentalist long before the term or the profession were in vogue.

---

[16] Now known as Zimbabwe.

And thus he could tell by the wrinkles and shape of that bizarre footstool what leg it was, the sex, the age, and what the beast probably weighed. We were impressed but knowing all of that didn't change things much. The stool remained an embarrassment in our sitting room.

Years later, my last close encounter with pachyderms was in Kitwan Game Park in the lowlands of Nepal, just above India. An old friend and I had decided to visit the Kitwan to see a part of Nepal that wasn't the Himalayas, where we had just spent twenty eight days trekking. Late one afternoon we mounted an elephant, not quite as big as Jumbo, and went sightseeing through the bush. We hoped to find the four-footed beasts that had given me my African nickname, *ekuni,* otherwise known as rhinoceros. I never admired rhinos and didn't particularly appreciate the association, but the African boys who named me said it was "because you never take no for an answer!" It was a dubious honorific.

So there we were out to find my shady namesakes and take some pictures. It was a good time of the day because the rhinoceri were foraging for their dinner. Sure enough, we found a small herd of rhinos and the excitement began. Sitting high on the elephant's back, the rhinos couldn't see us or smell us or it would have provoked things. Rhinos are fairly low on brain power but have sufficient survival instinct to know not to bother elephants. These guys chose to graze peacefully, just feet away from us. All but one. Suddenly, a baby rhino broke loose from the herd and darted under our elephant's feet. There was a skirmish, and we nearly went down as our beast tried to avoid tripping over the thousand-pounder. Then mother rhino came thundering down upon us. Everyone went mad. The mammoths were irritated, we were petrified and our seat on top of the elephant was teetering. Fortunately for us, the baby rhino freed itself from the elephant's feet and went running in the opposite direction, like a young brat who knew he'd caused trouble. You could almost imagine a smirk on his face. There's no way to tell if rhinos laugh, but we figured it was just another case of a kid trying to annoy his parents. We didn't hang around to see if there were any repercussions, as our elephant beat a hasty retreat with us clutching beer bottles, cameras and makeshift saddle.

As the sun was setting, like modern day maharajahs we uncorked our Indian Tusker Beer and had sundowners on that elephant's back, not far from the legendary Shangri-la. It was a beer and a back to remember.

There was a big *oshana* on the eastern side of St. Mary's Mission. That's what they called a waterhole 'though the word isn't Kwanyama. *Oshanas* are similar to salt flats, sometimes quite large, with a flat hard surface that allows water to collect and remain for a long time. St. Mary's *oshana* was marked with scrub brush and grass in the dry season when it became a soccer pitch. The school boys would gather every afternoon for a rousing game that made you tired just watching. Like youth everywhere, they seemed never to tire from running around. In the Ovambo culture, it wasn't just the youth who never seemed to tire: it was all males and most of the females. I think all children must have been taught *never* to admit fatigue, for I never heard it spoken. For years, I would witness them dropping from exhaustion and never once did I hear the words *onda loloka* (I'm tired). Maybe that was considered a weakness. And so went the game of soccer, endlessly, tirelessly, on the *oshana*.

The southern end of the playing field was marked by one of the oldest trees in the neighborhood, said to be at least ninety years old. That's old today for trees in Ovamboland. To get that old, a tree had survived all kinds of abuse from drought to hacking, stripping for bark or cutting for firewood. I never fully understood why the African people didn't seem to take more care to preserve or protect the flora and fauna of their magnificent continent. Perhaps it was because there was so much of it; vast areas of Africa still remain virtually unused for a variety of reasons, even with a population of over a billion on a continent three-and-a half times the size of the United States. But the degradation of land and resources in Africa is increasingly becoming a problem while every year the San people (Bushmen) and others continue to use the ancient practice of burning the bush and savannah to promote new growth. They say hunting is only good when the game come to graze on the new growth, but burning it to get there makes for a harsh ecological cycle.

Beyond the old tree was a waterhole which fed into a man-made dam that provided water for the Mission. The water system was pretty simple: rainwater collected in the *oshana*, drained into the waterhole and was then pumped into an earthen dam, later to be filtered and stored for use by the Mission. The waterhole served like a coffee klatch for the animal kingdom: they gathered there every morning and evening without fail. This Starbucks-in-the-wild was visited twice daily by cattle, goats, donkeys and the occasional pig, all more or less shepherded by small herdboys. The locals didn't drink there because the water was polluted. There were notable exceptions such as when there was extreme drought when people had no choice—but that brought intestinal sickness. Much of the Third World routinely faces the dilemma of dying of thirst or drinking polluted water and dealing with diseases from that.

The ritual visit to the waterhole was one I never noticed when we lived there. In fact, not until many years later when my late wife and I returned did the subject ever arise. We had come to work for a year at St. Mary's, to rebuild the high school that had been destroyed in the war for independence. Being new to Africa, she was fascinated with everything, but had a special curiosity for the things no one else noticed and delighted in, what others considered were the insignificant details. Countless times, she would grab my arm and say "did you see that?" and it would be a tiny ant dragging his lunch home, a minuscule dandelion valiantly pushing its way through a crack in the pavement, the "cunning" weave in a headcloth, or a hidden flower growing out of a wall. At St. Mary's, she would perch herself in the window of our makeshift kitchen, a hundred yards west of the big waterhole, and there she would note things that for years had passed me by. Hours would fly by as she took note, carefully keeping all the details in her memory. When I popped in for a quick lunch she would tell me how the entire morning had transpired: who came first to the waterhole, then second, then third, and so on. She could report if there had been any skirmishes and on occasion whose ox got gored. She even kept track of which herdboys went AWOL that morning (usually to hunt wild berries or play games with other herdboys). Truth be told, her mornings usually sounded more exciting than mine, and her power of observation identified a veritable hierarchy of waterhole goers.

The ways of the waterhole were known instinctively by every African boy. Being a herdboy was a rite of passage. They drank it in with their mother's milk or had it beaten into them by an elder's knobkerrie at about age seven. And so I was a late learner about the ritual at the waterhole, which went as follows: first came the cattle, known as oxen in Africa. Americans call them bulls, cows and heifers. Egrets came with them, white spindly-legged birds that planted themselves on the backs of the cattle, especially in the rainy season. These funny creatures feasted topside on bugs and vermin and made an amusing sight, perched up there on top of the beast. There must have been a symbiosis because I never saw an ox try to toss them off. Among the cattle, true to the ways of the world, the bulls came first, giving way to those with the largest horns. Several herds might arrive at the same time, which didn't seem to matter unless one of them belonged to the Headman. That one always went first and everyone knew it. Sometimes there was drama in the first act when two herds arrived at the same time. That's when the herdboys were inclined to take leave of things. Maybe it was their ancient way of playing itself out which was not to compete against a neighbor. In traditional Africa, the community always came first before the individual. It was a nice principle in theory but not a workable way to run a waterhole. So there was no way to guess which herd would yield and it seemed to depend on the size of the lead ox and how well he could bluff. Not unlike other bullies, if he bellowed loud enough to scare off his opponents and kept advancing, he got the spoils. Getting to that point could become a lengthy affair, taking up to half an hour or more. It was a sure way for a foul-tempered stud to goad his neighbor.

Once it was established which herd went first, the rest followed in good order, as if rehearsed for a thousand years. Once in the water, they bellowed triumphantly and stood their ground. They cooled in it, defecated in it, drank, stood some more, and let out great bovine burps. Having seen at least that much of the parade, I often wondered if the lead bulls shat in the water just to give the losers a comeuppance. They seemed to enjoy being the biggest, fattest and meanest on the block. It took up to five years to get so big but only seconds to lose it all by rifle shot or knife, as most of them would, sooner or later. Cattle were the chief symbol of wealth, yet few died of old age. Interesting…

Next to the waterhole came the goats, much lower in the animal kingdom. Neither the people nor the land nor their bovine relatives liked them much. For one thing, they had bad eating habits. They not only ate what was above the ground but pulled the roots out and ate them as well. The best way to clean weeds out of a garden was to invite a herd of goats in. In the dry season, that happened routinely at the Mission. Herdboys navigated the entire goat herd into the Mission compound and ran off for the day. The goats then ransacked trees, bushes, flowers, and even low hanging clothes lines. Protests to priest and headmen followed, which produced a few heated announcements in church but not much else.

In addition to having bad table manners and being willing to eat anything, goats have a distinct odor, at times offensive. It was rumored that cattle farmers in South Africa were changing to goat production because they were so robust and less expensive to keep but their greatest problem was breeding out the disgusting smell. To their credit and probably their survival, goats are wily and can out-manoever larger animals at the waterhole and almost anywhere else. Herdboys too. Eventually their time came at the waterhole to drop bee bee crap in the water and stir it up with their tiny hooves. Maybe that was their way of getting even with the whole universe. Herdboys, also close to the bottom of the human food chain, generally had contempt for goats because they were unruly and didn't follow traffic signals, knobkerrie or not. They seemed to be more stupid than the larger beasts.

Then came the pigs, if there were any. By the time the pigs made it to the water, the herdboys were usually gathering cattle and heading homeward. Belching and bellowing, the herd announced the homeward trail. Remarkably, each herdboy knew exactly which cattle were his, called each by name, and knew where to hurl the knobkerrie when one strayed. It was amazing how those little kids could command a herd of beasts many times their size. They had an inborn understanding of what made the animals tick and could get them to the waterhole and back with little more than a stick and a whistle.

Donkeys filled in the rest, wandering to and fro and acting the dumbest of all. Actually, they were quite handy beasts of burden, not all that dumb, and used for transport, plowing and hauling.

And so would go the theatrics of the waterhole. My late wife would sit in her window and watch the parade by the hour. She caught every nuance, even the occasional dogfight in the middle of it all. How did I never notice it? I lived next to that waterhole for eight years and never took notice of things so mundane and yet so extraordinary. I am reminded of Andrew's words, "all of life is holy."

She also knew an awful lot about dandelions and ladybugs and other tiny things...

Southern Africa[17] sits, for the most part, like a baker's loaf—on a high plateau with fairly steep to gently tapered sides all around. It is said the high plateau accounts for a lot of its dramatic weather which tends to move from east to west, like the great monsoon patterns of India. The most uncomfortable months usually last from September until the rains come; in a good year, that would be in December. Before the rains, man and beast swelter, temperature and humidity go up and life can be unbearable. Things like air conditioners and fans were unheard of when we lived there. So was electricity. During those months, tempers flared and fights were common.

---

[17] Not to be confused with the nation of South Africa. Southern Africa comprises upward of a dozen countries.

In the olden days, animal sacrifices were offered to jolly up the god of rain. By name, that was Kalunga. Actually, Kalunga was in charge of everything. Traditionally, the Ovambo people didn't have a Greek panoply of gods to look after mortal concerns. Kalunga ruled the roost, so to speak, and was believed to know how to make it rain. When the Christian missionaries came, Kalunga was stripped of everything but his name and given new responsibilities, which raised a serious question for me. If the Christian God was still Kalunga, what changed other than a name? The missionaries hoped what changed was the traditional *understanding* of Kalunga, from a deity that needed placating to a better one of love and compassion. The early missionaries must have thought they had a better deal to offer the Africans, which surely they would be quick to see: replace their traditional divine overseer who didn't care too much what people did, as long as they didn't annoy him, with one who was into everyone's business every moment of every day, sort of like a kindly Constant Inspector, benevolent but always there. As things turned out, the African people didn't see that as much of a deal but didn't say so. Early on I had a hunch that maybe traditional thinking hadn't shifted all that much.[18] It never occurred to the early missionaries, nor to me that African Traditional Religion was buried so deep in the soul of Africa that Christian concepts of God simply could not supplant it. As remote as Kalunga traditionally was believed to be from day-to-day life, there was a busy spirit world going on at all times, which is why traditional African belief regards all of life as holy. The spiritual realm made it so, and Kalunga was behind it all.

Since there was no service for rain-making in the Prayer Book, the Church didn't get involved other than the occasional prayer. Who knows if the traditional sacrifices worked or not? For that matter, who knows if they didn't? Placebos might work in all sorts of situations. The only counsel I ever received on the subject of rain-making was from a bishop who had served many years in Africa. He was famous for saying, *"Gentlemen, never pray for rain until you see the clouds!"* And then there

---

[18] This hunch became the basis of a social anthropology research project at Rhodes University, some years later which was eventually published as an M.A. Thesis.

is always that fall-back smart-aleck retort when clergy are asked to do something about the weather, (and I have used many times), "I'm in sales, not management!"

During the season of swelter, nights were miserable. We slept in the buff and sweated through the night. Dawn brought little relief; more likely, it was exhaustion and crankiness from a wretched night's sleep. The days weren't as bad—somehow it seemed more natural to sweat standing up. Fortunately, the mosquitoes didn't come before the rains, but when the rains came, so did the "mozzies," bringing malaria with them, absolutely without fail. The Africans called malaria "the fever," which was an understatement. The several times I suffered from it, my fever went above 104 and I thought I was dying. The worst kind is known medically as *falciparum* and is usually fatal. Africans have simply learned to live and die with malaria. Everyone has it at one time or another, sometimes annually. Unfortunately, it is endemic in the Third World and there is no sure way to avoid it. The world of pharmaceutical magic still has no prophylactic that guarantees complete immunity. [19]

Lives that malaria didn't claim, drought often would. Some years it never rained as it should. That's when life turned hard and the ensuing drought was cruel to every living thing. Crops failed, people and cattle starved and died. In those days, there were no relief agencies or emergency feeding schemes to come to the rescue, and unknown to most of the world, death stalked Africa. Such ravages of extreme weather in Africa and elsewhere still occur with regularity and generally go unnoticed by the rest of the world, never make the front page of a single newspaper outside of Africa. Fortunately, today the United Nations and other international food organizations are alert to these emergencies in providing publicity and relief.

The house we lived in at the Mission looked like something out of a nineteenth century explorer's sketchbook. One of the oldest on the Mission, it could have been a double for Karen Blixen's 1890

---

[19] The World Health Organization estimated that in 2010 there were 291 million cases of malaria, resulting in almost a million deaths. Other estimates go as high as 550 million, a large portion of those with the deadly strain of *falciparum*.

home in Kenya, made famous by the film "Out of Africa." Built in the shape of a huge U, each room had only screens in the windows for ventilation, which allowed the comforting sound of a chiming clock in the living room to be heard in every room. This colossal house had a thatched roof eighteen inches thick which made it a wonderful weather station of sorts. The walls were also eighteen inches thick and made of mud by a technique known as *pise de terre*, or 'rammed earth'. This involved compressing between two forms mud mixed with straw and sometimes soil from anthills which, when dry, produced a very hard wall. I remember cutting a doorway through a wall to add a room. It required a primitive cross-cut saw which we made out of barbed, and eight hours to saw the doorway. That mud wall, having "cured" for forty years, was as hard as concrete.

The huge thatched roof rested on massive beams that required an entire tree for one beam. The thatching of heavy reeds and grass was estimated to be at least forty years old and so thick that in the heaviest of storms all we heard was rain water pouring off the sides. The roof looked all the more impressive because of its steep pitch, which was said to be the influence of the early Finnish Lutheran missionaries. High pitched roofs were the only ones they knew how to make in Finland, designed them to keep snow off the roof. In Africa, they looked good but were totally impractical in a country where it never snowed;[20] they required excessive building material, but provided great overhanging eaves. Our house had a seven-foot eave all 'round, which provided a dry refuge from almost any thunderstorm. Many a night, children and adults huddled under that protection and with wide eyes watched the heavenly fireworks. I have fond memories of carrying each of our kids out under the great eaves to make tentative friendship with thunder and lightning. We would all jump and laugh nervously with the deafening cracks of lightning, followed by long drum rolls that rumbled for miles across the African bush. The entire countryside would light up for a moment, and then a deluge would follow. Mother Nature entertained us

---

[20] Contrary to what Westerners might think parts of Africa do get snow, but not in South West Africa (Namibia)

well under the great eaves of our African home. The great pitched roof also provided space for a small zoo. A simple layer of palm mats served as the ceiling, and from the noises above that we figured the attic was home to snakes, lizards, bats and owls. Mice probably provided food for them all.

The Kwanyama had wonderful names for thunder and lightning: they called the one *"ngunguma"* and the other *"pwalakata."* Merely pronouncing the words suggested what they represented. It's called *onomatopoeias,* when a word sounds like what it is describing. Learning that in high school English never made much of an impression on me, but it sure did in this African language. Thunder sounded like *ngunguma,* and the crackling of lightning sounded just like *pwalakata.* It was the same with the name of their wild turkey, a Ground Hornbill generally revered or feared throughout Africa. They called that big bird an *"epumumu"* because of its doleful wail. That wild turkey was sometimes eaten but not for thanksgiving; there is no day of thanksgiving observed in Africa, despite Africans' natural, almost childlike, attitude of thankfulness.

Sometimes lightning struck people that stood out in the rain, and herdboys were especially vulnerable. Remarkably, some that were struck lived, but not usually. The story was told of a man who was hit by a bolt of lightning that went right through him, knocked him out but left only a burn mark where it hit. When he came to, he got up and walked away. That was the exception, and the story was probably embellished with every telling.

One of the more dramatic things that came with a good rain year was the *efundja*. These were floods of Biblical proportions that could turn vast areas of the country into a challenge fit for Noah. The source of the floods was the Kunene River that snaked down through Angola and made its way into western Ovamboland. When the Kunene burst its banks hundreds of miles to the north, the flood water could take weeks to reach Ovamboland. It would start slowly with flood waters creeping silently down, and when it arrived the water could be three feet deep. Huts dissolved and harvests could be destroyed overnight as the waters advanced. Mud brick buildings simply melted away. Cattle got confused and lost and many would die. Native granaries would collapse and food supplies would be destroyed. Roads would become impassable unless in a high enough wheelbase so the engine didn't die. If that happened, as it did on occasion, water would get sucked up the exhaust pipe into the engine, a big mess would ensue and Mac, the jack-of-all-trades, would not be happy.

Driving in the flood was a harrowing experience. It was imperative to find the track *(spoor),* and to do that, someone had to venture on foot ahead of the vehicle. That didn't work if the water was too deep or the road too obscure. Generally, the *efundja* was a sticky wicket for the missionaries, who were the only ones with vehicles—most everyone else went on foot and didn't get stuck.

My worst experience of the *efundja* happened on the Onekwaya road. It was one I had traveled so many times I thought I knew it in my sleep. But this time when we set out for Onekwaya there was no road to be seen, just water for miles and miles. Trees, high fields, and a few buildings here and there were the only guides we had, and that was usually sufficient, Along with my faithful companion, Denys, one of our major donors from England was with me, an elderly doctor intent on seeing Onekwaya, which was one of the major outstations. On the road I thought I knew so well, we got hopelessly lost and things quickly went from bad to worse. The Landrover got mired in mud with the water still rising. Digging the mud away from the wheels was usually tried first, but in this case it was useless. We tried for hours shoving branches under the wheels to help with traction but that too failed. In four hours we had only managed to make things worse. Then the perfect solution appeared on the horizon: a man plowing with a team of oxen—the next best thing to horsepower, or so we thought. But eight strong oxen couldn't move us either.

Darkness was approaching, and we had no provisions for a night in the swamp, neither food nor bedding. I had fears of our benefactor's support drying up a lot faster than the flood. Mosquitoes smelled our blood and called their buddies. We slept in the vehicle without pillows or blankets and little else but biting mosquitoes. It was a night to remember, as I do these many years later. By morning, word of our plight had reached Odibo, and the big lorry came to our rescue with steel cable to pull us out. When the misadventure was over, our British donor, well into his seventies, said he thought the whole thing was a hoot. I guess everything depends on the way you look at it.

Without the *efundja*, a normal season brought eight to ten inches of rain. If the rains came late, they could spoil the harvest, and an early rain could mess up planting or cause the grain to sprout too soon. The Ovambo people lived with the disappointment of delayed seasons for so many generations they were stoical about nature. Outsiders misunderstood this: they judged the men lazy for not getting to their plows sooner. But those men weren't lazy, they knew to wait upon nature before plowing and sowing too soon. Traditional wisdom ought not to be confused with laziness, but Westerners still do this all the time in the Third World. But the Westerners have graduated somewhat: the enlightened ones now call traditional wisdom "indigenous technology," the locals call it common sense. Such common sense taught the Ovamboes to build large granaries out of huge palm baskets, suspend them off the ground and mud the inside to protect the stored grain. A good year's harvest could feed a family for at least two years, depending on the size of the garden.

We grew to appreciate the drama of weather in Africa, thunderstorms and lightning that cracked so loudly you stopped breathing. They now call those heavy rains monsoons after the terminology of India, but they really don't compare with the monsoons of the sub-continent. An Indian monsoon can dump over twelve inches of rain in an hour, Ovamboland might get that much in a season. The rainmaker in Ovamboland was more likely to be stubborn than generous.

After a thunderstorm, the countryside was magical. The air was fresh and smelled newly made, and you could hear voices over the countryside chattering about what the rains had brought, for good or ill. Children came out to play in puddles and squealed with delight over creatures the rain had coaxed out of hiding, like the dung beetles that could roll a ball of ox dung many times their size. They would back up to it with their tiny feet and push, and the dung ball would go ambling this way and that, like a lopsided beachball. Or the *shongololos*, little black millipedes that would roll themselves into a ball if you touched them. And the more evasive *cicadas* that would strike up a deafening chorus like tiny, unrelenting castanets, a noise that could be overwhelming at night. It would echo off the walls and get amplified under the eaves and make a helluva racket. It led to my undoing late one night after a storm when the *cicadas* were especially noisy. In a state of sleepy exasperation I marched out with spade in hand to put an end to it. In my sleepy stupor, I attacked, thrusting the spade into the wet ground to catch them before they could escape into their tunnels. Aiming at their tunnels and thrusting again and again—each time they were too fast and I never got a one. Meanwhile, my wife was standing at the window watching this ridiculous performance. With no obvious explanation as to why I was out there, she thought my hinges were broken. Softly she called my name, not sure of my mental state. When I realized I was being watched, it all became very funny. I returned to bed feeling dumb and outwitted. My unsuccessful bout with the *cicadas* became a very funny family story.

There were other neat things that followed thunderstorms, like the dams and *oshanas* that filled with water and overnight had thousands of croaking frogs and water beetles and crickets to serenade us to sleep. It was a sound so completely African. Sometimes I miss it, especially living where it hardly ever rains and we never hear frogs or water beetles. Plants also did their thing after a good storm: water lilies on the deeper waters and indigenous bulbs that seemed long dead suddenly sprung into flower and the *embe* trees brought forth millions of nostril-stopper seeds. African children were fascinated with these bright red bee-bee sized seeds and had the bizarre habit of pushing them up their nose. Getting them out caused frequent seasonal problems at the Mission Hospital.

Cattle and people were happiest when it rained and the land would laugh and sing; the ox and the plow would find favor with the fields, and the plowing season would begin. And magically, the whole countryside would turn bright with a tender yellow green that almost hurt the eyes. I remember it as if it was yesterday.

An average year of eight to ten inches of rain would generally produce a fair harvest, provided those eight to ten inches didn't all come too soon to germinate the seeds early or too late to nurture them to full harvest. Nature could be tricky and so would be the planting cycle. Farmers in America have Uncle Sam at their back to compensate them for *not* sowing or to make up for a bad year—a luxury that exists probably no other place in the world and certainly not in the Third World. In Africa, even feeding schemes are not readily or reliably available, which means starvation or malnutrition are common occurrences.

The traditional Ovambo staple crop was sorghum, sometimes called millet, a bee-bee sized grain with a rich bronze color, which looks much like corn when growing. My first experience of millet was as a kid when I had a regular summer job at a granary, unloading 50-ton railroad cars of the stuff. Colossal railroad cars were filled to the top with the grain, so deep I could literally drown in it and it would take a full day's work to unload the stuff. Other names for this amazing grain are milo, durra, Egyptian millet, great millet, kaffir corn and solam. I've no idea how the ancients came to settle on this grain as their staple crop in Ovamboland, but it was a brilliant decision...like those 'ancients' who knew nothing before Western technology arrived. Sorghum has for centuries been the most important staple food for millions of poor people in the semi-arid regions of Africa and Asia.[21] It's rich in protein, low in carbohydrates, high in vitamins and minerals and much more nourishing and wholesome than the corn that we know from our midwestern breadbasket. Consequently, in earlier days high blood pressure and obesity were unheard of in Ovamboland. But not so, after the later introduction of corn, which brought numerous health problems into the country.

Harvest time always felt like a special time for me. Late in summer it came, in May or June, when the heat got mellow and the leaves turned yellow and a full moon rose in the east. The season was crowned with

---

[21] Sorghum is the third most important cereal crop grown in the United States and the fifth most important in the world. In 2010, Nigeria was the world's largest producer of grain sorghum, followed by the United States and India. (Wikipedia)

that huge harvest moon and the countryside would turn to singing. They had harvesting parties and threshing parties when all the neighbors would gather in each others' gardens and work around the clock until the harvest was in. It was a communal affair with much work, somehow made easier by the singing of their souls as only Africans could. During the season, we would hear the distant singing all through the night and until that family's harvest was ready to be stored.

The threshing floor, where the heads of grain were stomped to release the grain, was carefully prepared in advance by plastering it with soil taken from an ant-hill and mud. This produced a smooth, hard-surfaced floor for the work of threshing and stomping. Men and women did the hard work of harvesting and threshing, followed by winnowing, usually done by the women. The grain was then stored in huge baskets, mud-plastered on the inside to keep the grain from leaking out and rodents from burrowing in. Finally, when the grain was to be eaten, it was pounded with 'stomping sticks' into a fine powder, then to become their staple porridge—'oshifima' it was called, and our family loved it. The stalks that remained in the field were either used for thatching or fed to the cattle; and the land was left fallow until another season. It was a pattern of life that knew more generations than we probably could count, and it had served the people well. Many a time I reflected on that simple fact and wondered if we have really made life better with the introduction of Western foods and Western diets and the health problems that have come with them. It always made me wonder what true 'development' should be about. Many years later when I worked for a short time for World Neighbors, I would learn more.[22]

---

[22] Unfortunately, World Neighbors as a development agency no longer exists. The organization was founded on the belief that exporting money and technology from the West often was not the most helpful thing to do, and that solutions to developmental problems in the Third World often can be solved by traditional "indigenous" knowledge and wisdom.

"What's That You Said, Archbishop?"

There were two reasons we had to leave our beloved home at Odibo after almost eight idyllic years. Both were man-made and both very much against our will. In the years we had been there, we had seen St. Mary's grow from a derelict, almost forgotten Mission Station, to a thriving center that included a growing hospital, a primary school for more than a thousand learners, a high school, a seminary with ten young men in training, and the Great Church of St. Mary that had over fifty far-flung bush churches and schools. The central hospital was the mother hen for a number of bush clinics. Much had been accomplished during those happy years, and much of that was because we had developed a large base of donors in America, a source hitherto untouched before us.

Basically, the causes of our departure late in the year of '69 had to do with what I will sum up as the Gospel, the government, and the blundering of the Anglican Church and all of it needs a little background information.

The South West African Peoples Organization (SWAPO) had been founded some years before we moved to Ovamboland and I am proud to say that one of our priests was behind the birth of this political movement. That was Theofelus Hamutumbangela, who was somewhat of a combative character with a fierce sense of right and wrong and was ready to fight for it at the slightest provocation, and there were plenty of those in his day. Father Theofelus is commemorated by a huge statue that stands today in front of Parliament Building in the capital. By the mid-sixties, the political organization Hamutumbangela had helped into existence had that same fierce opposition to the systematic injustice being inflicted on the country by the South African government. Not surprisingly it became a scorpion in their bed, so to speak, one which had begun striking back at the horrible injustices of the *apartheid* government.

The Anglican Church was quietly supportive of SWAPO and consequently was held responsible for much of the "native unrest" as the South African government crudely phrased it. It was believed the unrest was the result of supporting SWAPO and teaching Africans about the dignity of humanity; how to read, write and speak English; how to ask "why" and how to find their own honor as human beings. So the government's hammer fell frequently, usually at the hands of the South African Police or Defense Force.

By the mid-sixties the "Boers" (as the African people described the South African government, a term of derision among Africans to this day) had moved into Ovamboland in a big way. It began with the construction of a major airport at Oshakati, some seventy-five miles from Odibo, with a runway big enough to take C-130s. I don't recall if there was an official justification for the airport, but with it came a gravel highway with extremely wide shoulders. One rationale for that was in case the government had to bring in bulldozers. Bulldozers? For what? We figured the real reason was in the event the government had to fly in with heavy airplanes and armaments they could land on the gravel highway in case there was war. This frenzy of anxiety was just the introit to what followed when war did break out within a few years to come.

My part of the story goes roughly like this. Along with a heavy influx of South African Police and their bedfellows, the Defense Force, came helicopters. Such a flying contraption had never before been seen in the skies of Ovamboland. We figured the government got the idea of using them from watching the war waged in Vietnam. This contraption was an uncanny weapon of war: it could hover in mid-air, swoop low to drop gunfire or propaganda, still lower to kidnap and kill. In time, the South Africans did all that and more. The local people became terrified at the sound of a chopper. So did all of us at the Mission, for we knew by then that we were regarded as suspect on some occasions and the enemy on others. As the Archdeacon of Ovamboland, I represented the Anglican Church throughout the area and its 50,000 members, not to mention all who lived at the Mission. Africans were being abducted, intimidated and disappearing and the very least I should do was lodge an official protest. So off I went to their headquarters at Oshakati to call upon the head of police action in the North, a crusty old Afrikaner known as Colonel Pretorius. I was a little surprised to learn he knew all about me before we met. This was unsettling. One thing the South

African government was good at was espionage. They had stooges and informers everywhere, and the Anglican Church was fairly easy to identify—we were the ones who spoke and taught English, the ones who were always complaining about *apartheid,* and the ones who apparently were colorblind in our relations with the Africans. "Natives" and "kaffirs" were the preferred terms of derogation used by all who were pro-government. We regarded them as brothers and sisters of equal dignity and deserving of the same things as whites, but we were reading from a totally different book of life.

So, Colonel Pretorius knew all about me. Another chilling thought that occurred to me later was that he even knew I was coming to see him that troubling day in late '69. He sat rigidly behind his desk and heard me out as I laid out complaints about the way the people were being treated by his men. Of course he feigned to know nothing of this and therefore could disbelieve as much of it as he chose, which was all of it. "Father", he said in retort, "these are difficult days here in the country and we need your help to find the troublemakers. We are here to help the people and the way we will do that is by finding those who are stirring up the people. It's just a handful of malcontents and they will be found and punished. And you must help us do that!" *"Ja meneer"* was what he wanted to hear from me ("yes sir"). *"Roll over and be a nice chap for us now won't you Father".* But by that time I was so angry I was shaking and so was he, only he had the upper hand and the trump card in the deck. My permit to reside in the "Native Territory" had to be renewed from time to time. Hitherto it had been little more than a formality, but not after he played his trump card. Sure enough, shortly after my clash with Pretorius, there arose a "problem" with my permit to reside in Ovamboland, and it would no longer be renewed automatically. In fact, it was not to be renewed at all! There was no recourse to that decision which came from the top, in Pretoria. That was the official reason for our departure from our beloved home at St. Mary's. As quickly and simply as that.

The other reason is more sordid and no less painful because it involved a colleague. The name of my eventual nemesis was Colin O'Brian Winter. Originally from England, he had been the Dean of the little Cathedral of St. George in Windhoek (which had the dubious distinction of being the smallest Anglican Cathedral in the world). Those were the days after our much loved Bishop Robert Mize, now years away from the Kansas cornfields, had been deported. His major offense had been chronic color blindness in an *apartheid* state. He had been unabashedly forthright in doing illegal things like letting Africans eat at his table, sleep under his roof and become his friends. All of this led to his deportation in 1968, which was a terrible loss for the diocese and the African people. Shortly thereafter, there followed a frenzy of talk about who the next bishop would be and I found myself in a very difficult position. In any election for bishop, the Ovambo people, who constituted the majority of the diocese, would line up solidly behind me because they knew and trusted me, having lived among them for years. But if I were elected we would have to leave Ovamboland and go to live in the capital city of Windhoek, hundreds of miles away. We couldn't face the possibility of leaving Ovamboland and the people we loved so I refused to be considered for bishop.

Then followed another frenzy of talk about dividing the country into two dioceses, making Ovamboland the northernmost diocese with me as bishop. That had great appeal but was unrealistic because the remainder of the country didn't have enough members or resources to constitute a viable diocese. Through all of this, Colin Winter was positioning himself for the upcoming election and in due course was elected bishop, whereupon something mysterious came to pass: he became a stranger to us all. He became suspicious of me, with a paranoid notion that they hadn't elected me because the northern territory was going to revolt and split the diocese in two. Before this, he had had nothing to do with Ovamboland, having visited only once. Suddenly, he presented himself as the champion of the oppressed people of Ovamboland, and I was the one who had oppressed them. It was all laughable, but it made for serious trouble. He became resentful of the supporters we had in the United States and resentful that I spoke the language and loved and knew the people of Ovamboland. In his confusion, he concluded I was disloyal and probably needed to leave his diocese. I was heartsick and overwhelmed by all of this and didn't know what to do. Then, from an unexpected source, the Archbishop of Cape Town helped me out.[23] His Grace, Robert Selby Taylor, had been informed of these troubles in the household and called me to visit him at Bishopscourt in Cape Town. It was an ominous invitation.

Just vaguely I remember the meeting, for this whole thing had developed such an air of unreality about it. To anyone else it might have looked comical, and it probably had some amusing moments. One of those may have been when the Archbishop (a bachelor) and I dined alone in his immense formal dining room, making polite chit chat at opposite ends of his huge table, a good fifteen feet apart. We then retired to the "Smoker," (aka Library) lit up cigars and sipped brandy in a lot of silence. In the course of the cigars, civility and silence he made it very clear why I had been summoned to Bishopscourt. The upshot of it came in one simple sentence, spoken in his deep Oxford accent. "Shannon, I regret to have to say this…(long episcopal pause) but one of you will have to go." He didn't need to say which one because he didn't have to: a bishop always trumps an archdeacon, regardless of the facts. It was an impossible conundrum. Sad and heartbroken, I returned to Odibo for the last time, to tell Mondi and the family we would have to leave St. Mary's. Anger, despair, and sadness descended upon us for the next few months as we slowly uprooted ourselves from the happy life we had known there. Our last week was the most wrenching of all. For five days, we sat under the big *embe* tree outside our home and listened to speeches and singing from hundreds who had come from miles around to bid us farewell. We felt blacklisted!

It was a painful farewell. The final irony was that had the Church waited, the civil authorities would have done its dirty work: my permit to remain in Ovamboland had already been revoked by the government. Thus it was that we entered a period of feeling unwanted, evicted, and betrayed by Church and State, not knowing what the future held.

---

[23] The Archbishop of Cape Town is the primate responsible for the entire Church of the Province of Southern Africa, which comprises a number of countries and a great number of dioceses, including Namibia..

Meanwhile, Jacob was having his own tribulations in another part of Africa. He had grown in the ranks of SWAPO to become Secretary General and in that capacity had become one of their chief spokesmen. I would like to think that his schooling at St. Mary's Mission School had helped develop his oratorical skills. He became noted for his ability to speak convincingly in simple plain language.

Jacob's lifelong passion was for education. He had reiterated on many occasions that SWAPO leadership was not overly committed to an armed liberation struggle although he had to go soft on that point to receive recognition and material support from the Organization of African Unity. But Jacob Kuhangwa was more committed to the education of political refugees than to a bloody fight. He repeatedly stressed that an independent Namibia would require well-educated people to govern it competently, underscoring that Namibians in exile should seek education rather than military training. This put him on a collision course with other SWAPO leaders. One of them was Louis Nelengani, who had received guerrilla training in the Soviet Union. Kuhangwa had received his further education in the United States and was no friend of the Soviet Union or the communist system. Nelengani, on the other hand, was known to hate the United States, the capitalist system and everything associated with the West. Namibians in exile found themselves divided between them. Things came to a tragic head in Dar es Salaam when Nelengani attacked Kuhangwa with a butcher knife, stabbing him in the back and severing his spinal cord. Jacob would spend the rest of his life in a wheelchair, and Nelengani would die several years later by the violence he had embraced.

Jacob had been true to his earliest dream as a young boy—to get education and to help others do likewise —but he had paid a price for his dream. He believed that education was the key to the eventual liberation of his people: education of global leaders, education of business leaders to realize that morals and ethics play a key part in the health of any work force; and education of his own people to be able to take charge of their own destiny. Jacob didn't live to see it all happen but he saw signs of a new day soon to dawn for his country.

This stranger was the stranger who had brought us to Africa. But for that one brief meeting in our New York City apartment, I would never see him again. Yet I owe him much. Without his brief cameo appearance in my life, we would never have ventured to Africa. Without his passionate spirit for justice my own spirit may never have been kindled as it was. And without our meeting, my own life would have been the poorer for not having fallen in love with Africa and the people of the Third World.

Chapter Five

Massacre

Perhaps there is a divine irony that Jacob Kuhangwa was so frequently called to follow in the footsteps of his Biblical namesake. Many thousands of years before, God spoke to that other Jacob at crucial junctions, telling him to lead his people away from a life of servitude to become a people who ceased to bow down to earthly powers.[24] And so it was for this Jacob, in leading his people through great tribulations to freedom. Much of his time was required at SWAPO headquarters in Lusaka. The number of refugees from South West Africa was increasing dramatically and safe locations were in short supply. One camp became famous. The following are the details of that camp as related by Jacob Kuhangwa years later. In relating the story, Jacob made it clear this event was one with the events that destroyed most of St. Mary's Mission—High School, Seminary, Hospital, residences and hostels. This was Jacob's report:

> "Cassinga was an abandoned mining town in southern Angola and had been chosen by SWAPO to be a regional camp for refugees coming out of Namibia. It was selected because it was 250 kilometers from the war zone in Ovamboland and was offered by the Angolan government; most importantly, it was remote and situated next to a river.

---

[24] See "The Gifts of the Jews", p. 89-90.

It became a semi-permanent settlement for non-combatants who fled the terror in Namibia. But it was nonetheless a place of uneasy refuge because Angola was also in the grip of a civil war at the time. SWAPO code named the place "Moscow". Soon, upwards of 4,000 Namibian refugees lived there under the command of SWAPO military leaders. Entire families dwelled there. They had schools for the children and a wide variety of activities to make the community productive and self-supporting. They also had a bush clinic with a few foreign doctors. One was a young German neurosurgeon from Berlin.[25]

The South African Defense Force, like the apartheid government it defended, had spies everywhere and was aware of virtually everything that went on at Cassinga. The practice of using paid informers to infiltrate SWAPO was one of the things that made the Struggle so ugly and dangerous for Namibians. That practice set brother against brother, children against parents, and family against family. No other practice sowed as much terror throughout the country and it took years after Independence to purge the bitter suspicion left throughout the country. Cassinga was not heavily armed, except for some hand weapons, a few grenades and an old anti-aircraft canon. "Operation Reindeer" took place on May 4, 1978 and was South Africa's secret military operation to wipe out Cassinga. It involved a combat force of over 2,000 troops with helicopters, jet bombers and reconnaissance planes. Quoting from South African military records, the objective was "to kill or capture Dino Hamaambo (the Base Commander) and as many terrorists (their terminology) as possible; to destroy ammunition, equipment and weapons, and to capture documents"

Every day began an 8:00 am sharp at Cassinga. Men, women and children lined up on the parade ground for daily

---

[25] Many years later, that same German surgeon, Dr. Fred Gartner, would save my life after a fall from a high scaffold during the rebuilding of St. Mary's High School.

instructions. That was the perfect time for an aerial attack. According to records, it took place in four phases. At 8:05 four Canberra bombers flying low, dropped fragmentation bombs. These were ugly bombs, designed to maim any human target. They are called 'dirty bombs' and considered illegal under the Geneva Convention, but such details didn't stop Operation Reindeer. With the first bombing, the parade ground was mayhem: women and children screaming, trying to run for cover, blood and body parts everywhere, surrounded by deafening noise, smoke and screaming. And suddenly it got eerily quiet but only for a moment, until four more bombers flew low, dropping thousand pound bombs that destroyed the buildings and made craters in the earth. Then more ominous quiet, pierced with screams of the dying. As survivors crawled from cover hoping it was over, came the most brutal blow of all: four Mirage jets flew low and strafed the survivors with rockets. After this, as if they needed more, six planes flew over and dropped four companies of paratroopers to lead a land attack on whoever was still alive. It was over in less than three hours. It is a miracle anyone survived but some did to tell this story.

The South Africans' grotesque report said it was like shooting fish in a barrel. It was celebrated and treated lightly on South African television. One South African source reported 1,000 dead, 240 wounded, and 200 captured. A report in "Namibian Woman" broke down the figures more accurately: 'On that day, South African troops murdered 298 children, 147 elderly and handicapped, and 170 women; over 1,000 were wounded and another 300 abducted by the invading forces. Word of the slaughter reached the United Nations Headquarters in New York within 24 hours, and recriminations and excuses from South Africa followed. Nothing much came of it in the end. Meanwhile at Cassinga, the dead were so many they made two mass graves to bury them. A crude epitaph was scraped into the huge cement slab over one mass grave: 'We Shall Remember Them'..." This was Jacob's official report of the incident.

Twenty five years later, in 2004, I visited the site, along with a truck-load of Ovamboes who had lost family members at Cassinga. Ladened with excited passengers and not much else, we left St. Mary's heading north. We hoped to make the 250 kilometer journey in one day, spend the night, and return the next day. In fact, it was about to become a trip with monumental delays and we made none of our time targets. It started at the Angola border where we were told our papers were not in order. Nor a good omen. We needed additional documentation from the Namibian side to enter Angola. Back to the other side for a two-hour wait in the queues. With the new documents in hand we returned to the Angolan authorities. Ah, this time we were told we needed "additional" documentation to verify that the truck we were driving really belonged to us, that the engine was not stolen, the vehicle was fully insured, and that it had a valid license. In the banana republic that Angola was at the time, who were these guys kidding! But back to Namibia to the Regional Office where our humiliation was only beginning. We arrived fifteen minutes before lunch time and were told nothing would happen for the next hour and a half, as they "dined". In fact, the young officials in the office were surly enough to send the message that we might not even get the documentation after lunch if they didn't feel like it or were otherwise too busy. It was hot and we had limited supplies of food and water, just enough for the road and were running low on patience. After a leisurely lunch break, the young officials wandered into the office, picking their teeth, and asked what we wanted, acting as if they had never seen us before. Having explained it all before lunch, we related it all one more time. As if not hearing a word spoken, one of them intoned, "And another thing, you will have to remove your vehicle from this parking area: kindly observe this is for official vehicles only. You are not official. You can park down there", pointing his finger a good hundred yards away. I began to wonder if Cassinga was worth it...

By the time we got our papers in order and presented ourselves to the Angolan authorities, the day was shot. The next best thing was to make for Namakunde, a miserable little dorp I had known from the sixties. We hoped to sleep there and move early the next morning. No such luck. In beautiful downtown Namakunde, there was neither hotel nor motel, neither camp site nor tent site. The place barely existed. We had no choice but to press on over the worst roads in all of Africa. What gave them that distinction was a combination of the last season's flood waters, makeshift bridges, levees that had collapsed and gargantuan trucks that left ruts deep enough to swallow our truck or turn it over. Trucks were notoriously big in Angola: instead of the usual double axle on a big rig, they would have three and sometimes four.

The journey was made slower because none of us knew where we were going; that meant constant stops to ask the locals. Usually we got one of three pieces of advice from the highway consultants: "You're hopelessly lost so turn around," "No, not this road…the other one", or "You're okay." Naturally, the last one was heard the least. Just before sunset we bumbled into the general vicinity of Cassinga. In the fading light of sunset, we could hardly find what remained of the bombed out buildings, covered with forest and bush. The locals revered the area and had left it alone for the decades. Roads and trails had disappeared and we wandered aimlessly on foot through waist-high bush. Only days later did we realize that entire area was still heavily mined from the days of the Struggle. Thirty-two feet had been walking over unexploded land mines buried in the undergrowth. It was a miracle we came out alive.

Using flashlights and torches, at last we stumbled onto the parade ground, recognizable only by the remains of a few buildings that outlined the area. Brave slogans of a bygone war were visible on the few crumbled remains, graffiti hastily written to stoke up those going forth to their destiny. Forth to fight an enemy so big and strong and distant, they were doomed from the start. The odds were much worse than David and Goliath. That faded graffiti was probably a talisman for the young Namibians rushing forth into the gunfire of attacking aircraft.

Hardly a word was spoken as we walked the area, each of us dealing with our own imagination of what it must have been like. It was a long, solemn moment. There were tears, quiet weeping and blank stares of disbelief, like people whose thoughts had suddenly left them. Then the biggest shock of all: we stumbled upon the mass grave. It was the moment we all had secretly dreaded and hoped somehow wouldn't happen. It really was there, just as the stories had said. It was the size of a large swimming pool, covered with a concrete slap, holding hundreds of bodies. Scratched into the slab and barely visible were the words, "Always Remember Them", and I wondered about that. I wondered why the place was such a mess; why there was bush and trees of twenty five years' growth; why there were no signs or markers to say "This Was the Mighty Cassinga;" why the huge gravestone was deteriorating? I wondered, is this the way they got remembered? And I felt very sad, like wailing, but I didn't. Why had the Namibian government allowed this site to deteriorate? Why wasn't it a national shrine? I still don't have answers to those questions. But then, maybe I do. Maybe this memory was just too painful and humiliating to hang onto. Later, we were told a group of officials from Namibia had paid a visit to the site on Cassinga Day a few years prior. There's been nothing since. Maybe the best way to remember Cassinga is to forget it. Some memories are just too painful to remember.

We were exhausted and emotionally drained from our visit to the killing field. It was dark, we were without food or bedding, with no place to lay our heads, and we didn't seem to care, nothing seemed to matter. I decided we would drive all night to the border post and wait for the gate to open the next morning. It was dark now and I just wanted to get out of there. And then a wonderful thing happened, and we were more than ready for even a small wonderful thing. We were told to drive to a nearby village, named Chimakela, where we could spend the night, and the local people proceeded to guide our truck through the bush. Angels had come to our rescue from the death camp that was

Cassinga. Chimakela resembled the sleepy old Portuguese station it had once been, run-down but with warm hospitality. We could have cared less about its physical appearance.

Now, well and truly lost somewhere in Angola, we were taken to the village leader who was a tall gracious man with the unlikely name of Galliano. He spoke just enough Kwanyama to understand our situation and insisted on feeding us in his own house. He then topped off his hospitality with bottled Angolan beer which really made him the hero of the day. After meal and malt, Galliano the Great insisted he would find beds for us, and in less than half an hour he came forth with simple rubber mattresses, blankets and pillows. I shall never forget Galliano's hospitality.

The next morning, as our tank was perilously low, our angel-host gave us enough petrol to make it back to Namibia. I thought it was ironic that Angola, one of the major oil-producing nations in Africa, had not one roadside amenity or petrol station in all that lonely road.

It's interesting what we do with memories, even the collective ones. If we're insecure, perhaps we exaggerate them. If we're secure, we may remember them. But if we're too wounded to face them, then maybe we just let them slip away so they don't hurt us anymore. Maybe Cassinga needs to slip away quietly into the forest it once was, before the days too painful to remember.

It was good to get back to Odibo…and some of us will never forget Cassinga.

Chapter Six

Getting Kicked Around...and Out

We left South West Africa in late 1969 amidst political and ecclesiastical turmoil. Politically, things continued to get worse. It was clear to everyone who thought deeply about the situation that a violent denouement was approaching the country. SWAPO's influence continued to grow as the South African Defense Force tried to stamp it out. "The Struggle" was an insurgency that would continue for another twenty years. The strategy of boycotting South Africa's economy to bring about political change was still a hard sell internationally. Western leaders and politicians continued to be ill-informed of what was taking place under the *apartheid* regime and reluctant to believe that boycotts could change anything. The truth was that Western investors in the South African economy chose to turn a blind eye and not get involved. Nelson Mandela and his inner circle had been locked up for life on Robbin Island, and his efforts had been deliberately misunderstood by some Western leaders. President Reagan and Prime Minister Thatcher continued to call all those pressing for change "terrorists"and chose to believe the South African government propaganda that said they knew what was best for the Africans. Desmond Tutu hadn't yet arrived on the scene and was living in Geneva and working for the World Council of Churches.

The next two years would be a new adventure for us in every way. We left our home and work in the all black area of Ovamboland

and headed to Grahamstown, a town in South Africa, where I would do postgraduate work at whites-only Rhodes University and teach daughters of wealthy white South Africans in a prestigious Anglican institution, the Diocesan School for Girls. It would be an eye-opening experience. DSG, as the school was called, catered to affluent farmers and professionals in the Eastern Cape. Beyond duties at DSG, my time would be spent working on a social anthropology research degree. Although so totally different from what we had known thus far, remarkably, these would be halcyon days for us.

Grahamstown had an illustrious history. Situated in the Eastern Cape Province of South Africa, it was one of the most English towns in South Africa. The Anglican Cathedral sat at one end of the town, Rhodes University at the other, joined by High Street, lined with quaint shops that could have come right out of London. The town was named after a British colonel and founded as a British military outpost in 1812, about the time Napoleon was preparing for victory in St. Petersburg. Further afield, around the same time the thirteen colonies were about to declare war on Great Britain in what has been called the "second war of independence," It was the season of conquest and it was no coincidence Great Britain had chosen this part of South Africa. The British Empire wanted to establish influence over the Xhosa nation whose lands lay just to the east. In just a few generations, this great nation would produce a host of world-class leaders, including Nelson Mandela and Desmond Tutu. In 1820, the British government moved 4,000 colonists into the area in an effort to secure this outpost against the Afrikaner Boers. It would become the largest British settlement in Africa. These 1820 settlers, as they came to be known, would become a continuing thorn in the side of the Boers.

Grahamstown developed as the focal point for the 1820 settlers. Ironically it came to be known as 'The City of Saints' because of a vibrant spirit of evangelism during its heyday, then home to more than forty religious buildings. The story is told of the Royal Engineers in 1846 in need of building materials. They sent word to Cape Town requesting a machinist's vice be sent to them from the government stores. A reply came back "Buy vice locally". The response from Grahamstown was "No vice in Grahamstown".[26]

The Diocesan School for Girls was founded in 1874 and became the training ground for many of the grand dames of British South African society. There was more than a little irony with us going there; for us, nothing could have been more of a contrast from our last eight years.

My attachment to the School came about in a strange way. I was planning on some time for academic reflection at Rhodes University, and the only housing we could find for our large brood was at the Diocesan School for Girls, but there was a catch to it. The housing would be free if I served as Chaplain. What was provided was an historic building known as "The Grange," a rambling old structure which looked like it had been built in 1820, old but clean and sparkling white all over from many coats of whitewash. It had dozens of rooms, some of them used by the Music Department, the remainder for us. The toilets were a particular amusement. They consisted of two bathrooms, one on each end of the house, both arranged with a long row of toilets, dormitory style, from the days when the building had been used as a dormitory. Our large brood never lacked for a toilet. We came to love the drafty old building with high ceilings, hardwood floors, two fireplaces and huge windows. It sat on the school grounds, high upon a lawn that overlooked the school pool and the little town of Grahamstown.

We would miss our home in Ovamboland but find fulfilment here in other ways. As we now lived with the daughters of the privileged, we would see firsthand how the other side lived. I can't say 'other half' because the black-white ratio was about one-to-twenty. The only contact many of these white girls had with Africans was as house boys or gardeners or perhaps drivers. Not surprisingly, therefore, most of the girls knew nothing about the African people and were gullible to fables and irrationality of every sort. Some of them believed that to touch an implement used by an African or to come in contact with their sweat

---

[26] By the time we arrived, there was scant evidence of any vibrant spirit of evangelism nor a preponderance of churches. Religiously, the town was solidly and stolidly Anglican.

would in some manner taint you or turn you black. Many believed Africans were sub-human and incapable of intelligent thought. And alas, this was the mentality that the *apartheid* policy appealed to and created.

They were good girls from good families that went to church every week and said their prayers every night. But they had been shielded from Africa as perhaps their parents had been, deprived of learning about their black neighbors and left to learn by old wives' tales and bizarre stories handed down. They had doubts and fears of the unknown surrounding them to an unhealthy degree. It was astonishing to meet families that had lived in Africa for generations who had such little knowledge of their African neighbors, and sad to see the degree of ignorance these privileged girls had about the people in whose land they lived. I would learn it was more than naive ignorance: it was a deliberate religious teaching that had brought this about. They had been taught that God had created an inferior subservient race. This was pure Calvinist theology upon which the Dutch Reformed Church was established. I tried to broaden their horizon but couldn't broaden their understanding. It was a closed system, comfortable and confined, walled off in its own fantasy world.

One Sunday I was invited by Father Dhlamini, the neighboring African priest, to visit his parish church. I was thrilled to get outside the white Grahamstown ghetto. His parish was in a nearby Township designated for the Xhosa people. It was a traditional Anglican service, with singing for which the Xhosa people are famous, after which I was asked to say a few words. That consisted of greeting them, expressing appreciation to be among them, telling them they were special in God's eyes, and thanking them for their warm African welcome. Following the service, I had tea and cold drinks with the congregation, exchanged greetings and departed. I returned home feeling like I had made connection with the real Africa that morning, and nostalgic for life among the African people which we no longer had.

Later that afternoon, a stranger knocked on our door. He was a handsome young Afrikaner, well groomed in typical South African dress of the day, khaki shorts, knee socks, and a white rugby shirt. In a pleasant tone of voice he asked if I would please come to his *baakie* (pick-up) for a chat. I thought it a bit strange but he seemed sincere enough and so I went along. But then it became apparent what was coming down: he knew I had visited the local African church which was in the non-white township. (I was aware that might be an issue, since I had not obtained a permit to visit outside the white area). He wanted to know what I said to the congregation. "What did you say to those people? he asked. "I greeted them, told them God was on their side and blessed them—pretty innocent stuff, or so I thought." "What do you mean saying God is on their side?" he wanted to know. "Well, God is for all of us, don't you know?" "No!" he spat out with anger. "God is not for everybody the same and we don't think the African has God's blessing like we do! You have no business telling kaffirs those things!" With his limited English he continued, "God mean that all kaffirs should be servants." I was shocked to hear out loud such a bold statement of what I suspected most Afrikaners thought anyway, There was a long silence during which I thought of all sorts of openers like *"Well guess what, bozo, we are all God's children"* or *"Then why are you so out-numbered in this land that is their land...you will have too many servants!"* But I kept quiet. And then he lectured me in mangled English: "Padre, you understand the kaffir not like me and you; he don't think much 'cause he got only small brain. They's limited to what they understand, like little children. Pas op Padre, you got no business going visit them and definitely not locations or townships 'round Grahamstown. You know you must have official permit to go there, don't you?" I think you not do this again!" I was too angry to speak and wanted to question his own mental capacity. Then there was a dramatic shift: he got friendly and tried a new canard, saying he looked forward to more chats in the future. I didn't, but there would be more nonetheless. I learned later this charming young man was from the Special Branch, the intelligence wing of the government, that lived in the shadows and spied on people, especially Anglican clergy with American accents. Vanny van der Merwe's buddies. The Special Branch operated by night and with lethal force against Africans. This handsome young man and I would meet again.

My work with the girls was not always frustrating and we had some good times together. Living on the School grounds made it easy for the girls to drop in just to chat, a few times to babysit, and sometimes for more serious conversation. Often they would come over to listen to music or picnic on our large lawn. "Jesus Christ Superstar" was the popular favorite then and they knew all the lyrics. I wondered who Jesus was to those white, naive, *apartheid*-observing girls. He had certainly been converted into a white Caucasian, fair haired and blue eyed, like a typical Afrikaner. Maybe we all domesticate Jesus so he looks like our coeval. I knew it was impossible for them to recognize Jesus in a black person, ever to see him in the poor and down-trodden around them, and more's the pity. They were simply a product of a society that had built a wall of ignorance and prejudice around them and had bent the world to suit their reality.

Some months later, I had coffee with Father Dhlamini from the neighboring township. We talked about his ministry and how things were going for his parish. Poverty and the ever-present oppression of *apartheid* inevitably came up in any conversation across racial lines, as it did with us. He recited the usual litany of woes suffered by non-Europeans, of how people were routinely jailed for minor pass law violations, of almost nightly police raids looking for political agitators, of the indignities of being called 'boy' by the whites and having to use separate public facilities, and where there were none, how they had to cope however they could. He talked about the appalling living conditions in his township where their meagre electricity supply was habitually cut off and water restricted to one spigot for an entire street. I felt frustration and sorrow for him and those who had to put up with such treatment, simply because of skin color. That night my thoughts were all about, "How long, O Lord? How long!"

The next afternoon, the pleasant young man without a name came to call on me again. I wasn't surprised. All smiles, he suggested we go for a drive which I reluctantly agreed to. It wasn't a drive at all but another interrogation in his *baakie*. Surprise! He knew of my coffee with Father Dhlamini. He knew where we met but he didn't know what we had talked about. That was the subject of an intense conversation he was determined to have. "What you talk about with the Domine? (He refused to call him Father, using the Afrikaans title for minister). "Why you want to see him?" "How come you know him?" "How well you know him, do you talk to him reglar?" "You must know he's a trouble-maker in this dorp. He get members of his church worked up and we watch 'cause they's up to mischief." Who was up to greater mischief, I thought to myself, when the South African government was oppressing helpless and harmless non-whites by the thousands every day. I remained quiet as he continued, "Padre, you Residence Permit you live in Grahamstown and teach at DSG, you know that?" *Of course I did, you idiot*, was what I wanted to say. "Yes sir" I replied. "Then you better not visit the kaffirs no more but stick to you work here in town. Pas op, Padre, you could get into big trouble." I'd heard that line before and had a good idea what it meant. I remained quiet. And then he got down to business with somewhat of a prepared speech. He said, "You know, Father, they's harmful elements in Suid Africa (Afrikaans, pron. "sayd" Africa) today that are trying to give the government a bad name and disturb our peace. We pretty sure these bad elements come from outside Suid Africa, probably other African countries. Theys communists and want to mess up Suid Africa's rule of law. You are new to Suid Africa and must watch out for these people. We have nice country and we intend to keep it that way." I was not that new to South Africa and had lived under their evil system of government for almost a decade and had to disagree with most of what he said, but I did so silently. So I sat and listened, having decided attempting to converse with the Special Branch about anything would be counter-productive.

We parted with an insincere handshake. I would never see him again but alas, he would see me—just one more time.

In the classroom we spent hours discussing ethical issues and challenges with a little bit of Biblical history thrown in, but we never discussed *apartheid* head on. I sensed that could have caused a major upheaval within the school, which I did not need. The discussions we had on truth and justice made it fairly obvious official government policy was wrong in every way, but I avoided asking if they thought *apartheid* was wrong, because in a vacuum of thought they probably would have said it wasn't. These girls in their mid-teens didn't actually live in a vacuum but in a land of dark make-believe, astonishingly able to dissociate themselves from the reality of their country when talking about justice and fair play. For them, the theoretical and the actual never made contact. By an unspoken societal fear, whites were discouraged from straying too far from the *apartheid* party line. Such social pressure, subtle but strong, meant going along to get along, which is what the majority of well-meaning white South Africans did. The unspoken mantra was, "whatever you do or say, don't make waves!"

These not-so-innocent girls had been raised in a society that was basically *laissez-faire* and they enjoyed the good life they had inherited. That required having plenty of African help around as servants, house-boys, gardeners, cooks, and drivers. Yet despite this overwhelming presence of blacks in all walks of their lives, the average white knew very little about Africans. It 'simply wasn't done' to become too friendly with the help other than as superiors who gave the orders. For an African to speak to a white as an equal was considered "cheeky" for which they often got a beating, though the African might have a university degree and the white person barely literate. Africans knew their place and whites, even the good-hearted ones, made damn sure they did. For me to witness black-white encounters invariably made me cringe with embarrassment for the blacks or fume inwardly about the white attitude of superiority. The racial barrier that existed meant that none of the girls would know any African on a personal basis as an individual like themselves with emotions and dreams, hopes and fears. This, of course was the intention of government policy from the beginning. Any human understanding of the African was denied them by the law of the land. *Apartheid*, "separate development," had won the day for at least two generations to come.

Consequently, there were days when I wondered what I was doing at the Girls' School. My work at Rhodes saved many a day from despondency. I buried myself in a study that focused on how well Christianity had been assimilated by the Ovambo people. I could just as well have researched how well it had penetrated the *whites* in South Africa. My supervisor, Professor Calvin Cook, had a keen mind that added a lot of stimulation to the project and kept me challenged. It was only in hindsight and through this time of study that I came to see centuries of Christian mission to Africa in a wholly new way, how it had shaped both black and white society, in many ways not always to the good. I was beginning to learn that black Africa was remarkably resilient when it came to changing its ancient world view and spirituality. I would come to wonder if Christianity had ever been on the right track with its approach to "heathen religions." In short, I would discover that devout Ovambo Christians still held many of the beliefs of their forefathers and that many of them were not in conflict with Christian teaching. Perhaps for them, becoming a Christian was more like taking out a second life insurance policy that didn't cancel or alter the original. [27]

The exercise of my priesthood took a back seat in those days, aside from serving as Chaplain at the Girls' School. It took a sudden leap out of the back seat the day the Dean of the Cathedral invited me to participate in a dialogue on the subject of violence. It was to be in the form of a sermon at Sunday Evensong, a popular weekly Cathedral service. The invitation sounded interesting if a little ominous, for this was not a subject openly discussed in public by anyone. The Dean had invited David Hamer, the Chaplain of St. Paul's Theological College and a good friend, to be my counterpart. Both of us believed that violence was seldom right or justified except in trying to stop a greater violence, and our opposition to violence in general made this a difficult assignment. But given the political situation in South Africa we felt there was too much at stake not to use the occasion to speak out. The format we settled on was a dialogue sermon that involved reading passages from the Bible, notably those from the Prophets which spoke against injustice and oppression, and to intersperse (contrast) them with selected *apartheid* laws. It was gutsy, if not foolish of us, but we were determined not to make this simply an intellectual or philosophical presentation. We thought the two sources, the Biblical Prophets and the South African laws, could best speak for themselves without much

---

[27] See "Postscript" for further discussion of this point.

personal comment from us. I suspect we were also thinking that, should trouble follow, we could claim we were only reading from reliable sources. It would later turn out that reasoning wasn't worth much to the authorities.

It was a chilling exercise to put the two sources side by side: the words of the Prophets and the *apartheid* laws of the land. Anyone with a modest knowledge of the Old Testament would be aware of the stern condemnation the Prophets had for the unjust practices of their day. For them, to serve God meant to act with justice. They were fearless in speaking truth to power, in condemning kings and rulers, often at great personal suffering and sacrifice. We didn't wish to repeat their example, but thought the relevance of their utterances was perfectly on target. We also understood that using the Bible to challenge the South African government was probably a risky thing to do, since they had an entirely different way of understanding Holy Writ.

That difference had long been a point of contention among Christians, and not only in South Africa. Anglicans have always understood Scripture not simply by what is written but also as being informed and interpreted by tradition and reason. We therefore admit to error and contradiction in the Bible and do not believe it to be the infallible Word of God, but rather a compilation of writings by fallible and sinful individuals, collected over many centuries. Such an approach is radically different from that of the Calvinist tradition of the Afrikaner Dutch Reformed Church, which was the State Church in South Africa.

Calvinism was officially adopted by the Dutch Reformed Church in the Netherlands in 1571, the mother church of the Dutch Reformed Church in South Africa. John Calvin was an influential leader in Geneva in the sixteenth century, who insisted that people be kept under close watch for their own moral benefit and that crimes should be severely punished. His brand of Christianity had a hard edge to it and was a harbinger of things to come in South Africa, centuries later.

One of the basic tenets of classical Calvinism, sometimes referred to as the Reformed Tradition, maintains that salvation is by grace alone and that God chooses some to be saved, but not all. The saved are commonly referred to as "the elect". Africans were not believed to be among the elect but were created as a lesser servant class, destined to be "hewers of wood and drawers of water." For the Afrikaner, this had its basis in a literal understanding of passages from the Book of Joshua (9:9-21).[28]Another tenet of Calvinism is the belief that the Bible is the infallible Word of God. Practically speaking, this amounts to a kind of fundamentalism that believes Scripture means exactly what it says in every instance. Error and contradiction within the Bible are neither admitted nor explained. Thus, in the above passage when the Book of Joshua speaks of one group becoming servants of another because of treachery and deceit, by a remarkable stretch of logic Afrikaners took this to mean God *created* the African to serve them. They believed this arrangement was God's will and the divine order for the creation and that it was not an issue of justice or morality at all. Using this strange logic, it was an easy step to use the Bible to justify the *apartheid* policy of Afrikaner nationalism. Thus, at the behest of the National Party in power a theological justification for *apartheid* was devised by South African Reformed theologians. Such an interpretation was quickly condemned by all Reformed Churches outside South Africa but the intransigence of the South African State Church over this issue led to their expulsion from the World Council of Churches. Their response to that action was to regard themselves as the victim of deliberate worldwide misunderstanding; they subsequently referred to themselves as the "skunk of the world".

It was against this backdrop that David and I stepped into in our public dialogue.

The first law to be presented was the Criminal Law Amendment Act of 1953 which gave draconian powers to the government. It had been passed in response to a non-violent demonstration in 1952 organized by the African National Congress (ANC) against specific *apartheid* laws. That campaign had been directed by a very young Nelson Mandela

---

[28] This passage describes a meeting between two tribes, the latter pretending to be subject to the former in order to save themselves. Whereupon the former appoint them to be "hewers of wood and drawers of water," as a servant race forever. A literal interpretation holds this to be a permanent arrangement when most likely it was not meant to be interpreted that way.

and his colleagues. It had recruited volunteers to refuse to carry passes, defy 'European only' signs in public places, and enter restricted areas. The plan, similar to that used by Gandhi in South Africa thirty years prior, was to clog the judicial process with arrests and detentions. The campaign succeeded fairly well, and by the end of that year 5,000 had gone to jail and over 8,000 had been arrested. It did clog the judicial system. But the State had to act to stop this interference, and thus enacted a law which stated *"Any person who in any way whatsoever advises, encourages, incites, commands, aids or procures any other person or uses language calculated to cause any other person to commit an offense by way of protest against any law shall be guilty of an offense."* Passive resistance against any law would thus be illegal—there was no legal way left for non-whites to protest against injustice.

We read the law, the details of which were probably news to most listeners, and followed it with words from the Prophets: *"Is it just a slight thing that you fill the land with violence…I will punish all who oppress with violence…" "Do not oppress the widow, the fatherless or the poor, for great wrath will come from the Lord."* [29] The South African government was one of the most violent in the so-called free world, and it was our aim to present that fact to the congregation. But alas, systematic violence would only get worse for the next three decades, as it got more legalized.

Twenty-five years after that campaign, Nelson Mandela would refuse freedom from prison because he and the ANC would not renounce their violence. In what would become a famous response: he said it was *the South African government* that needed to renounce their greater violence, a systemic violence woven into a myriad of laws that propped up the *apartheid* state. *Then* the ANC would follow suit.

Contract labor was the next subject of the evening. Having personally witnessed the disintegrating effects of migrant labor on African life among the mine workers and the devastation it caused to their families back home, I had some personal experience of this. Under the Contract Labour Laws contract workers were designated as "labour

---

[29] Ezekiel 8:17, Jeremiah 30:20, Zechariah 7:10.

units" rather than as human beings. That alone was a telling statement. Contract labor was indentured and in effect owned by the employer. This law meant (1) contracts were for eighteen to thirty six months at a time and visits home were not permitted; (2) shifts were long, and at the discretion of the employer, could be up to twelve hours a day, seven days a week; (3) visits by wives and families were not permitted; (4) pay could not be negotiated and employers were free to pay whatever they wished; (5) living quarters were crude and often mere slums; (6) diet and medical services depended on the employer; and (7) African labor unions were illegal. In terms of this law, an African worker had no recourse to abuse or human rights violations. It was a legalized form of slavery.

Having read the law and its application, portions of the Book of Lamentations were read: *"We have become as orphans, fatherless, and our mothers like widows…with a yoke on our necks we are hard driven, weary and given no rest".* [30] The Cathedral was eerily quiet. I must admit to being pretty up-tight by this point.

Next came the Group Areas Act. That was the law that had taken the house of Jacob's granny from her and caused untold suffering throughout the land. The law authorized the government to expropriate African lands and farms and assign them to Europeans, forcibly moving the African inhabitants to designated "group areas". The law was implemented ostensibly for slum clearance but in practice it was used to procure fertile African land for white development. Sheer greed motivated many of the removals. Having read the law, we quoted more of the Old Testament: *"Woe to those who covet fields and seize them and houses and take them away, that oppress a man and his house, a man and his inheritance…" "You who trample upon the needy and bring the poor of the land to an end…behold the days of judgment are coming."* [31]

Then came the Sabotage Act of 1962, one of the most egregious of all laws. This Act allowed for detention up to ninety days, without trial or charges, and defined sabotage so broadly as to include labor strikes

---

[30] Lamentations 5:3-5.
[31] Amos 8:4, 11; Micah 2:1; Lamentations 5:4

and almost everything else. Terrorism and sabotage were defined as *any act that endangered the law and order, public safety, health or the movement of traffic, that jeopardized the supply of fuel, food, water, light and power, or hindered medical services, anyone who trespassed on any land or building or destroyed private or public property.* The word of a local policeman was enough to bring charges which could carry the death penalty.

We joined it with the reading of the Terrorism Act of 1967. This law allowed for the detention of anyone by a policeman of the rank of lieutenant colonel or higher for almost any common criminal behavior, or the mere suspicion of such. People could be held indefinitely with no visitors allowed, and the public not allowed information about those being held, including their identity. This law meant that people could simply disappear for official reasons and many did.

We ended with words from Isaiah: *"Woe to those who decree iniquitous decrees, to those who keep writing oppressive laws to turn away the needy from justice and rob the poor of my people of their right…what will you do on the day of punishment, to whom will you flee for help and where will you leave your wealth?"*[32] We ended the evening's presentation with a general question, "Is this the kind of country you want South Africa to be? And with words from Hosea, *"Hear the word of the Lord…the Lord is angry with the inhabitants of the land (because) there is no kindness, no knowledge of God in the land…(but) there is lying, killing, stealing… and murder follows murder."*[33] These haunting questions could call into question the exploits of a lifetime, all of them done *within the law.*

The Cathedral was quiet for a long time. We were realizing the seriousness of what we had just done, but feeling we had done what was needed. I no longer cared what the government response might be. We had presented the harsh realities of an *apartheid* nation that believed in God and said their prayers, but also believed that God had created the African as inferior and therefore a servant. What *would* they say

---

[32] Isaiah 10:1-3
[33] Hosea 4:1.

on the day of judgment, which the Afrikaner most assuredly believed would come?

The average South African had little or no knowledge of these laws. They lived in fear, simply knowing the Police and the State were dreaded authorities to be avoided at all costs, and they were probably looking after things as best they could. The popular mantra of the common man was "Don't ask questions."

There was little comment following the Service, except for the few who congratulated us and commended the presentation. That was mostly the university crowd. Everyone else was too frightened to speak because we were all being watched. My handsome young interrogator from the Special Branch, along with his friends, sat in the front row taking notes. Newspaper journalists were there too. The one reported to the authorities, the other to the press. Neither report was favorable the next day. Although there was little fall-out that evening, there was plenty the next morning. One regional newspaper headlined in bold type:

"ANGLICANS WARN OF VIOLENCE" [34]

The article went on to report:

Violence in South Africa was not so much necessary as inevitable and inescapable, two Anglican priests said in a dialogue, the first of a Lenten series in Grahamstown Cathedral...in one of the most controversial public discussions heard by the congregation they said violence was the sole basis of the security of the State. Defining violence as the unlawful exercise of physical force or intimidation by a show of physical force, Father Mallory cited three laws by which the solidarity of the State was secured by violence.."

"The Chief Interrogation Officer in South Africa, Major T.J. Swanepoel, as quoted as saying in 1969, 'in many ways

---

[34] The East London Daily Dispatch, March 3, 1971.

our methods are the same as the communists but for different reasons…"

"The two priests said non-violent resistance or non- violent cooperation as practiced by Martin Luther King and Gandhi was based on fundamentally Christian principles…They said that violence remained violence even if it was legalized. South Africans had reached a crossroads. They had this choice: either a non-violent solution had to be found or white South Africa faced non-existence, the priests said."

"Father Mallory said the only hope lay in people recognizing the situation and trying to do something about ending it. If South Africans were to avoid a violent confrontation they must try to build deep friendships across the colour line. [35]

We had endeavored to point out that the only difference between the two forms of violence was that one was legalized, the other was not.

The Friday evening after the debate, the South African Broadcasting Company news program "Current Affairs" (which was a propaganda tool of the government) gave us one final kick with this misguided comment, *"It is said that we are persecuting Clergy. We do not do that, but two young Anglican Clergy in Grahamstown, who spoke about violence in South Africa should be careful and mind their language."*

---

[35] The East London Dispatch was one of the most liberal and courageous newspapers in South Africa at the time. Investigative journalism was virtually non-existent because of State security restrictions. Neverthelesss, the editor of the Daily Dispatch, Donald Woods, was an exception. He had several scrapes with the Security Police and on numerous occasions ruffled the feathers of then Prime minister B.J. Vorster in frank face-to-face exchanges regarding the content of Dispatch editorials. In the seventies, Woods was placed under a five-year house arrest. He was subjected to increasing harassment and his phone was tapped. In 1978 he and his family fled the country and were granted political asylum in Great Britain. Years later, Richard Attenborough produced an award-winning film "Cry Freedom" which told Woods' story and that of Steve Biko, an African who died at the hands of the South African Police.

In the end, we were just two guys in clerical collars pissing in the wind and crying in the wilderness. It would be another *twenty years* before any significant change would even be considered by the National Party. That would come as the result of many more years of sustained international pressure, boycotts and the eventual realization that the white government was fighting a losing battle.

By now, my police dossier was thick with unfavorable reports. They dated from Tsumeb, to Ovamboland, to Grahamstown, and now this. I had indeed been Peck's Bad Boy! In retrospect, however, I believe it was all in the service of truth and justice as my conscience had directed me. I expected serious repercussions, but surprisingly this last time I wasn't visited by the handsome young man from the Special Branch. I was informed by Registered Post. The official letter was to inform me that I was now regarded as an enemy of the state, a troublemaker, formally declared a "Prohibited Immigrant" and given ninety days to leave the country. To be sure, it was an inconvenience but not that surprising. Greater than the inconvenience was the honor to join the ranks of many others who had faced similar action.

We would soon be leaving South Africa for the last time and sailing up the east coast of Africa to a newly independent African country.

We had completed nine years working in Africa when the South African government handed us our walking papers. Discouraged and disgusted by our forced departure from the people and country we had grown to love, the central question was where to go. Returning home to the United States was not an option we yet wanted to consider. Idealists like us were still needed in Africa. They usually came as Peace Corps volunteers, who also were not welcome in South Africa. These were perceived as a hippie bunch from the land of quasi-democracy and freedom, who would only make trouble for the South African way of life. Peace Corps workers were scattered around the tiny neighboring country of Lesotho, where we could have gone but for the fact that Lesotho is surrounded by South Africa and carefully watched from over the border. Lesotho is a small independent country, known before independence as Basutoland. South Africa treated it as little more than a pawn and a ready source for mine labor. South West Africa fared no better. There, in the land of our adoption, so to speak, *apartheid* was still in full swing, which meant we couldn't return there either. That country was still decades away from its independence when it would become the Republic of Namibia; but it was nevertheless the birthplace of four of our kids and so they would theoretically have a claim to live there. Legally they were citizens but officially we were Prohibited Immigrants—"P.I's." It was time to pack the bags.

Chapter Seven

Things Fall Apart

Not only was *apartheid* stupid and immoral, it was doomed to fail eventually, but that time was still years away. Elsewhere in Africa, people were getting the message that it was time for self-rule, time to bid farewell to colonial powers that had over-stayed a dubious welcome. Steadily the winds of change had been blowing from Cape Town to Cairo, as the British Prime Minister had predicted, and most of Africa was now free of colonialism. Unfortunately, it would be years before many of those newly-minted countries would be truly free from the colonial mentality they had inherited, which would have to be out-grown over decades of independence. Colonialism would continue to cling like a patina of the past. We wanted the experience of living in one of those countries, preferably one without the patina. The Episcopal Church still funded a select few possible positions, one of them being a posting to Makerere University in Uganda. That was a two-year lectureship in the Department of Religious Studies and Philosophy in the Faculty of Arts. The position also administered a University Diploma in Theology that catered to over five hundred students from seminaries and theological colleges throughout Uganda, Kenya, Tanzania and Zambia. The position was ours for the taking and we jumped at the chance.

Setting our sights on East Africa kindled a new excitement. Most of our worldly goods had been crated and were in the hands of the shippers. We and a big white Kombi were in our own hands and must have seemed like amateurs the way we fumbled around, cramming stuff into every available space. We were each a bundle of anxiety, probably feeling both good and not so good, for the next great unknown up ahead. This time I had no wisdom or imagination, real or pretended, to suggest what we would be moving to. My batting average wasn't too good at this point, but the family was still of good cheer. Once loaded, we headed west to Cape Town, a good thousand miles away where we would board our ship to East Africa. Heading west had always meant going home to Ovamboland. Now it meant going into another unknown. God was probably laughing.

We drove the coastal route which went through the Tsitsikama Forest, famous to all forest lovers, and Plettenberg Bay, famous to all surfers—a world-class surfing hang out. The first night we bedded down in the forgettable town of Humansdorp, memorable only for a funeral home named Human & Pitt. We thought that very funny, how two guys with names like that could end up in the burial business. The next day took us through the little town of George, which would have its name changed after independence. That might be just as well: it was George III after whom the town was named, obviously by the British, who must have thought he was a good guy. However, there's another side to his story. He was a warring king, in Africa and elsewhere around the world, most notoriously in the American colonies. George III is the one who put a price on the head of every British subject who defected to the New World. It is commonly believed he eventually went mad and messed things up at home as well. I'm sure the good people of the City of George, in South Africa, knew none of this.

As we motored through that little English town I recalled a funny story that had circulated among the bishops for years. It was about the Dean of the Cathedral who lived next door to his superior, the Bishop of George, whom he could not stand. As it happened, both dog and bishop were named Hunter, and the Dean would take great glee when walking his dog on the homeward stretch to shout, loud enough for the bishop to hear 'most every time, "Hunter, get inside you miserable dog, INSIDE!" Very funny.

We crept into Cape Town feeling a bit tentative and eventually made our way to the appointed dock where we handed over the VW Kombi to disappear into the bowels of the ship, and ourselves to our quarters. Fortunately it was a familiar ship, one of the Lloyd Tristino fleet we had sailed twice before from Africa to Europe. This time we would stop half way there, in the Port of Mombasa. And then it hit us. As we stood in silence on the deck and saw Table Mountain for the last time, we realized we were saying goodbye to southern Africa where four of us had been born and all of us had spent many years of our lives. None of us had any experience saying a goodbye as big as that. It wasn't exactly like old Abraham and Sarah saying goodbye to their Biblical homeland, but almost. We were heading again into a wilderness we did not know, to a people and culture we did not know, and there to pitch our tent and make a home in a land we did not know. I'm not exactly sure how we got through that moment.

The trip took a week, sailing northward into the Indian Ocean, beginning with the roiling excitement of sailing between two oceans. At the southern tip of Africa, the Atlantic and Indian Oceans meet at what is known as the Cape of Good Hope, so named because ancient mariners used to have bad things happen to them there. A lot of hope was often all that got them through. It's also sometimes called the Cape of Storms. Apparently, problems can arise when the warm Agulhas Current from the Indian Ocean meets the cold Benguela Current of the Atlantic. The Cape of Good Hope is also said to be the legendary home of The Flying Dutchman, the ship of Wagnerian opera fame that was manned by a damned crew of ghostly sailors. There was no evidence of ghost ships but we were too sick to see much of anything for the several hours the two oceans met and mixed. Our huge ship was tossed about like a bathtub toy for most of the morning, not knowing which way to roll.

First stop after South Africa was Beira, the second largest city in Mozambique. Like Angola, that country was under the laid-back administration of the Portuguese. One of the useless things I remember from that stop was the huge cashew trees from which they made a powerful hooch, the local white lightning that probably helped make life livable for the locals. The rest of the crop they peddled abroad as expensive cocktail nuts in chic bars and upscale parties. From Beira, we chugged up the coast to Dar es Salaam, capital of Tanzania. In just a few years that capital would be moved to a forlorn place known as Dodoma, out in the middle of nowhere, supposedly to start all over again after independence. Its wise president, Julius Nyerere, chose for Tanzania to remain non-aligned politically, which made him and his country suspect in Washington. America never seems to know what to do with countries that choose to be in the middle of the road, so to speak, preferring friendships with everyone. In this case, Nyerere was wise, but he paid for it in the way the United States treated Tanzania— more as a stranger than a friend. Dar es Salaam was the largest and richest city in East Africa and the jumping-off point to the neighboring island of Zanzibar.

A few days later we reached our destination as we sailed into Mombasa, second largest city in Kenya and their principal port. The place had an illustrious history that included the migration of tens of thousands of Indians and Chinese coming as laborers in the early 1900s, many to become permanent residents of East Africa. It also had a mystique about it, in part from centuries of Arab traders and their mysterious-looking dhows that plied the waters between Arabia and Africa.

We were hardly veterans of disembarkation, but we did have some experience of the process. This time, we were driving that big white VW Kombi, which was our home on wheels for now. Like a big family rag doll, it gave a degree of security, 'though we had no idea where to drive it or which way. Just keep that vehicle on the 'wrong' side of the road, as Americans would say, which meant the left-hand side, true for all of Africa. By now, we were thoroughly familiar with that peculiarity, which didn't seem at all peculiar to us. Most of our junk had been shipped ahead, which meant a minimum of fussing with Customs and Immigration. In a matter of hours we were through that and heading off to find the big city of Mombasa, which wasn't all that big. The main street still had that colonial patina about it, with lush trees and vegetation, shops, bicycles and rickshaws everywhere pulled by men in white jallabias. Over the main street was an arch of fake elephant tusks, hardly to match the golden arches of St. Louis but still impressive for gawking tourists on a first visit. More like a town than a city, Mombasa had a distinct Arab and Muslim character, displaying mosques and Arab dress everywhere. This was a new experience for us, never having seen a mosque in southern Africa, nor Arab dress. But we were now approaching that geographical divide that cuts Africa into two parts: the Arab-Muslim north and the Bantu-Christian south. The Sahalian countries of the Sahara Desert are roughly the dividing line. Uganda and Kenya were just south of the divide. Kenya probably has as many Muslims as Christians by now.

We left Mombasa on the only road out and began a gentle climb northeast which wound its way to Nairobi, three hundred miles away. Lush equatorial vegetation was everywhere, a thrilling change from the harsh savannah of southern Africa. We reached the capital of Nairobi by afternoon and spent the night in a western-style hotel with a distinctly new feel. Part of that was being in the first independent African country we had ever experienced. It was also equatorial and had an altitude of over four thousand feet, both of which were new to us. Not surprisingly, Nairobi (and most of Kenya) still had a residue of British colonialism, which gave it a grace and gentleness despite the bitter days of the Mau Mau that finally brought about independence in 1963.

On a fresh, cool morning we headed for Kampala, capital of Uganda, which Churchill once called the "Pearl of the Nile." This was real excitement, heading for our new home! Halfway there, just north of Lake Nakuru and west of the Great Rift Valley, we made an historic stop for a photo op, the photo long since having disappeared. There our clan stood on the equator, half of us in the northern hemisphere and half in the south. We all thought that great fun to be hemispheres apart for the moment. In another hundred miles, we would cross into Uganda at a little town known as Tororo. At the border, the wide Kenya highway would taper down to a thin ribbon of two lanes, generally in poor condition. Going into Uganda was easy but leaving over that same border in less than a year would be a harrowing experience. That would be in the dark days of Idi Amin when we were traveling to Mombasa for a Christmas holiday. I was asked my profession and replied "Minister". We were about to be flagged through when one of the Ugandans hesitated and asked "Minister of what?" When I replied "religion" he ordered everything out of the car, everything off the top, "Everything!" Being a political minister would have got me through. Little did we know that first day we crossed the border what lay ahead of us in this "independent" Uganda.

Politically, Uganda was no longer under the British Empire nor was it yet a truly democratic republic, though it pretended to be. It had regressed since its independence in 1962, when the country was ruled by the King of the Baganda, known as the Kabaka and John Milton Obote served as Prime Minister. Obote was a graduate of Makerere University and a socialist political leader who helped in the birthing of the new republic. All was well in the beginning, but in 1966 things came apart. Obote was implicated in a gold smuggling plot and when Parliament demanded an investigation he suspended the constitution and declared himself President. Notwithstanding all of that, Uganda was still an independent African country, albeit under questionable leadership. Not knowing such details, we naively grabbed the offer to go there (but probably would have gone anyway).

We had thought the move to East Africa would be a propitious one. I relished the opportunity for a few years in the academic environment of Makerere, known throughout most of Africa for its standard of excellence. The University was legendary for producing some of Africa's finest doctors, lawyers, academics, and teachers; that much we knew. What we didn't know was the difficulty the next two years would hold. Had we known in advance how rough the road was going to be, we may not have accepted the offer. Maybe it's good that adventure and foresight are usually on opposite sides of life's toughest experiences. Blithely, we looked forward to the changes we knew were coming, the others were beyond our imagining.

One of the changes we anticipated was living where Africans were in the majority and made most of the decisions, notwithstanding the small pockets of colonial mentality here and there.[36] Then there was the huge topographical change. Far from the wide open spaces of Southern Africa and the big sky country we knew so well, we would now be living in dense equatorial jungle, right on the equator. The city of Kampala, our new home, seemed to know only perpetual springtime with predictable moderate temperatures. Culturally we would be living in a part of Africa that was famous for one of the noble tribes of Africa, the Baganda, for whom the country was named. The Baganda had a rich history in the life of Church and State, a fact we would come to appreciate.

In 1894, Great Britain bestowed upon Uganda the 'honor' of being a Protectorate but kept it snugly under colonial control until independence, just nine years before our arrival. Thus, during the colonial era it was officially known as the British Protectorate of Uganda, a designation that differed only in theory from that of neighboring Kenya, which was regarded as a Colony. Technically, a Protectorate retained a degree of self-administration, but Uganda nevertheless had all the characteristics of a colonial hangout. Despite being a Protectorate, the British had managed to install their own administration and ruled it virtually as a Colony. That meant appearing to govern through the sovereignty of Mutesa II, King of the Baganda. So much for the protection of Pax Britannia—it came with a price.

Early in 1971, we arrived with less than perfect timing. Two weeks prior, the head of the Ugandan Army General Idi Amin, had staged a *coup d'etat* and was waiting to greet us, so to speak. Churchill's Pearl of the Nile was about to lose some of its luster and the whole country would soon be in chaos. Uganda had been suffering from several years of poor leadership under Obote. He was out of the country at the time, making it easy for General Amin to seize power.

President Obote was, in fact, in faraway Singapore, attending the Commonwealth Conference, by now little more than a formality for the remnants of the rapidly fading British Empire. It was far enough away for Obote's top General to stray from the barracks and make

---

[36] While it was true that in South Africa Africans were in the majority, but the whites still had the upper hand and ruled the country as if they were the majority.

mischief. The *coup* came as no surprise to most of the country. Amin and Obote were from widely differing tribal groups with an ill wind blowing between them. Obote had open disdain for Amin's West Nile tribe which made the revolt even easier; and the fact that Obote had become an iron-fisted ruler made it necessary.

Idi Amin Dada had visions of grandeur that were shared by few—he was not known for having much common sense or leadership ability. In 1946, he had joined the British colonial regiment known as the King's African Rifles, where he served as a cook. His experience of the world consisted of one tour of Kenya while serving in the British Regiment, and a short time in England. Eventually he held the rank of Major General in the post-colonial Ugandan Army, and somewhat incredulously he became its commander, although everyone knew he was a dubious pick to head the Army or hold the rank of General. Both the position and the rank were responsibilities far above any ability he might have possessed. The British had sent him to the prestigious Sandhurst Academy in England to give him a touch of panache, but alas, he needed more than a touch; he needed a basic education which he did not have beyond the fourth grade. One British officer once said of him, "Idi Amin is a good rugby player but virtually bone from the neck up and needs things explained in words of one letter." In short, General Amin was an embarrassment. But he had "those Sandhurst years", as the British would say, which with some skullduggery and his unbridled ambition got him into higher ranks in the Ugandan Army. His many and severe shortcomings would soon become a public embarrassment for the country, eventually to be played out on an international stage.

How ever did the Pearl of the Nile fall into the hands of a man with so many deficits? It couldn't have been for lack of well-educated Ugandan leaders or the enterprising Asian community of roughly 80,000. The answer lay just beneath the surface of polite society in a simmering wrath of the noble Baganda people. Churning away in the bowels of the most influential and best educated people in the country was a hatred for President Milton Obote that was deep and unrelenting. It began in 1966, when Obote staged a *coup* that overthrew King

Mutesa II; that was bad, but the worst was to follow a few years later when Obote committed the unforgivable sin that sealed his fate.

It happened on this wise. During some local unrest involving the Baganda people, Obote had banished their King into exile in England. Banishing an African commoner from his people is probably the worst thing that could happen anywhere in Africa; but banishing a distinguished king is unthinkable. The logic is as follows. Every African believes that only by being connected to tribe and family does one really exist. The individual thus derives *being* by virtue of *belonging*. This makes a nice idea which Westerners muse over and tinker with but is a totally foreign concept to Western thought and social organization. And it is another of the many ways in which the Western world continues to misunderstand Africans. A gem of West African wisdom puts it in five words: "*I am because we are,*" and that can speak for all of Africa. Nice thought but hardly a Western one, so committed to individualism are we.

So, by Obote removing the Kabaka from his people and sending him into exile, their king in essence ceased to be. Moreover, they now had no king! To compound the insult, the Kabaka languished in poverty in England and eventually died in the slums of East London. It was a shameful moment for Uganda and all of Africa, brought about by one of their own, a power hungry opportunist. The sentiment of the Baganda people was shame on Obote and everlasting shame on his kith and kin. This despicable deed had to be vindicated sooner or later and that time had finally come. Though the Baganda probably loathed Amin for the coarse fellow that he was, he was more acceptable than Milton Obote and they would cooperate with his *coup d'etat.*[37]

Uganda was still a pleasant place to be on the African Continent, but that's rather like saying the voyage on the Titanic was wonderful while it lasted. The Pearl of the Nile was about to be thrown before swine, and all of Uganda would suffer in indescribable ways. We could know nothing of what was coming and were determined to enjoy our

---

[37] When Amin's brutal regime was at its worst, the Baganda still refused to consider a return of President Obote, who was then in exile.

chance to live there. Small wonder the British liked it there so much: it had everything Kenya had and more. The capital city of Kampala was physically an idyllic place. Built on seven hills, two of those would become very familiar: one where Makerere University was situated and the other where we would be living. Our house on Kololo Hill was a pleasant two-storied utilitarian structure with concrete floors and a red tiled roof. The British had constructed dozens of these buildings for university housing. Ours was surrounded with a modestly tamed jungle. Vegetation was everywhere, growing by the minute, so green it could almost dazzle the eyes. Things seemed to grow overnight entangling the city with lush flowering trees, vines, and flowers, with green grass everywhere, maintained by afternoon thundershowers almost on a daily basis. Physically it felt like we had arrived in paradise. It was the best of Hawaii without the humidity.

I was intrigued that our street was named after the little known Prince Albert, Queen Victoria's Royal Consort. While it is true that Victoria loved him with an everlasting passion and forever grieved his early death, Albert was her husband for a mere eighteen years. But this young German, also Victoria's cousin, spent those years busily producing nine children by her. Just like African families. That may have been Albert's only claim to fame—he was a great royal stud. At any rate, he got a pretty street in Kampala named after him, just like everything else in the British Empire got named after someone or something back in jolly old England. When the British messed around with the local language, sometimes the results were quite funny; so rather than fuss overmuch with the local names, they just substituted English ones. In Malawi, they tried to go native and named the principal lake "Nyasa." The only trouble with that is that in the local language, *"nyasa"* means lake; hence, they ended up with such foolishness as Lake Nyasa, which in the local language meant "Lake Lake." This of course made the locals laugh hysterically. As far as I can tell, with few exceptions, the British did not distinguish themselves as gifted linguists anywhere in Africa, figuring, I suppose, that everyone ought to speak the King's (or Queen's) English and none other,—Cambridge or Oxford accent preferred.

When it came to naming, Queen Victoria fared better by far than her Consort: she got her name on the largest lake in East Africa, known to this day as Lake Victoria which borders on Uganda, Kenya and Tanzania. A little further downstream, she managed to get her name on the famous Victoria Falls in Zambia/Zimbabwe. It's interesting that in all the years since the independence of these countries, neither Lake Victoria nor Victoria Falls have been renamed with an African name. The Africanizing of most place and country names was a natural outcome of independence, but probably an insult to all who thought the British Empire had discovered Africa and produced the golden years of its history.

We soon discovered a disconcerting presence on beautiful Prince Albert Drive on lovely Kololo Hill. Located only doors from our house was the Command Post, the principal residence of General Amin and his many wives. What luck. We had to drive past the Command Post several times a day, for virtually everything: taking the kids to school in the morning, going to work at Makerere, coming home at noonday for lunch, and at the end of the day. Sometimes in the evening we would take another more complicated route to avoid the Command Post stress but that one had unpleasant military roadblocks. The Command Post looked ominous enough, with a sentry booth at the entrance attended by uniformed soldiers armed with rifles and what-have-you. Barbed wire guarded the rest of the place, which sat high atop the hill side of the road with plenty of glass and eyes spying down on the rest of us. It was scary at best and at times terrifying.

One of those times came when we had a visitor from the United States. She was an inveterate taker of photos and loved to wander about with her camera. Wander she would, but this time we warned her emphatically not to take the camera or go walking near the Command Post. She ignored every word we said and went for a morning walk, intent on taking pictures of the Command Post. Before long, we got a frantic message that our guest was being held by the sentries. She had wandered by and taken their picture and now there was big trouble. The guards went berserk and demanded to see her passport which she refused to give them because it was tucked into her underwear. Next came the camera. They yanked the film out and proceeded to inspect it, and finding no pictures on the film thought they were being tricked. All of this transpired without a word of English spoken except by our guest, who was speaking it at great volume and using many ill-advised words. Fortunately, the soldiers didn't understand a thing she said. Finally, one of Amin's younger wives who knew a bit of English came to the gate and untangled things. Our guest returned home with camera empty of film and highly irritated she didn't get her pictures. That wasn't the only thing she didn't get; we heaved a sigh of relief when she departed the next day.

It seems we had many foreign visitors and they were all interesting. Like Desmond Tutu. He was then working for the World Council of Church in Geneva, and was responsible for the Theological Education Fund. My position at Makerere was a recipient of those funds so it was Desmond's job to visit us from time to time. This was long before he was a bishop and the shade of purple trimmed his balding head. His first visit to us was memorable. The bedrooms in our house were on the second floor and Desmond's was right next to ours. The first morning of his stay I awoke early to a strange *thump, thump, thump* and thought I was dreaming of Ovamboland. We had heard it for years—the waking sound of the young girls pounding grain for their breakfast meal. But it wasn't Ovamboland, it was Kampala where they didn't pound grain for their morning meal. At breakfast, I mentioned the strange thumping sound to Desmond, and he replied with his typical giggle, "Oh, that was me! I was running in place as I do every morning when I say my prayers," Many years later, when I took up early morning jogging, I would often do the same, but not in the bedroom.

Our arrival in Kampala coincided with the annual celebration of Robert Burns' birthday, the poetic patron saint of Scotland. "Bobby Burns Day," as it was called by the Scottish locals, was a red-letter celebration and we were invited to the Scots' annual dinner at the Grand Hotel. This was one of the premier hotels where a good meal could still be had with dancing to a live band. They played mellow golden oldies, and in the stressful months to come, to keep body and soul together we would indulge ourselves with dinner and dancing to what sounded like Glenn Miller.

The Bobby Burns observance was another eye-opener. It would become an eye-closer for this crowd before the evening was over. Gallons of Scotch whiskey would be consumed by hundreds of Scots who showed up for this bacchanalian festival. We were told that in Scotland, Burns Night is like a second national holiday, celebrated every January 25th without fail. It was just as sacred an event in colonial Africa. We had discovered that Scots were everywhere in Africa where the Union Jack was flying and some where it was not. I figured their migration south was because of the weather in Scotland, cold and foul most of the time; any place south would be an improvement. Since most of Her Majesty's Empire was in the sun-drenched parts of the Southern Hemisphere, so were the Scots, and Uganda was no exception.[38]

The Grand Hotel dining room was filled to capacity with Scots speaking in thick accents made thicker by Scotch malt. The supper began with the traditional Selkirk Grace, followed by toasts. And then more toasts. Then came the piping in of the haggis, which was treated like a Scottish version of the Holy Grail. We had no idea what haggis was; our host tried to explain as delicately as possible that it was a mixture of chopped guts and blood, not to be confused with corned beef hash. I would have taken the hash any day. This haggis was cooked in a gut that looked like a bloated stomach when they brought it in. It looked awful to us, the uninitiated, but we didn't say so. Before the haggis was ritually punctured or "killed" as they said, Robert Burns' famous "Address to a Haggis" was recited. This was an impressive moment. The Great Scot who presided over things recited this very long poem from memory, well after consuming many a tot of Scotch whiskey. I sat in amazement as this guy remembered his lines. It went on and on and I wouldn't have known if he had missed entire stanzas. When we got around to eating the sacred haggis, it tasted like hell, which may be why it's eaten in a state of inebriation, washed down with great swills

---

[38] It's interesting to note that the only parts of the old British Empire to the north of England were Scotland and Canada.

of whiskey, neat. Hours later, the evening concluded with a few final toasts and a slurred singing of Auld Lang Syne. It was an unforgettable introduction to a part of life in Kampala. Bacchus would have been proud of this orgy.

The next introduction to Uganda came a few days later. It was of a much more serious nature, a command performance at my new place of work. By tradition, the President of Uganda is the Chancellor of the University and technically the final authority over everyone teaching or attending. That now included me. So, by the strangest of quirks, Idi Amin had become my boss! It was a Friday, and the Office of the President had summoned all faculty members to be at the University at 6:30 pm sharp, no exceptions.

It was a dark omen that the first event I was to attend at Makerere had nothing to do with academics or the university. It was to hear Amin tell us what the *coup* was about. I remember it was a fairly relaxed meeting with a fair amount of laughter. I wondered months later if that could have been gallows humor in the making. Amin's boyish playfulness was entertaining, but made it hard to take him seriously in his attempt to persuade us that all would be well under his "temporary" leadership. In so many words, he told us that in ninety days he would do the necessary house cleaning which he thought the country needed. That sounded reasonable enough, especially the ninety day part. Or so we thought.

In retrospect, it's hard to believe Amin really said that and harder still that we believed him. We were sitting on our brains that evening and hoping for the best, which is probably what folks do in a *coup d'etat*. There were the wise among us who knew better but kept quiet. They were the ones who had been through this before when Obote seized power, four years prior. Within weeks the country would experience the harsh truth of Lord Acton's immortal words about absolute power corrupting absolutely. Ninety days came and went and the schoolboy dictator was beginning to enjoy being the sovereign leader of Uganda. He now had absolute power. He may have been low on brains but he had the survival instincts of a panther and would soon wield power in animal fashion. Before long, we would learn that the only thing he had going for him when he spoke to the Makerere faculty that fateful evening was a boyish grin and the barrel of a gun. And to think we had believed him.

What comic irony this had all become! At last, we had the opportunity to live in an independent African country and work with some of Africa's brightest, but this wasn't what we had in mind. The palace coup that had brought this bumpkin to power began messing things up for everyone. Fortunately, Amin didn't begin his brutal house cleaning at Makerere. That fine University didn't need its house cleaned by him or anyone else. It was doing quite well what it had done for many years as the premier college of East Africa. The Department of Religious Studies and Philosophy was running smoothly, with nothing more than the usual faculty squabbles over which books to require, what syllabus to adopt, or who gets the better office. I learned that academics avoid the public eye by burying themselves in academia, which was what was about to happen on Makerere Hill. There, everyone would soon hunker down and hope for the best. Except for the occasional sound of gunfire in the city or unsettling reports in the news, life at Makerere would go on much as usual. For a while.

My new boss was John Mbiti, a small Kenyan gentleman with an amazing intellect and known internationally for his seminal work in the field of African Traditional Religion. After eight years in the bush with respite of a break at Rhodes, it felt good to be back in an academic setting. I had time to read, plan classes, mix with colleagues and generally learn what would be required of me in the new academic year. I would be expected to supervise a few graduate programs, teach two courses and supervise the Diploma in Theology. African Traditional Religion was still a relatively new field of serious study, having been debunked by Western scholars and missionaries of earlier generations. It was an eye-opener for me to discover the many ways in which the traditional religion of Africa and Christianity *could* have come together to reinforce each other. Unfortunately, the chasm between the two was already so great that many Africans had abandoned traditional Christianity for African interpretations found in the rapidly growing indigenous church movement. Membership of indigenous churches already numbered in the tens of millions as the movement expanded throughout Africa. Sadly, much of Christianity still denies any validity to traditional religious beliefs condemning them as "heathen".

I was enjoying the chance to mix with African students but found it a little daunting to face a lecture hall filled with black faces looking bored but respectful. The previous year had been a classroom filled with white faces looking bored but respectful. On the one hand, not much had changed while on the other, a great deal had.

I also found time to read political science which was especially germane to our situation. In that field, Ali Mazrui, a Kenyan, was the hottest thing going at Makerere because he was challenging what was happening in the country. Ali was fearless in stirring the pot in the classroom and in public lectures and it amazed us he wasn't silenced by the regime. He was, in effect, when he was exiled and soon after that offered an appointment at the University of Michigan and disappeared.

Administering the Diploma in Theology meant keeping track of several hundred students in twelve theological colleges and seminaries in Uganda, Kenya, Tanzania and Zambia. There was enough paperwork involved to replenish a small forest. Those taking the two-year course were theological students chosen by their institutions to do the University Diploma. My job was to be the liaison with their institution, set final exams and work with the external examiners who descended on Makerere once a year.

The job also involved periodically visiting each of the participating institutions which gave me a chance to see some of East Africa I would never have seen—places like Kipalapala, Zanzibar, Nakuru, Mbale, Tabora, Mbarara and many more exotically named places not in the ordinary tourist guidebook. Initially, travel was easy between the various countries until Amin alienated himself from Kenya and Tanzania to the point where the borders were closed. The East African Community would eventually break up during his time as military dictator, thanks mainly to his ineptitude.

Colleagues in the Department were an interesting lot. Abu Yassir was a Sudanese Arab from Khartoum and responsible for the limited number of Islamic studies in the Department. He was married to a gal from Ohio and as time went by we would spend more and more time with them. Professor John Mbiti, the head of the department, was also an Anglican priest and married to a Swiss miss by the name of Verena. We enjoyed them but had little social time together. Four other expatriates included a neurotic spinster who had been away from England so long she didn't know where she belonged; an eccentric French Canadian who taught philosophy and climbed Mount Kilimanjaro every year until he went goofy on his last climb; another Canadian philosopher and a German Lutheran who was probably the brightest guy among us. He taught New Testament and is remembered for saying publicly that Amin ought to be shot. *"SHOT"*, he would shout in his German accent, *"as you would do to a mad dog!"* No one we knew rose to the suggestion though in time there were numerous assassination attempts which all failed. Panthers are wily at surviving.

One colleague had become heavily involved in Christian efforts to bring about a peace accord for the war that had been raging in southern Sudan for seventeen years. The grievances behind the war were many but chiefly they were race, religion and politics (what else is there?). The Sudan is an enormous country, situated immediately north of Uganda. In addition to being Africa's largest country comprising over a million square miles, it also contains the world's largest desert, the Sahara, which spans the continent and stretches across twelve nations in a vast region known as the Sahel. The Sahara is sometimes referred to as the divide between the Islamic Arab countries of North Africa and the Christian Bantu people to the south known as sub-Saharan Africa. That divide, also a racial and religious one, has been the genesis of age-old conflicts in the Sudan. This war was already seventeen years old with no signs of weakening.

The northern city of Khartoum was the capital and seat of government, then entirely under the control of the Arab Sudanese, who were largely Islamic. The southern parts of the country consisted of many African tribes that were largely Christian. The ensuing tension between them went back to the days of the British presence prior to independence in 1953. (Southern Sudan would become Africa's newest independent nation in 2011, at a time of huge oil discoveries in the region that would enflame relations with its northern neighbor to the point of an undeclared war). The frictions of race and religion had been exacerbated by the northern government that routinely persecuted and abused the south, driving tens of thousands of southern Sudanese refugees into neighboring countries. Uganda took the brunt of that.

My colleague, Margaret, loved the excitement of intrigue and one of her preoccupations was the conflict in the southern Sudan. In a moment of inattention she got me involved in the British Church Missionary Society's efforts to coordinate relief and aid to the south. I wasn't sure what useful part I could play in support of the effort, but my sentiments and support were for the southerners who were at a disadvantage in every way. For years, the peace process had been a prolonged effort of one step forward and two back. Colonel Joseph Lagu became a key figure in that war.

Colonel Lagu had defected from the Sudanese army in 1963 and joined the South Sudan resistance movement against the government, subsequently founding the military wing of the movement, known as the Anyanya. By 1968, Lagu was commander of the entire southern resistance, known as the South Sudan Liberation Movement. Lagu would frequently slip into Uganda to keep in touch with Sudanese refugees and freedom fighters and help with relief and aid to his beleaguered countrymen. Having met him on a previous occasion, one day Margaret brought him to our home for an unexpected meeting. During the visit my colleague, Abu Yassir, dropped by the house for a friendly visit. Abu Yassir was Arab, from Khartoum, and heavily involved in the Sudanese government with which Lagu was in deadly conflict. Both men knew of each other and were arch-enemies. We were good friends with Abu Yassir and his American wife, with whom we had spent many pleasant hours together. But not today.

So there sat Lagu in our lounge, out of sight from the front door, where Abu Yassir stood. I mumbled a lame excuse to Yassir that I was busy and he needed to come back later. It was an uncharacteristic snub and we both knew it. He was curious and with a typical wry smile and winking eye didn't move from the door. *Oh my God, I thought, what now?* With Abu Yassir not moving, I panicked that Lagu would come to see what had delayed me at the door. "So, who do you not want me to see in there"Abu Yassir asked. I lied and told him the Bishop had come to see me, which was excuse enough for him to leave. I have re-lived the terror of that moment many times and have no idea what would have happened had the two of them met in my house, but it would not have been pleasant.

Our next door neighbors on Prince Albert Drive were David and Catherine Kisumba. David was an orthopedic surgeon and Catherine a pharmacist, both trained in Canada. David practiced and taught at Mulago Hospital, Catherine had her own pharmacy in town. Dr. and Mrs. Kisumba were a handsome Baganda couple. Whenever they had a weekend free they would drive home to their village, drop their Western lifestyle and live like traditional Baganda. But that was a far cry from what we might think of as "going native." Baganda culture had a touch of elegance throughout: customs, cuisine, dress, manners, poise and behavior, they were known for it all. Traditional Baganda cuisine, for instance, had dozens of delectable dishes, the women's attire no less impressive. But keeping in touch with the family and the village was more important than the Western scientific professions they practiced in the city the rest of the week, so off they would go and we would miss them on weekends.

Our eldest son and theirs were about the same age. Like most kids in Africa, they had a keen interest in soccer which they played fairly well until ours broke his leg. Dr. Kisumba set the bones and plastered him up with a hip cast that slowed him down for weeks. Thinking he could play soccer with a cast, four weeks later he broke both cast and leg a second time and was in it for twice as long as he should have been! One of his Christmas gifts that year was to be the removal of the cast. The day came, I had been instructed on how to get the thing off, and the family stood 'round waiting with great expectation. It was a messy process for an amateur but eventually the cast came off. The little guy's muscles had been inactive so long he couldn't stand or walk on the leg for days. Some Christmas gift. We all felt terrible.

My contract with the University was for two years, with the possibility of extending. That was the usual arrangement for expatriate staff. Traditionally a lot of the faculty were recruited from Great Britain. We thought the British a funny lot on how they looked upon their two year hitch as a very temporary residency. They would visit our house and express great surprise that we had hung our pictures. "Well of course, why not?" To which they would reply, "Blimy mate, we're only here for two years, it's not even worth unpacking all that stuff!"And they would live with empty, bare walls. For those who didn't unpack their stuff, it seemed like a metaphor for their life, not wanting to settle down in an alien and very un-British environment. Is it worth settling down and investing in a place for "only two years"? Or is two years so temporary that it's just a time out from the main event of life? It seemed unfortunate that to some the fantastic opportunity to live two years in Uganda would not be worth hanging pictures and making a home of it. To some it was just a time out to be endured. As it would turn out, It was a time to be endured for all of us.

I think our arrival made a statement to the contrary. Our dwindling worldly goods arrived in a huge wooden crate, measuring about five-by-seven feet. When it was completely empty (and every picture hung), we made a walk-in playhouse out of the crate, complete with a couple of windows and a door that could open and shut. The kids had a wonderful time with that playhouse....for what would turn out to be less than two years.

Our youngest was a little guy at the time. He attended the university nursery school in the mornings while his brother and sisters went to Kitante Primary School on a hill adjacent to Kololo. He was a happy kid and loved his nursery school. One day he came home and told us he had a girlfriend. "And what's her name?" we asked. He didn't really know but the next day he would point her out. When we got to his school and he was about to go through the gate he said, "There she is...she's the one with the black curly hair." Since he was one of only a few Caucasians in the school, we had a choice of about thirty who fit the description. Basic human attraction may be blind and innocent—if only the world could live that way...

Khartoum, Sudan

During a Spring Break we were invited to visit Abu Yassir and his family in Khartoum. In those days we thought nothing of packing up with five kids and flying off to some new part of Africa. It took two African taxis and a lot of struggling to get it all to the airport: two adults, five kids and fifteen pieces of luggage. Africans thought nothing of a family that size; Europeans, on the other hand were alarmed. We were too, when years later we would look back on the traveling we had done with a brood that size. We had one visitor from the United States who had a larger family and reported to us that someone back home once said to him, "Mister, they ought to shoot guys like you!" The comment didn't make us want to rush back to the States. But five kids and fifteen bags weren't a big deal in Africa, they just required room. And patience.

Driving the Entebbe Road to the airport was always a treat. There you could see all of Uganda in one form or another. An equatorial forest framed the road with colorful clothes, freshly washed and draped over bushes to dry on Africa's clothes line. There were cloth merchants with colors bright enough to hurt the eye, roadside shopkeepers peddling everything from meat and vegetables to bicycles and goats. The whole road pulsed with that African spirit that said it was good to be alive and blessed to be together. Happy buyers, if they were women, would stack the stuff on their heads and find an impossible balance. Men were more likely to sling their booty on the back of a bicycle or on top of a car, sometimes to include goats or chickens or an over-stuffed easy chair. We once saw a fully grown cow tied to the roof of a car.

We schlupped our stuff into the tiny Entebbe Airport whose innocence was marred by young soldiers carrying Russian semi-automatic rifles. They looked awkward and hardly knew what to do with themselves or their rifles but their presence wasn't questioned. General Amin's boy soldiers were everywhere, presumably to protect the country from some imaginary foe. In time, neighboring Tanzania would become a big foe because of Amin's provocations. Entebbe was the only airport in the country and resembled a small-town American airport in the fifties. Most of the runway was paved, the rest had potholes. Boeing 707's were the largest commercial planes around in those days and had to negotiate the potholes as best they could.

It can safely be said that throughout the colonial empire, the British left their mark essentially on paper and bureaucracy. It was as true in Uganda as it was throughout the faded Empire. Long before modern copiers were invented, forests of trees and oceans of ink were consumed producing bureaucratic forms for everything. Sometimes it was a withering sight. I remember going into government offices in Uganda for this or that and seeing stacks of forms, permits, reports and what-have-you from bygone years. In every government building there were mountains of this stuff, bound in bundles with red tape and stacked floor to ceiling, wherever there wasn't a window. Ugandans had been taught by the British to save anything that resembled a government form but the practice got out of hand and never came to an end. Leaving the country involved a marathon of bureaucratic procedures and paperwork, sometimes in quadruplicate. God alone knows if anyone read it or where it all went. We had to run this gauntlet just to travel to next-door Sudan.

Amin's under-employed soldiers paced lazily around the airport occasionally upsetting someone and asking for cigarettes. Flies pestered the rest of us. I had moments wondering why we were dragging ourselves off to Khartoum to spend a week in a place where the average temperature was over 110 and we would not know a soul except the Abu Yassirs. But it was an invitation to visit a traditional Arab family and a rare opportunity to live for a few days in a Sudanese Arab village, in a country that fascinated me because of its strangeness.

Our arrival at the dusty little airport in Khartoum is but a hazy memory. I was too overwhelmed just taking in the sights, sounds and smells, the details of it all have faded. I do remember our host wasn't there to meet us and we had to negotiate a taxi to get us to a local hotel. Hardly anyone spoke English, and no one seemed much interested in our lot except to stare at us and probably wonder why we were there. There were moments when I did too. It didn't help matters that my wife was wearing a knee-length skirt entirely too tight and short for Arab sensibilities and Sharia law. We didn't know that at the time, but were quickly informed by all sorts of body signals and hand waving. Fortunately, she had brought a long wrap-around skirt which quickly amended things. Our eldest daughter, twelve at the time, has uncomplimentary memories of the place: "Like a town out of the Wild West, uncivilized, crude and primitive!" The hotel we were taken to was a fair-sized colonial building beyond run-down. With not a trace of once-glorious days under the British, it was now a dingy hovel with high ceilings, tile floors that were badly broken, and old men lazing about trying to keep cool.[39] Flies buzzed lazily in the subdued light of the lounge. But we were grateful to find the old place at least to give some shade while we waited for our host. The heat was worse than anything we had yet experienced in Africa, almost too hot for the flies that were circling slower than usual. A noisy ceiling fan spun a losing battle to improve things.

With some difficulty, we managed to engage the hotel manager as our interpreter and an ancient crank phone to contact our host. Finally, Abu Yassir arrived with two old cars, and we made our way through the dusty streets of the city to a neighboring village. In those days, only the main street of Khartoum was paved and it was a city of a few thousand traditional dwellings. Today Khartoum is a bustling metropolis of well over five million, with paved highways and roads, modern hotels and skyscrapers, chic shops and restaurants, thanks chiefly to the discovery of oil and foreign aid.

We drove to an ancient village that rose right out of the desert. It looked like Arab civilization had lived on that spot for centuries. The houses had flat roofs and mud walls, most with surrounding patios enclosed by low mud walls. They were simple earthen dwellings that probably couldn't be improved much by modern architecture, for they were cool in summer and warm in winter, inexpensive to build and could easily withstand the annual rainfall of a few inches or less.

---

[39] Another daughter, slightly younger, remembers this hotel with admiration, "huge and stately, a veritable oasis in the desert!"

After the customary welcome of many words and movements, we were introduced to our sleeping quarters, all dark rooms, men on one side, women on the other. Traditional Arab households are physically divided down the middle—the men relaxed and visited, ate and slept on one side, with benefit of a patio, the women and children on the other side, with their own patio, kitchen and food storage. Naturally they expected our family to fit into that time-honored arrangement, probably thinking the whole world lived that way. We obliged, divided up our stuff, and went to our respective quarters. One of the degradations Arab women had to endure in this male-dominated society included having to parade through the men's quarters whenever they left or entered the house. Was that for inspection purposes? We never knew. With divided sleeping quarters, we never figured out how couples got together, but there was ample evidence they did. Despite the inferior status assigned to women, from the laughter and conversation we heard through the wall, they seemed to have more fun. In a man's presence, there would never be such laughter or conversation: women and children knew their place and it was to be quiet and servile. At meal time, food was delivered to the men on huge brass trays with an impressive array of tasty dishes. We were beginning to think that Arab cuisine, like Ugandan, was so much more interesting and varied than standard Western fare.

One story translated from the women's side was unforgettable. North Sudanese cooking made use of many spices, some of them exotic and notoriously hot. In the right proportions they produced some of the tastiest food in the world, and the Sudanese women were masters of the art. But after years of adding spices and tasting hot food, their taste buds simply wore out; when that happened, they had a solution to the problem that was all but unbelievable. When the older women could no longer feel the sensation of hot spices in their mouth, they resorted to their eyes: they would break the hottest spices and rub them under their eyelids to feel the sensation of heat! Amazing what humans will do for their fix.

It was the middle of summer, and in our flat-roofed house the heat was intolerable and air conditioning unheard of. (Those lucky enough to have electricity generally had a single light bulb hanging from the ceiling and nothing more). Over time, this culture, like all desert dwellers, had learned to bend with the heat. From midday to about four in the afternoon all shops and businesses closed for an extended siesta. Actually they weren't sleeping all that time, just staying behind shutters waiting for the worst heat to pass. Not me. I wanted the experience of walking on a street in Khartoum in the noonday sun, maybe just once. I ventured forth and not a thing was moving except a stray dog and me—and the dog was looking for shade. Feeling a little smug, I sang to myself Noel Coward's famous comedy, "Mad Dogs and Englishmen Go Out In The Noonday Sun". And it was so, except I didn't even see an Englishman. I passed a shop where the elderly owner was sitting quietly on his stoep waiting for the sun to pass. I greeted him and to my amazement he spoke perfect English with a slightly cultured British accent, obviously from a time long passed. Apparently pleased to be able to use his English he went on to say how much better things were under the British, lo those many years past. "Everything was more predictable, more organized, more regimented." We talked a little about that, and it was obvious he longed for those days when his life was more certain under British rule. Ah yes, how that Imperial Presence lived on, but only selectively and in the memories of the elderly.

Night came, and we were taken to visit relatives for a family celebration. The occasion was an engagement party for a bride of fourteen and a man of fifty two. She would be his third wife. To us it was an unhappy event, cruel and inhumane, but to Arab Muslim society it was normative. In traditional Arab society, as in much of the world still, marriage is not based on love but on an arrangement between a man and a girl's family and is a contract generally for life. The bride is bartered for a specified amount agreed upon by the family. We talked about this with our Western-educated host who lived in both worlds. It was hard for him to explain and he was almost embarrassed by our ignorance. Ironically, he had chosen to marry an independent, strong-willed and highly-educated girl from Ohio who wasn't about to adopt the Arab ways of his culture.

The next day was shopping at the bazaar, a huge open-air affair akin to an American street market. Abu Yassir's assignment was to buy *jalabias* for me and my two sons. This is a traditional Arab garment worn by men, basically a full length slip-over robe made of white sheet material, sometimes with fancy needle work on the sleeves and at the hem. It is practical in the heat, as little needs to be worn under it, a feature that fascinated the girls. The shopkeeper was charming but somewhat immovable. He stated his price, we countered, and then our host stepped in and made it clear he would do the bargaining. Finally, we arrived at a price and the old vendor proceeded to make our garments. In less than an hour, three *jalabias* were ready and we wore them home, feeling just a bit silly with what felt like a Halloween costume wrapped around us. I quickly got used to mine and wore it frequently, mainly at dinner parties, for the remainder of our time in Uganda. It felt good, and I relished the story of how it came about.

Another night the Abu Yassirs took us for a special treat. That evening was hosted by a senior military figure and the guests included professional people and academics from the university. We were seated on the patio of a large and lovely home, under a southern sky of night beauty and surrounded by stimulating conversation. Soon, a well known Sudanese musician joined the party and proceeded to work magic on his ten-stringed lute. The conversation quieted as he took us on a musical odyssey of the Sudan, beginning with the harvest music of the Dinka to the rich folk tunes of the Azande in the south to the Nuba, who divide north from south. We sat spellbound as he took us through the lyrical music of the Haquibah Muslim tradition. On and on he went, and we sat entranced. I wished I had a recorder, but it turned out most of this music was already available on professional recordings. We learned later that he was one of the Sudan's most popular recording artists, famous for his knowledge of the songs and musical traditions of that huge country.

Conversation was intermittent as the evening waxed mellow. We talked with a university professor who had all the right qualifications: a PhD in his field, he'd studied in the West and had great teaching experience. He was married to an attractive woman, also on the faculty with similar qualifications. And not in the hearing of his wife but without apology he said to us "If I had it to do over again, I would marry a barefoot peasant woman who knew nothing and had no education. That way, my life would be simpler and I would be more in control." We were stunned into silence. He wasn't kidding. That was one of those moments when we realized we would never understand some of Africa's cultures. We wondered what that said for the marriage of our good friend from Ohio who was highly educated and married to our host, a Sudanese Arab, equally educated.[40]

And so the evening passed as gently as the desert night breeze. We sat under a sky filled with the celestial wonder of the southern hemisphere. I could make out the Southern Cross and pondered the wonder of it all as the conversation went on, most of it in English, about politics and academia, shop talk among old friends. It was the impeccable hospitality of the Sudanese intelligentsia. But it was now well after ten and still there was no sign of dinner. We struggled to hold back the occasional yawn. We were in a culture where the evening meal is eaten as late as possible, when the heat has subsided. That would be eleven or later. Late nights made for late starts the next day, usually with a simple breakfast and a midday meal in the afternoon. In the world of the Sahara, the clock gets tipped at least four hours off from milder climes.

When dinner arrived, sometime after eleven, it was such an array of Sudanese cuisine, far more than we could even sample. Our taste buds were too sleepy, but we were humbled knowing many women had worked long hours preparing that feast. Just for us.

Two days before our scheduled departure from Khartoum, nature went wild. A Saharan sandstorm descended on the country and for thousands of miles to the west. We were told these things were monstrous in size and were regularly visited upon the Sahara, a desert large enough to cover a dozen countries. Sandstorms like this were of epic proportions and could last for days. Our hostess moved calmly about the house as if by habit, closing windows and doors and stuffing damp cloths around them, and we hunkered down to do not much of anything. It became harder to breathe and fine sand in the air gave the inside of the house an

---

[40] The Abu Yassirs are happily married and Sarah went on to become an Assistant Secretary General of the United Nations, responsible for one of its major programs.

amber haze that looked like an old faded photograph. This sandstorm would last five days, getting into millions of lungs and every nook and cranny for thousands of miles across Africa. Everywhere, life came to a standstill and there in the house we sat by the hour, sweating like pigs, on the verge of claustrophobia. Having windows and doors blanketed only made it more uncomfortable, but had they been open we would have choked and probably ceased to breathe. There had been a marked change in temperature from Kampala at 3500 feet to Khartoum in the desert at less than 1000 feet and now we felt the heat at its worst. The wind blew and blew and we could think only of getting out of the Sudan. Two days later, we sat at the airport waiting for our BOAC flight that never opened its doors. Virtually every flight had been cancelled. The grinding sand in the air made flying too much of a risk for the jet turbines. Human lungs as well, but we couldn't shut those down. Natural events like this, as well as grinding poverty, are why most people die in places like the Sudan before they reach the age of 60.

In desperation, we looked for another airline that could get us out. None were flying. I felt a panic like being the last one on a sinking ship but tried the stiff upper lip for the family's sake. Finally, we heard Alitalia was still flying, and we raced to their gate. There was only one plane leaving, and that would be the last chance of getting out. It was on a first-come, first-served basis with no assigned seats, but that didn't matter. Getting on that plane was the only thought in our minds and those of a few hundred others. It was bedlam, everyone pushing and screaming, Sudanese women balancing baskets and bundles on their heads, the stench of old sweat, heat, and dust. The panic of the crowd was palpable, and there we were, dealing with sharp elbows and dragging our kids through the midst of it trying to find seven seats. Finally, almost overcome by the screams and smells and the heat of a plane that had been sitting in the desert all day, there was a collective sigh of relief when the doors finally closed.

Our last glimpse of the Sudan was unforgettable. That weather-beaten Alitalia jet struggled to an altitude of 35,000 feet before we were out of that sandstorm. And I thought for a brief moment about the millions who live there and will never get out.

I had met a young Anglican priest by the name of Charles Dickens Mutesa, who was a youth worker for the central diocese in Kampala. I was intrigued by his name and he told me he was given it by his father, who had studied English literature and was enamored with the writings of Charles Dickens. Young Charles didn't know any more than that, nor who his namesake was. He didn't much like his name because his schoolmates used to call him "Charlie Dickey-Prickey." I understood his dis-ease. The name of Mutesa should have redeemed things for him for it spoke for itself: it was the royal name of the King at the time English missionaries arrived in 1870. King Mutesa was the head of the Baganda tribe, for whom the country had been named. Ugandans of other tribes have resented the name given the country ever since because there are dozens of other tribes in the country, but the Baganda have always fancied themselves a cut above the rest. The British, who named the place, must have thought so too.

Young Charles had a passion for youth work and was good at it, which is what caught my attention. My work at Makerere University didn't involve me in the church. Consequently I had no connections with the Anglican Church in Uganda, which made my connection with Charles all the more unlikely. I may have met him at the University Chapel, but the next thing I knew I was accompanying him on a trip to the Luwero Triangle which was a dangerous part of the country. It may have been Uganda's version of the Bermuda Triangle. Charles was on a mission to distribute Bibles in that area and asked if I would like to come along. Never had I been party to delivering Bibles, but I had heard intriguing stories of the Luwero Triangle and thought this might be my only chance to see it—as long as I didn't have to hand out Bibles. That just wasn't my thing; I have often found just reading it chore enough. But the Anglican Church in Uganda was solidly evangelical which meant they put the Bible before everything else which made them act more like Baptists than Anglicans. They had a tendency to take the Bible literally, like it was "Godspeak", believing, like fundamentalists, that God had written every word of it.

This Bible thing all started in East Africa in the late nineteenth century with the missionary work spearheaded by the Church Missionary

Society (CMS), the evangelical wing of the Church of England, and the polar-opposite of the Anglo Catholic branch. Evangelicals emphasize the Bible almost to the exclusion of everything else, placing lesser emphasis (or none at all) on the sacraments, vestments, liturgical practices, or even the theology that one might associate with "High Church" Anglicanism. I remember the beloved Archbishop Erica Sabiti, the head of the Church of Uganda, who never missed an opportunity to tell you about his conversion experience. It had occurred fifty years ago, but he would tell that story like it was yesterday. People would talk incessantly about the moment they had been "saved" and took a dim view of some of the things the rest of us might enjoy, like alcohol, dancing, playing cards and having a good time. When it came to worship, I found their services exceedingly dull. Services at the University Chapel were only moderately better.

My experience of Anglicanism, as observed in the Episcopal Church in the United States, had always been what used to be called "High Church" or Anglo-Catholic The emphasis was placed on rich and colorful liturgical services, a theology that was broad, inclusive and involved in the affairs of the world,, and clergy were addressed as "Father (not "Mr." or "Reverend") generally more closely related to the Roman Catholic Church than to other Protestant churches. Things were different in Uganda. I felt like a fish out of water, which makes my story of the Luwero Triangle visit with Charles all the more unlikely.

In his little Volkswagen bug, Charles and I set off, the back seat crammed with Bibles and tracts to hand out along the way. Charles called himself a Salesman for Jesus. I cringed a little at the thought, recalling another evangelical I had met in South Africa, a dentist, who was equally proud of his corny motto that hung in his office window, "Pulling for Christ." But it was comical being cooped up in Charles' VW with Godspeak and tracts—sort of like door-to-door bell-ringing evangelists. Definitely not my schtick!

The Luweru Triangle had been a dangerous place for years. Located north of the capital, the term commonly referred to an area renowned for the persecution of civilians during the Luwero War, which had been between the rebel National Resistance Army and the government of former President Milton Obote. Gross human rights abuses had been committed in the area by Obote's troops, which involved the removal of nearly three-quarters of a million people, forcing them into refugee camps. Infrastructures such as roads and communications suffered greatly and were in bad condition, if existing at all. Military roadblocks were everywhere, and travel was almost non-existent. And it was into *this* young Charles wanted to take us. I think he figured the Bibles would somehow keep us safe but I didn't share his faith or his optimism. But off we went.

The roads were atrocious, which slowed us almost to a creep as we dodged potholes and craters left by bombs and missiles that had shelled the area in an earlier day. And then came our first roadblock. Rifles and questions were on the ready: "Where are you going?" "Who's the *mzungu* with you?" "Don't you know it's dangerous to be on these roads?" "So, why are you here?" "Who gave you permission?" "What are those books in the back seat?" On and on the mindless chatter went, sometimes doubling back on itself. Charles smiled his way through the whole thing, I supposed giving them the right answers, though I had no knowledge at all of Luganda. I was the *mzungu* they were inquiring about, that much I knew. That's a Swahili word used all over East Africa, meaning 'white man.' Eventually, they waved us on.

As we passed through a small settlement of huts, villagers shouted to us, "Hey, *mzungu*, you're going the wrong way…this way…this way" they crowed. Charles didn't seem all that certain of the road so he took their advice, only to discover a few miles down the road they were playing us for the fool. When we turned around and came back their way, they brayed with laughter at our stupidity, collapsing on the ground with the success of their joke. Very funny.

Like virtually every road in Uganda, this one was filled with bicycles and pedestrians, most of them carrying huge loads of bananas. Uganda is a country addicted to bananas. They claim some sixty varieties grow there, and even the smallest homestead will have a few trees. As a staple food, it is said Ugandans eat an average of five to six hundred pounds per year, most of it in the form of *matoke,* which is a stiff porridge made from particular kinds of bananas, fairly tasty with a traditional peanut sauce. Not surprisingly, bananas are also used to make a local hooch known as *waragi*, a cultural form of gin more like white lightning. The *mazungu* discovered that mixed with lemonade it made a very pleasant drink and the supply was abundant. It became one of our favorite drinks—best vodka and tonic substitute in all of East Africa.

We saw raw evidence of the war. One account reported it must have ranked with the worst atrocities in human history when Obote's troops ravaged the countryside and slaughtered between 200,000 and 500,000 people before they were defeated. South Africa's so-called civilized government didn't kill numbers like that, they only persecuted them, denied them basic human rights and treated them as sub-human. But violence was violence: one form killed the body, the other killed the soul.

Charles grew quiet, which was unusual for him. I sensed he was worried. My God, (I thought), were we in over our heads, sitting here in this little bug of a car, two naive priests and a load of Bibles. We must have been a laughable sight but now the situation wasn't worth a smile. And then another roadblock, this time a big one. We were surrounded by young soldiers, some of them mere boys, all toting rifles pointed at us, like we were the enemy. *Good grief, now what!* Out came the same old questions, but this time Charles was prepared. He launched into his sales pitch: "Hey brother, have you met my friend Jesus?" That prompted a rifle in my face: "You mean this *mzungu*?" "No, No", Charles jumped in, "He's not Jesus. Jesus is black like us," he lied, I guess figuring it might gain us some favor. "Jesus is my best friend and he wants to be yours too." "He's a wonderful man and you should get to know him." And with that, like a traveling salesman right on cue, Charles whipped out his tracts and got the soldier's attention long enough for him to put down his rifle and take a look. I slid down in the seat as he carried on like a Pentecostal preacher, but if it could get us out of this jam I could go along with it. "You can read all about Jesus in this," Charles crooned, pointing to the tract and hoping to make nice long enough to get us through the bind. (Oh this is ever so clever, I thought, if a little devious). "Hey, all of you brothers, come and look at this," he sang out as he shoveled out handfuls of the things. And before long those soldiers were laughing, either with us or at us, and flagged us through without paying us any more attention. With my life depending on it, I doubt I could have pulled it off like Charles Dickens.

A little further on, we came on a wailing party. In a little village of only a few shacks, there had been a death, and everybody turned out to mourn for the dead and feel sorry for themselves. Africa does wakes really well, some of them lasting days, maybe even weeks, gathering huge crowds of friends and relations and passers-by wanting a good meal. This wailing party wasn't very big, which made me wonder why. Good priest that he was, Charles stopped to see if he could be of help. They explained to him the one who had died was a homosexual (they didn't use terms like "gay") and this young man whom everybody loved had contracted what they called the "homo disease" (later to be identified as HIV/AIDS) and so he was shunned and left alone to die. My heart sank. I knew the deplorable attitude towards gay people in Uganda generally, but here we were meeting it face to face. The people showed genuine sorrow but nobody would touch the dead body; it just lay there on a grass mat, lifeless, covered with a blanket. They had called the village authorities who said that since he was a homosexual and had died from the homo disease they couldn't help. Charles took charge and told them he would bury the body upon our return later that afternoon. I thought that was noble of him and told him so, considering the Church of Uganda had the same narrow judgmental attitudes as the rest of society.

As we continued on our way, Charles began to explain things. I knew approximately what he was going to say and didn't want to hear it, but there was no escaping the sermon about to come. I was doing a slow burn but kept quiet as Charles launched into his lecture like it had been well-rehearsed. He explained to me that the Bible says homosexuality is a sin and therefore people are to be condemned who practice such filthy, ungodly behavior. "Reverend, you know the Bible is quite clear on the subject, you should know that!" I did and it wasn't his interpretation by a long shot. It was all I could do to keep quiet as he droned on. "All of these sinful liberal ideas are coming into Uganda from the West and we must be on our guard against Satan's attacks." And reaching his apogee, he raised his voice to end the diatribe, almost abandoning the steering wheel, "In fact, many members of Ugandan Parliament want to make homosexuality an offense punishable by death." Wonder of wonders, I thought, when he told me he was sympathetic to their view but hadn't yet made up his mind. My heart sank. *Made up his mind? For God's sake, this isn't a matter of sin let alone criminality in this country or any other, and his Christian faith ought to be against the death penalty for anything!* For once, I maintained my silence, but I thought how tragic that this nice, intelligent young priest had such a twisted understanding of the Christian faith, the Bible, and most of life.

Much if not all of the Bible thumping on the issue of homosexuality in Uganda goes back to the original missionaries from England, whose evangelical influence continues throughout most of East Africa to this day. It was one of the things that made me uncomfortable around the Church of Uganda. They had almost a fundamentalist view of Scripture that allowed for very little interpretation or understanding beyond the written text, and frequently chosen passages at that. As a whole, the Church of Uganda knew little about any 'social gospel' and acted as though religion and politics probably aren't meant to mix. There were remarkable exceptions—courageous church leaders who spoke out against Amin's injustice and were being systematically eliminated, but they were not the majority. Those courageous bishops were disappearing at an alarming rate and being executed. Archbishop Janani Luwum, a happy friend to everyone, was assassinated by Amin personally, found later with four bullets in his head in the shape of a cross. All hell had broken loose in this 'Christian' nation as the faithful looked on in disbelief, powerless but defiant in their condemnation of what was happening.

Charles was right about one thing: there definitely *were* outside influences on the issue of homosexuality; but it was from evangelical and fundamentalist churches and individuals from the United States and other parts of the world who had pressed themselves upon Ugandans to sell their narrow-minded views. Some of those outsiders had even influenced members of the Ugandan Parliament to criminalize homosexuality, at the same time that foreign governments the world over were condemning such efforts. I sat and listened to Charles' rant on the subject, not knowing where to jump in. I was facing pretty much a closed mind on the subject. "God has told us in the Bible and the Word of God never lies" Charles repeated. It was significant, I thought, that not once did he ask what I thought about it. Maybe he was afraid I would come out with that "liberal theology" of the West they were warned about; but he couldn't have thought I agreed with him.

Finally I did speak. "Charles, there is another way to look at this, you know." By this time he was ready for the fight. "What other way?" he demanded his voice raising. "Well", I demurred, "God has created all kinds of human differences and the same is true in sexuality. God created homosexuality and it isn't a sin," I argued, now *my* voice raising. "Reverend" he said, (and that misused title always riled me) now repeating himself, "The Bible is very clear on this subject and being a teacher you should know that!" I sensed it was time to leave this discussion for another day and said so. Charles agreed we would discuss it later, when we were not on a potholed road in the Luwero Triangle, dodging soldiers and roadblocks. Definitely not a good time or place for this discussion. But I wondered to myself what was the use of further discussion anyway—the Church of Uganda was so brainwashed into such evangelical/fundamentalist views that conversation and logic wouldn't change things. And sadly, the law was enacted in Uganda: if you were gay, you could die by the hand of the State and the law of the land.

We reached our destination and distributed the Bibles as planned, without fanfare. The tracts went with them. The return trip to Kampala was surprisingly uneventful and since we were leaving the area, there were no roadblocks or soldiers to contend with. The trip was pretty quiet. It gave me time to think about things, about how out of step the Anglican Church of Uganda was with the Anglican Church worldwide. They had come under the heavy influence of the evangelical Church Missionary Society in the beginning, and the seed had been planted for a simplistic "Bible Belt" kind of faith. I didn't know it then, but the move to criminalize homosexuality would carry forth into the next century and be a live issue, even as tens of thousands of gay Ugandans were hounded and persecuted by Church and State.

We stopped by the roadside to pick up a poor cripple who was walking with a leg twisted around a battered old walking stick which had obviously been his surrogate leg for many years. Good for Charles. In spite of his narrow views on sexuality and a few other things, he was a loving and caring priest. As the crippled man settled into the back seat, we talked a little with him, asking how he was. "Hey man" he said with a touch of enthusiasm, "God woke me up this morning and gave me another day to live, so I'm blessed!" It warmed my heart to hear such a childlike faith in a man who must have had many sorrows. Charles joined in the chorus praising God for his goodness, though the man seemed to have had an unequal share of it. "Yes brother, life is a blessing filled with blessings abounding" he replied. This was the other side of their simple evangelical faith that could judge and condemn on the one hand and be so wonderfully childlike on the other. With a little wonder I remained quiet, still troubled by the events of the day: the violence of the armed roadblocks and the violence of a religion that was so harsh and judgmental. I had seen enough for one day.

It had taken years of my adulthood to grow in my understanding of homosexuality, then to grow from acceptance to appreciation of those different from me. Today I had met with the prejudice of an entire nation that still had nothing but harsh judgment, condemnation, and persecution for those same people I had come to love and it was a depressing thought. As I lay on my pillow, I ended the day wondering how long it would take for the world to grow in acceptance and openness towards all people.

That night I had two dreams. The first was a nightmare. I saw two of the African countries I had now lived in and what the misuse of religion had done in each of them. In the dream I saw South Africa like a big church, with crowds of religious people going in and reading their Bibles, saying prayers and singing hymns and shouting "Amen." Then, when they went out of the church, they mistreated their black neighbors in all manner of ways. It was like their religion hadn't done anything to make them good to their neighbors. But they told me that

God and country and *apartheid* was what they believed in and what God wanted them to do. Then I saw Uganda and all of its religious people in another huge church building. In that dream I saw these millions of Christians [41] lining up to persecute and even kill some of their own people because they were homosexuals and they said it was God's will they should die. It was a terrible nightmare that woke me with an equal mix of sadness and anger.

But then I had another dream that swept all of that away. In it I saw, like the Book of Revelation said, "a new heaven and a new earth" being formed where there was love and acceptance and appreciation for one another, where people of all races and tribes and peoples and tongues, of all sexual orientation or none, gathered in harmony to celebrate life and each other. And there was singing and dancing and freedom and happiness. Then I awoke and for a moment had a good feeling that maybe, someday, some way, God's Kingdom will come and that may not be through any Church or Temple or organized religion. It made me wonder if maybe God's Kingdom will someday come in the spirit and heart of every one of us by a spiritual revolution when people are tired and worn out by prejudice and religion and war, Churches and Temples.

To end this sorry chapter, in 2014 Nigeria criminalized gay marriage and banned organizations that help gay people or fight HIV/AIDS. The Same Sex Marriage Prohibition Act called the "Jail the Gays Bill" became law in early 2014. Some ninety-eight percent of Nigerians polled said that homosexuality should not be tolerated and that this is a law that is in line with the people's religious inclination. I find it curious that Nigeria is another of the countries that was first introduced to Christianity by Bible-thumping evangelicals who taught the people to read the Bible literally and without interpretation or adaptation. With such narrow and selective reading of Scripture, they looked for passages that served their purposes, in which homosexuality was condemned and those practicing it were stoned to death. I wonder if there is a connection with those African countries that had an evangelical Christian beginning.

---

[41] Uganda is said to be numerically the most Christian country in all of Africa if not the world, with a Christian population over 90%.

On our return to Kampala, Charles Dickens the priest, didn't stop in the village to bury the dead gay man and I knew why…

Archbishop, You Said *What?*

In the sixth month of 1972, the strangest experience of my life was about to happen. It began with murmurs at a conference at Makerere earlier that year. Attendees from Botswana happened to mention they would be electing a bishop later that year. I couldn't have been less interested, but felt I had to carry on idle conversation with compatriots from Southern Africa. Their conversation had nothing to do with me but I remembered the discussion. Months later, I received the strangest message from the Archbishop of Central Africa to say my name was "under consideration" for bishop of a new diocese about to be formed in the newly independent Republic of Botswana. Out of the blue this came. "Would you be interested" the Archbishop asked. WHY would I be interested?!! Furthermore, they hadn't even asked if I wanted to be "under consideration." In an effort to be polite and at least honor the question, I told the Archbishop such a thing was not in my game plan but that I would think about it for a month or so. Fortunately, there was a spring break at Makerere which coincided with a short furlough back to the States.

During that furlough we discussed the Archbishop's preposterous suggestion with friends and family *ad nauseum*. Although we hadn't found that independent African country we had hoped for, we were tired and didn't really want to extend our time in Africa. I recall telling folks we needed to get back to the States so our children could learn the Pledge of Allegiance before adulthood. So we were fishing for opinions that would support our sentiments and found an abundance. In a word, they all said it's time to come home! We thought so too. When we left the States to return to Uganda, it was with the firm resolve to say no to the Archbishop. I would complete my contract with the University and leave Africa within the coming year. Orders and decision were in tack. On our return we stopped in Zurich for several days to visit seminary friends, and over many a glass of Jack Daniels we reviewed our decision. They also told me what I wanted to hear. So before we departed Zurich I sent a cable to the Archbishop declining any further consideration.

Pleased with our decision, we returned to Uganda ready to complete the academic year and return to the U.S. We were so certain of our decision that we left our two eldest girls in the U.S. with grandparents.

And then it happened. One morning, while listening to the news on my car radio, like a thunderbolt out of nowhere the BBC reported I had been elected Bishop of Botswana at a meeting held in Bulawayo days before. [42] I pulled to the side of the road in complete panic. *How could this be? What had happened? Why did they do this to me?* I have since described feeling like Job, Jeremiah, and Jonah: in the ancient stories, the first one suffered, the second protested and the third tried to run away. I rushed home and dumped the news on my wife, and together we telephoned the Archbishop in Malawi. Miraculously, we got through but the connection was faint. My first words were "Your Grace, didn't you receive my cable from Switzerland?" I was stupefied by his reply: "*What cable?*" was all he said in a deep, sonorous voice. My heart sank. The Archbishop then explained that on the Feast of St. John the Baptist, June 24th, 1972, in Bulawayo, Southern Rhodesia, I was duly elected the first Bishop of Botswana, and he expected me to accept the election. But I hadn't accepted and in a moment of fantasy thought there might yet be a bargaining chip in there somewhere. So I demurred, whereupon the Archbishop requested I fly to Malawi to meet with him and the other bishops of Central Africa to "discuss this matter."

---

[42] There was a touch of humor in the midst of it all. What the BBC actually reported was that a "Black Texan" had been elected. They got the Texan part right in that I was born there and assumed the rest: that I must be black to be elected to a black African country!

It was a hassle getting a flight out of troubled Uganda, a harbinger of things to come. When I arrived in Malawi and met that august body, they and the deep, sonorous voice made it emphatic they did not want to go through another election. "Clearly," the Archbishop said, "you were the unanimous choice of the Elective Assembly." That didn't make me feel any better. Then they sat in silence, looking my way and waiting for a reply. I knew their predictable advice was that my election must be "of the Holy Spirit." I thought that was probably a bunch of baloney but feeling somewhat trapped, reluctantly consented, thereby signing on for an unknown number of years in Africa. And that's how I became a very reluctant and very young bishop of an African country I had never seen nor visited. Whenever it's convenient, Anglicans and Episcopalians love to say, "It's of the Holy Spirit," but many times I have wondered.

Things had been growing tense in Uganda as reports of lawlessness continued to mount. Amin's troops seemed out of control. It was in those days we learned what a kondo was. In the early seventies they may have had condos in the United States; they had a different kind in Uganda, not the kind you could live in but the kind you feared. Kondos were young bandits, frequently petty thieves, who would kill for a chicken or a loaf of bread. They were often Amin's soldiers who were increasingly roaming about making mischief; more likely, kondos were just young school boys looking for food for their hungry family. Community outrage had grown so intense at the overall violence in the country that these kids would sometimes be stoned to death by their neighbors. We were living in a cradle of equatorial beauty with beautiful people held captive by a renegade military with violence covering the earth. It was as if the entire country was berserk. No one knew what the morrow would bring, but one thing was certain: it would be more fear and uncertainty.

It was said that as a student Milton Obote was influenced by the writings of John Milton, the seventeenth century poet who wrote the epic poem, "Paradise Lost." Uganda was about to become that paradise lost. John Milton's namesake had begun that process, and Idi Amin was about to complete it. People were beginning to speak in hushed tones, telling tales of violence, of people disappearing. I began to wonder if our move from *apartheid* South Africa had made any difference in the scale of human justice. We had exchanged one form of tyranny and terror for another. The Pearl was being trampled upon by swine, and it was beginning to look like nothing could save Uganda from plunging headlong into bloodshed and chaos.

It was ironic that South Africa and Uganda had so much of the natural beauty of Africa and yet both were blighted by evil leaders. It seemed there was no way out for either country. The Ugandan strong man was getting more brutal, and that smiling boyish face hid the mind of a psychopath with neither conscience nor morals. He was now killing at random and no one felt safe. My daily drive to work included dropping the kids off at their schools and then a straight run to Makerere Hill. The days came when that's all I did because of random roadblocks and military harassment that frequently ended in bloodshed. Uganda had become a very dangerous place to live, and we started considering our options.

As events went from bad to worse, Amin lowered his guns on the two groups he hated most: the Asians and the academics. He loathed the Asians because they were generally better educated than the Africans and were successful in business. He hated the academic community because many of them were not afraid to speak out against his brutal rule. They were also a constant reminder to Amin that he had little education. He was about to come for Makerere, but first he would deal with the Asian community. In one edict he ordered all 80,000 Asians to leave the country *within ninety days.* They would have to find countries that would grant them asylum, anyplace. It didn't matter that most of them were third and fourth generation Ugandans. What to do with homes, households, generations of possessions, lands, shops, friendships? Amin had gone crazy and rumors were spreading that syphilis was attacking his brain. Open persecution began of Asian shop keepers and tradesmen, engineers, doctors, and research scientists. With the Asians gone, the backbone of Uganda's economy would soon disappear. It was a heart-rending ninety days as the expatriate community watched with horror and sorrow. Tens of thousands of Ugandan citizens were forced to look for a new home elsewhere.

One of those who went through it described it in these words:

> We'd grown up assuming our country was safe. Now we were aware that it wasn't. Young African boys were harassing Indians like us. Mum heard a story about at African man, who in the middle of a busy bazaar, starting cutting Indian peoples' arms. He hadn't been caught and no one knew who he was. After that our parents didn't let us go out after sunset. General Amin said we were bloodsuckers. He claimed we were exploiting native Ugandans, while keeping a stranglehold on the economy. He ignored the fact that our industry and entrepreneurial efforts had made Uganda's economy stronger than it would have been otherwise. Indians controlled the majority of businesses, such as factories, sugar cane plantations, tea estates, agriculture, construction, textiles and cotton gins. We were the backbone of Uganda's economy…Amin claimed that we'd refused to integrate with the black community. But we were a minority, unpopular among the native Ugandans, who resented our success. Our departure would signal the downfall of Uganda's economy… Most of the Asians were Gujarati Indians and Pakistanis. We'd lived in this country for decades. We were second, third and fourth generation Ugandan residents. This was the only home we knew. ("Out of Uganda in 90 Days", Urmila Patel, 2014)

The brightest and best of the Asian community went to Canada. That government was one of the first to offer visas, transportation, and a home to the dispossessed, and by their generosity Canada got the pick of the lot. Most of the remainder went to the United Kingdom, others wandered the earth, looking for a place to call home. It was a time of great sadness that left a permanent scar on Uganda.

Next came the academics. Most were expatriates, like us, and had already returned to their home countries. We arranged for our family to fly to Malawi and wait for me to finish my contract. I would join them at the end of the academic year, now only months away. It was a difficult goodbye, filled with conflicting thoughts and emotions, many of them too frightening to express. Once they arrived in Malawi, the family would be in the hands of a Canadian couple, missionaries to Central Africa who were staying at Lake Malawi for a time. As for me? Would I be safe? Would things work out as we had planned? What would happen to those of us remaining at Makerere? No one knew and we dared not ponder those questions.

I moved in with the Abu Yassirs who lived on campus and have only blurred memories of those next few months. I was sleep walking through the days until I could shake off the nightmare and be gone. Those of us living on campus didn't venture off the hill for anything. By now, Amin's troops were crazed with killing and realized they could help themselves to anything they wanted, including the University. We knew that but tried not to think about it. We also knew that colleagues were disappearing on a daily basis. One day, soldiers marched the Vice Chancellor out of his office and he was never seen again. We developed a bunker mentality to get through each day. By night we used a bottle of scotch and talked late into the night. It was destructive but therapeutic. In a crazy way, it felt like we were doing something about the situation just to talk. Fortunately, Abu Yassir had good connections with the Sudanese Embassy, which kept the supply of scotch flowing.

My flight out of the nightmare was scheduled for early the next morning. Abu Yassir offered to drive me to Entebbe, which was noble because he was risking his life, but Arabs were faring better than the rest of us for some reason. It may have been because it was assumed most of them were Muslim, like Amin. The big buffoon had the crazy notion of making Uganda an Islamic State when over ninety percent of the population was Christian, and a mere five percent Muslim. Whatever his religion, I was glad to have Abu Yassir as a friend, and a good one he was.

The road to the airport had become a gauntlet of death. Roadblocks littered the once-peaceful sixty kilometer road to Entebbe. Stories abounded of brutal things happening at those stops—people and vehicles were disappearing. Life and limb could disappear at the whim of boy soldiers if they didn't like something about you. But there was no other way to get to the airport that we knew of.

The first roadblock came up just outside the city. Questions and searches. The questions made no sense. "Where are you going?" "Why?" "Who gave you permission for this?" "What's your name?" "What country do you come from?" "Why is that?" "Where are you going?" "Why?" "You have a very nice car" (*Oh my God, now do we lose the car? This is just the first roadblock..good thing we left early*). We cleared that one with only loss of time. Number two was just up ahead. They flagged us through. I wondered why that was. Ten minutes later, another roadblock, this time we got searched. "Everything out of the car!" "Why are you carrying a suitcase?" "Open it!" "Where are you going?" "Why?" "You don't like it in our country?" "Why is that?" "What's your name?" "You leave the suitcase here!" We argued gently over that issue and they let us keep the bag. Thank God! "You give me this wrist watch!" On and on the nonsense went. Then, as if they tired of their sport, they let us go—on to the next roadblock. When the airport was almost in sight we were stopped one last time. This time was almost our undoing. We were taken from the car, searched, interrogated, stripped, and made to squat by the roadside while the boy soldiers amused themselves with jokes and laughter, undoubtedly at our expense. I was beginning to wonder if I would get out of the country at all and had given up the idea of catching a plane. Now I worried about coming out of it alive. Miraculously, after what seemed like forever, the boys in uniform returned and told us to get dressed and go. No explanation of anything, which was fine with me.

Such was the measure of intimidation that went on day and night in the Uganda of those days. The Pearl of the Nile had been trampled underfoot in pig shit by the mindless beasts of General Amin's army.

As I sat nervously waiting to board my plane, I savored the memory of my last night in Uganda, which had been crazy but delicious. That night, we had cooked up an idea that could have got us all shot. It was late, we had sipped our scotch and discussed how bad things were, and decided, one more time, we should all get out of Uganda and leave it to its demons. But before we left, with mischievous glee we thought why not put the best thing in the country on the auction block. Why not put Makerere University up for sale? It sounded like a great idea to those of us sipping scotch so we made a plan. Abu Yassir's wife found some old sheets which were sacrificed to the cause. Out of them we made a huge banner, long enough to hang between the two Roman columns in front of the Faculty of Arts. On the banner in bold black letters we wrote, **UNIVERSITY FOR SALE**, ever so proud of ourselves. It was a drizzling night which was an added challenge to stringing this thing between the columns without a ladder. Without a flashlight and without much of anything else, include brains, I volunteered to shinny up the columns to tie the rope. By midnight, we got it hung without incident or shooting. As we drove off campus the next morning on the way to airport, it was still there. It felt like a last laugh.

I was on my way to Malawi and freedom and a happy family relaxing by the lake.

(Amin's rule was characterized by gross human rights abuse, political repression, ethnic persecution, extra-judicial killings, nepotism, corruption, and gross economic mismanagement. The number of people killed as a result of his regime is estimated by international observers and human rights groups to range from 100,000 to 500,000. In 1977, after the last two British diplomats withdrew from Uganda, Amin declared he had beaten the British and added "CBE" for "Conqueror of the British Empire" to his title. He then had Radio Uganda announce his full title: "His Excellency President for Life, Field Marshal Alhaji Dr. Idi Amin Dada, VC, DSO, MC, CBE.")

What more can be said...the last King of Scotland?

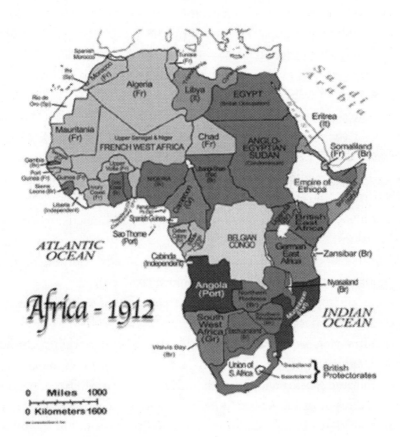

Colonial Africa

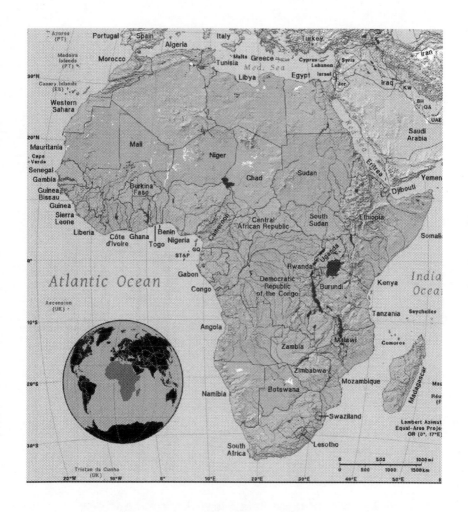

Sovereign Countries of Africa, 20th Century

Size of United States Relative to African Continent

Author's Home in Ovamboland
(St. Mary's Mission, Odibo)

The Efundja
Flood waters from Angola during rainy season.

The Old Lorry - "Onkwanime"

Preparing Grain Basket for Annual Harvest

Winnowing Millet Harvest

Stomping Grain for Cooking

Sifting Stomped Grain

Sir Seretse and Lady Ruth Celebrating
a Happy Moment

Reverend Professor John Mbiti,
Chairman, Department of Religious Studies & Philosophy
Makerere University, Kampala, Uganda

Nelson ("Madiba") Mandela
First President of Democratic Republic of South Africa

John Mwafangejo as a Young Boy
(later to become a foremost artist of Namibia)

Heraldic seal, Diocese of Botswana

Chapter Eight

On the Road Again

H aving spent almost twelve years in three countries and finding nothing but harsh laws and cruel treatment, we were tired of looking in Africa for a haven of peace where human rights would be the norm. We were tired of everything but still loved Africa and the thought of leaving was enough to hold us back. Now we had reason not to leave: this 'calling' to Botswana. I figured it was at least a pretty good excuse for staying in Africa, even if it wasn't our idea. We knew there was still much good to be found in Africa, not least the phenomenal spirit of the African people, their culture and their joy. Unbeknown to us at this point, just ahead of us we would be finding some of Africa's greatest successes. But alas, even today people in the Western world tend to look upon Africa with pessimism, unable to believe that anything good can come out of the dark continent of Joseph Conrad's cynical writing.

Malawi wasn't a paragon of democracy, but it was at peace with itself. Known in colonial days as Nyasaland, this slender country was almost a forgotten remnant of the colonial era. It was exotic in appearance but with limited natural resources that consisted of a lake that stretched the length of the country. In an earlier day Nyasaland was fondly nicknamed "The Warm Heart of Africa". The British had administered the country until independence in 1964, when it became Malawi and Dr. Hastings Banda became its first president. Banda was Malawian, a European trained medical doctor, having worked in the West African country of Ghana until

1958, when he was persuaded to return home to work for the national cause. Upon independence, he was elected president. Banda moved quickly to insure there would be no political opposition to his leadership by declaring a one-party government and himself as life president. And for almost thirty years he presided over a rigid authoritarian regime. For reasons that are not clear, early on he made the unfortunate decision to maintain diplomatic relations with South Africa during the *apartheid* era. That decision severely strained relations with surrounding African countries.[43]

Much of life in Malawi centered around the lake that gave the country its colonial name of Nyasaland, which translated meant "Lakeland". Locals still laughed at the joke on the British who named the lake "Lake Nyasa" (meaning "Lake Lake"). It was on the shores of this lake where our family would put itself back together. We had decided meanwhile that I would stay behind in Uganda to finish the academic year and my contract with the university.

Upon arrival my wife's first experience suggested they were not yet in a totally free society. As she entered the terminal with many children in tow, she was greeted by an official who told her the length of her dress was "unacceptable." Her first thought was, what police state are we in now? It wasn't a serious encounter however, just a silly quirk by order of the president that women's dress lengths had to be close to ankle-length. Fortunately, she had been warned in advance that too much feminine leg showing caused anxiety in Malawi, and with a piece of African cloth she made an instant African skirt. Welcome to Malawi!

Months later, the reunion of our family was memorable. I had flown from Entebbe, leaving behind a national tragedy. Just stepping into the fresh air of Malawi felt good.

---

[43] During the *apartheid* era, not one other African country had official diplomatic ties with South Africa, which meant that South African Airways was not allowed to land anyplace in Africa. The Spanish Canary Islands off of West Africa was as close as they could land to refuel. In time, South African planes were equipped with over-sized tanks to enable them to fly non-stop from Johannesburg to Rio de Janeiro. On occasion, emergency landings were permitted. In the sixties, we were on one such when we were forced to land in Ghana. The reception we got was somewhat less than friendly.

We drove through the colonial town of Blantyre, which never actually became the capital although it was the commercial center of the country. Founded in 1876 by Church of Scotland missionaries and named after a town by the same name in Scotland, Blantyre had managed to keep its name through independence. It is a little known fact that Blantyre is one of the oldest urban centers in east, central and southern Africa, pre-dating all of today's major cities in Kenya, Zambia, Zimbabwe, and South Africa. However, cities in those countries quickly developed into metropolitan centers whereas Blantyre never did, due in large part to the lack of vision of its first president and the sleepy pace he set for the country. When we arrived, the town still had a dominant colonial presence. Jacaranda trees were in full bloom, characteristic of much of the British Empire, with green corrugated iron roofs, wide comfortable verandahs and a pace that was slow enough for morning tea and afternoon coffee—still served by African help, as in the days of old.

The countryside was idyllic, with peaceful pastoral scenes of herdsmen and cattle, women hoeing crops, children playing happily in small villages, and the smell of springtime everywhere. Never out of sight was the lake which generated its own life with the primitive fishing industry that had sustained the country for generations. It felt good to be back in rural Africa where life was routine, peaceful, pastoral, and predictable. Simply to drive through it was therapeutic. At least we were now physically in the ecclesiastical province where I would soon be serving as bishop. That was known as the Province of Central Africa and consisted of four countries: Malawi, Zambia, Southern Rhodesia, and Botswana, geographically one of the largest Anglican provinces in the world.[44]

---

[44] In a few years' time, I would attend the Lambeth Conference in England as the Bishop of Botswana. Lambeth is a meeting of all the world's Anglican Bishops held every ten years. The sprawling Province of Central Africa had a total of only six bishops representing tens of thousands of members. At the opening service, when the American Bishops filed in, they numbered over a hundred, filled half the sanctuary and represented a fraction of the Central African membership. We chuckled.

We headed towards the eastern shore of Lake Nyasa which bordered on Tanzania, formerly Tanganyika and a part of German East Africa until 1964 when it became the Republic of Tanzania. Our destination was Malindi where there was a little Anglican mission station on a dusty road beside the lake. Malindi was a traditional African village. It had scattered thatched huts and children, goats and cattle everywhere. Its main boast was the sleepy mission station with a little church, a smaller clinic, a school and not much else. It had no resident missionaries but served as an ideal place for R & R, our design for the next month. An elderly Canadian couple were there temporarily to help, old enough to be the grandparents our kids would never get to know. We had a thatched cottage, not quite big enough for us all, nestled on the shore of the lake where the sounds were magical. Many nights we would drift off to sleep to the sound of gently lapping water only a few steps away.

The terrors of Uganda now seemed far enough away, but the memories were still close enough to scare up a few nightmares. We were in another world—one country and a thousand miles away, in a lazy backwater of the last century. We had traded the bogus independence of Uganda for the sleepy independence of Malawi. While it was refreshing, it was strikingly different from the three previous countries where we had experienced so much human rights abuse. It was as much of a holiday as we could make it, and it felt good.

Malawi was without violence and without much else as well. By maintaining diplomatic relations with South Africa, President Banda had chosen to follow a political course that was out of step with the rest of Africa. This would cause enormous strain with neighboring Tanzania and its president, Julius Nyerere, who was a close friend of the presidents of Zambia and Botswana. Together with Kenneth Kaunda of Zambia and Sir Seretse Khama of Botswana, they were regarded as some of Africa's more creative and courageous political thinkers. Banda, on the other hand, would continue to press his will upon Malawi with such silly moves as lowering the hemline of women's skirts, taking personal responsibility for visas and passports and taking over several ministries of state. While it was a harmless environment, it was hardly an exciting one. Banda's grandfatherly rule of his self-designed one-party state would continue until the early nineties, when public pressure would force him to hold a referendum. In 1993 the country voted for a multi-party democracy and put an end to his presidency. By that time, much damage had been done and the country had sunk into such economic doldrums that it became one of Africa's least-developed countries, with a population mostly rural and an economy based heavily on traditional agriculture and fishing.

Even with a peaceful lake, warm water and a family that was thrilled to have me home again, I found it hard to settle down. We did playful things in the water like building rafts and having them sink and watching beautiful sunsets over the lake. But I couldn't relax. It was hard to process memories of Uganda while knowing ahead of us would be still greater challenges. We had little way of dealing with either. The horrors of Uganda would eventually take their place among the dark deeds of history we all try forget. The challenges ahead included moving our family thousands of miles to a new country, becoming the altogether-too-young first bishop of a newly independent African country, and learning a new African language. Setswana would be the language, and my only teacher was a basic grammar book, a dictionary, and a Setswana Prayer Book—no recordings to help with pronunciation, which was needed most.

Traveling from Malawi to Botswana involved going through Zambia and Southern Rhodesia. To do this by road would have been difficult, by rail impossible. Banda had seen to that. Kaunda and Nyerere shared a vision of a Tan-zam railway that would connect Central Africa with the Indian Ocean and provide a regular means of commerce for both countries. Tens of thousands of Chinese laborers were imported and hundreds of miles of rail were laid, but for a variety of reasons the project was never completed. It wouldn't have helped Malawi because of the troubled relationship Banda had with his neighbors. Nyerere's hatred of Banda over his connection with South Africa made it impossible for them to cooperate on anything, and relations with Zambia weren't much better.

Our destination was Salisbury, the major city of Southern Rhodesia, which could only be reached by air. Like the rest of Africa, the winds of change were blowing over this country too. But Southern Rhodesia was different. It was involved in a bitter political chess game that would get played out over the next two decades, and the gist of the problem was this: the Southern Rhodesian government was controlled largely by Ian Smith, Deputy Prime Minister of a conservative white government, who refused to set a timetable for the introduction of black majority rule, preliminary to independence from Great Britain. As talks to settle it repeatedly broke down, in 1965 Smith's white minority government unilaterally declared independence from Great Britain. This Unilateral Declaration of Independence—"UDI" as it became known—was quickly condemned by the United Nations and most of the free world, and Southern Rhodesia would endure years of economic sanctions and worldwide ostracism as a result. Smith was called by some of his critics an "unrepentant racist" because of his harsh attitude towards blacks and his unbending conviction they should not have majority rule under any circumstances.

Meanwhile, the winds of change continued to blow and black consciousness was growing among Southern Rhodesians. Men like Robert Mugabe and Joshua Nkomo were pressing for an independent Republic of Zimbabwe, the ancient name for the country. Whether Salisbury was therefore in Zimbabwe or Southern Rhodesia depended on who you talked to. At the time we arrived, for better or worse, the Anglican Church still raised the Commonwealth moniker of Southern Rhodesia. When full independence finally came in 1980, Southern Rhodesia became the Republic of Zimbabwe and the grand old British name of the city of Salisbury was changed to Harare ("hah-rah-ray"), along with name changes all over the country. It would eventually become the capital of the new republic.

With five restless children and an untold number of suitcases and bags resting precariously, we arrived in Salisbury on September 23, 1972, and were met by John Paul Burroughs who was the Bishop of Mashonaland. Burroughs was a tall, charming patrician with a refined Oxford accent that made me wonder what he was doing in Africa. Paul had one of the largest dioceses in Central Africa, loved the country and was devoted to his clergy. He and his equally charming wife, Beth, would be our hosts for the next few weeks. They were childless, but our brood more than filled any breach there might have been in their otherwise quiet household. In the halcyon days we were with them, Paul was wonderfully gracious in counseling and consoling me about what lay ahead for me. Usually, it was more of the latter. He was easily old enough to be my father, as were most of the bishops of the Province, which would often make me wonder what I was doing in this league.

African Cinderella

Botswana's history over the last 125 years holds many twists and turns. The modern period began in the stormy decade of the 1880s, which brought a rapacious era of political intrigue, plunder and possession by European powers in what has been called the "Scramble for Africa". Great Britain played a major role in laying claim to the greater parts of Africa, including modern-day Botswana. That acquisition started with the unbridled ambition of Cecil John Rhodes, remembered by history as a driving but ruthless force in shaping the future of Southern Africa. Rhodes was an English businessman, politician, mining magnate, and first chairman of the De Beers Mining empire which he helped found in 1880. At one time, De Beers marketed ninety percent of the world's rough diamonds, which made Rhodes the global diamond king for a time. He thought he had been made for that role and gloried in the power it brought him. He is also remembered by some as the "founder" of the countries of modern-day Zambia and Zimbabwe, which for a full hundred years bore his name as "Northern" and "Southern Rhodesia." Rhodes is famously quoted as saying, "I contend that we (the British) are the first race in the world and that the more of the world we inhabit the better it is for the human race...the absorption of the greater portions of the world under our rule simply will mean the end of all wars...(and) if there be a God, I think what he would like me to do is paint as much of the map of Africa British Red as possible."[45] As the chief architect of British policy in Southern Africa, he spent most of his life trying to make that happen.

---

[45] From "The Story of Africa", BBC World Service, June 13, 2009.

Western history books have made the embarrassing assertion that the British missionary heroes, David Livingston and Robert Moffat, were the first to discover Bechuanaland (modern day Botswana). Such are the mis-statements the West has continued to make about the Third World. What Livingston and Moffat "discovered" was a grand and lucrative opportunity for imperial acquisition. To see it from a secular point of view (instead of as "religious heroes"), their motives were considerably more than simply bringing Christianity to Africa. Along with religious motivations, Livingstone and Moffat clearly had imperialist aims as well in their plans for African expansion, but neither happened without resistance. Throughout the nineteenth century, the Batswana (people of Botswana) were wary of and hostile to changes they suspected were introduced by early missionaries. In 1878, the southern Batswana rose in arms to reject social and economic changes the missionary settlements were attempting to bring about. Tribesmen were interested in developing trade with the newcomers, but only on condition they would not preach a new religion or way of life, even as Livingstone was demanding the exercise of British power to protect what he called the "English route to the North". Such a route was key to the strategy Cecil John Rhodes had mapped out.

By 1884, Rhodes had narrowed his focus on Bechuanaland and declared, "Bechuanaland is the neck of the bottle and commands the route to the Zambezi. We must secure it, unless we are prepared to see the whole of the North pass out of our hands." It was an astonishing statement by any measure. Rhodes called Bechuanaland the key to his dream of a "Cape to Cairo" road for trade to the African interior reaching as far as the Suez Canal. In 1885, he managed to persuade Great Britain to declare Bechuanaland a British Protectorate. The inhabitants of the country had no part in that decision, but ultimately that would turn out to be a good thing for them. British missionaries in the area also had considerable influence in making it happen. Rhodes, on the other hand, would come to rue the day he made it happen.

The motives of early missionaries were never entirely pure, and some worked closely with colonial explorers and expansionists who had no religious leanings at all. Archbishop Tutu has made famous what many other Africans have voiced, that when the missionaries came to Africa they taught the Africans to close their eyes when they prayed. "When we closed them, we had the land and they had the Bible; but when we opened them, they had the land and we had the Bible!" Sadly, there is more truth than humor in that statement.

Things came to a head less than ten years after the British Protectorate was established, prompted by the rapacious greed of Cecil Rhodes. In 1888, he went on record as saying "If Bechuanaland is lost to us, British development in Africa is at an end," foreshadowing almost precisely what Winston Churchill would say about the Empire "losing India" on the eve of their independence. Possessed with a fear that Bechuanaland might slip through British hands, he pressed his government to have the entire territory annexed to the Cape Province of South Africa, which was firmly under British control. Word of Rhodes' wild-eyed plan filtered through Bechuanaland and reached the ear of Khama III, King of the Bamangwato people, the ruling tribe in the country. Khama the Great, as he came to be known, was a convert to Christianity, a wise and revered leader of his people, and undoubtedly the equal of Cecil Rhodes in matters of state and the game of life. The response of Khama to Rhodes' machinations set the stage for the future of the country and the shape of politics in southern Africa. What he did was a stroke of genius and a measure of who the Khamas were.

In typical African fashion, Khama took counsel with two other Batswana kings, Bathoen and Sebele, and the three of them came up with an unprecedented decision: they would go directly to the Empress of the British Empire, Queen Victoria herself, and ask for her intervention in the matter. It wasn't especially an astonishing decision for them to speak directly with the Queen because royalty always spoke directly to royalty. Their decision was astonishing because none of them had any idea where England was nor had they seen the ocean, not to mention sailing upon it for thirty days! But in the summer of 1895, the three African chieftains and their retinue set out for Cape Town—on horseback. None of them had ever traveled that far from home, and the new sights and scenes of the Western Cape must at times have been overwhelming. It has been said they maintained a regal detachment through it all, showing as little surprise as possible. When they reached Cape Town, their request for passage on a sailing ship to England must have caused the stir of the century. "Who are these black Africans from some far country who speak little English and no Afrikaans and want to sail to England? This is a preposterous idea! They have no idea what they are doing!" Preposterous idea perhaps, but they knew what they were doing. The stately manner of the three must have been the talk of the town. Khama the Great took charge and made their wishes known. It was clear this man was of royal bearing and doors seemed to open for him as he requested passage to England. And thus the three of them boarded a clipper ship and sailed for thirty days to Southampton, England.

It boggles the imagination to think of three African chieftains with their attendants, baggage, and food for the journey, making their way to England. There is no record of sea sickness or how the voyage went for them, but upon arrival, without fanfare, they made their way to Queen Victoria, who met with them in Windsor Castle. There they were greeted as royalty and had their time with the Empress [46] who expressed interest in what they had to say and promised to act. What they sought was the continued protection of the Crown as a British Protectorate and the assurance that their country wouldn't be annexed to South Africa under any circumstances. This assurance was granted them in exchange for a strip of territory along the eastern border of Bechuanaland for the construction of a railway to the north, the future Rhodesian Railway. When Rhodes learned he had been out-maneuvered on his own home ground and before the Queen of England, he showed his true colors with the vicious retort, "It is utterly humiliating to be beaten by those niggers." But beaten he was, and it ended his expansionist dream of annexing Bechuanaland to his empire. On the other side of the coin, Sir Charles Warren, who had spent much of his career in southern Africa chasing lingering Boers from Bechuanaland, was on record as

---

[46] The chiefs respectfully called her "Mosadinyana" the "Little Woman", who was greatly impressed by the African chiefs. As gifts, they presented the Queen with leopard skins and she gave each of them a Bible. In Khama's she had written, "The secret of Khama's greatness", presumably meaning his Christian faith.

saying of Khama the Great, "I look upon him as having been one of the big men of the nineteenth century." And Lord Lugard, who visited Khama's home town of Serowe in 1896 remarked, "Although I am not in favour of eating with black men…I know of no one else in Africa whom I would wish to ask for lunch, and treat as an honoured guest and be proud to entertain. He is such a gentleman." Some British, after all, were capable of non-racialism, albeit selectively.

In the early twentieth century pressure to annex the territory continued to come from politicians in the Cape and in Great Britain. In 1910, Lord Selbourne, representing the British government in South Africa declared, "the black man is absolutely incapable of rivaling the white man…and no one can have experience of the two races without feeling the intrinsic superiority of the white."[47] Despite such inflammatory statements, the British government held true to its pledge. The last time the matter came up was in 1935, when the British government confirmed that no transfer of sovereignty would take place without the agreement of the people of Bechuanaland. And that would never happen. Notwithstanding the final outcome, Professor Tom Tlou probably wrote the most insightful comment on why Britain took any interest at all in Bechuanaland: "British involvement in the Bechuanaland Protectorate was not so much that the interests of the Batswana were paramount in British strategy for Southern Africa, but rather they (the British) feared among other things the colonization of Botswana by the Germans from Namibia."[48] The Germans, of all things!

---

[47] Blood River p. 198.
[48] "Documents on Botswana History: How Rhodes Tried to Seize Ngamiland", from Botswana Notes and Records, 7, 1975, p. 61

Chapter Nine

No "How To" Manual Available

Our destination was Gaborone, the capital of Botswana, and the journey from Salisbury would take four days by train. In those days, it was the Rhodesian Railway which, despite political rancor and disagreement, continued to provide service all the way from Lusaka to Cape Town. That continued existence of the Rhodesian Railway was a remarkable thing in that it spanned a political spectrum from a fully independent Zambia, through the political battle zone of Southern Rhodesia, through non-racial Botswana, and ending in *apartheid* South Africa. Despite all the political exigencies of emerging independence, it was a luxury service. Necessity and politics made strange bed fellows.

The carriages that bore the proud symbol of Rhodesian Railways, we had seen before on the South African Railroad, traveling from Walvis Bay to Tsumeb. The cabins were of the same solid teak wood with walls of green leather paneling. The seats hadn't changed from those padded green leather cushions, which at night converted into comfortable beds, graced with starched linen sheets and dark blue blankets. Turning into bed was still a treat, but the dining car was my favorite. I have fond memories of playing the aristocrat, sitting at a magnificently laid table with starched linen table cloth and serviettes, sipping a favorite beverage as the train swayed gently and the sun set on the African plain, with occasional wild animals dashing across the horizon. Maybe I had a secret maharaja or big game hunter in me someplace, but it was a fun moment to imagine all sorts of things—the very last of them being a bishop. Dinner was impeccably served with royal elegance by African waiters. It was another world. This was one of the perks I would have as bishop, but only occasionally when I traveled to the northern-most town of Francistown. The train ride was invariably the most pleasant part of those trips.

Our journey to the capital would be interrupted. We received word we were to stop off at a place called Mmadinare (*"mad-din-nar-ee"*), several hundred miles north of our destination; there I was to study the language at a mission station, unhindered by affairs awaiting me in the capital. I greeted the news with minimal enthusiasm. Having a fits-and-starts journey from Uganda to our new home interrupted one more time felt like a delay we didn't need. But we had at least learned our first Setswana word: *Mmadinare* (and no, it isn't a misprint with that double "m"), which means *"mother of buffaloes"*. The village must have taken this name from an ancient time when those beasts were around because there are no buffaloes to be found anywhere in Botswana today. Such creatures are still quite numerous in other parts of Southern Africa, the Cape Buffalo being the best known, with huge curved horns that encircle the head. African buffalo have an unpredictable nature, stand as tall as six feet, weigh up to 2,000 pounds, and can be dangerous. They tend to live in swamps and flood plains, and just to complete your briefing on buffalo, they have few predators and are quite capable of defending themselves even against lions. Most of the big cats like cheetah and leopard give them wide berth which is probably why they are listed among the "Big Five" of African game.

The communal nature of African buffaloes is worth a digression in the story. They are apparently very altruistic in their behavior among themselves and the females exhibit a sort of voting behavior when they're together. It's been observed that during rest time a female will stand up, shuffle around a bit and sit back down, pointing in the direction she thinks the herd should next move—sort of a body movement of "read my lips." After an hour of this shuffling about, the females will up themselves and move the herd in the direction they alone have decided, sort of like "do as we say as well as do!" The decision of the herd to move is apparently without any hierarchy—just don't get mama mad. When being chased by predators, the herd sticks together, with calves gathered in the middle to make it difficult for the predator to attack a young one; when attacked, the herd will come to the rescue and engage in a kind of mob behavior to fight off the invader. African buffalo have been known to kill lion, chase them up trees, and in one instance a calf was recorded on film surviving an attack by a lion and a crocodile at the same time. Some tough creature.

Being a member of the "Big Five," the Cape Buffalo is unfortunately still greatly sought as a trophy, with some hunters paying over $10,000 for the chance. Hemingway, probably pandering to his insecurity complex, famously boasted shooting one in 1953, posing beside the downed beast.

But there were no longer buffalo within hundreds of miles of Mmadinare nor within memory of anyone living there. In fact, the place was fairly remote from everything, surrounded by a harsh landscape that only grazing goats could enjoy. The Mission had a church named after St. Peter, a clinic and a school and this little kingdom was presided over by a Motswana priest named Daniel Dhlodhlo. Daniel was married to a delightful roly-poly wife named Martha who smiled all the time and was dying to please. Father Daniel was an equally delightful soul, relaxed and lugubrious, also with a smile that covered his face and a ready laugh that filled whatever space needed filling. He would be my tutor, of sorts, for the next several weeks. The family would be the somewhat unwilling victims in this deal, with not much to do but wander aimlessly about the mission, read, sleep or play games. That limited variety got old pretty fast. The heat was at times unbearable, typical of early spring in southern Africa; many a night we would sleep on the concrete floor under our beds, where it was noticeably cooler. With Namibia next door to the west, we were no strangers to the weather, but that didn't make the days before the spring rains any easier. Massive thunder clouds would gather in the east and humidity rise to unbearable limits with nothing to follow, as the clouds dissipated or moved away. We had only our discomfort to worry about, the locals had the season's crops and the year's food supply to worry them. Without favorable rain, they wouldn't have enough food to last through the year. I had come to appreciate how years of this harsh experience made African men seem listless and idle to the outsider. Like their neighbors, the Namibians, the Batswana had also experienced the uncertainty of rain for so many generations that they were not about to leap to their plows at the first sign of rain clouds. Not infrequently, they faced an entire year of near-drought conditions when they could neither plow nor plant. Westerners, unable to understand the effect that could have on the head of a family, have often been critical of what they thought was just laziness.

In our early years in South West Africa we heard the story, possibly apocryphal, of a German farmer in the Otjiwarango district who got so frustrated with the clouds not delivering rain he took matters into his own hands: he procured some kind of pellets that, when fired into rain clouds, would get them to release their precipitation. At peak frustration, he fired several volleys into the clouds and produced so much rain it washed his farm away. Apparently the technology, if there was one, hadn't been very well tested. The local moral that surrounded that story was that one should put the pellets away and probably not mess with nature.

Halfway through our time at Mmadinare, we were invited to visit Sister Pippa [49] who ran a tiny clinic at a forgotten place named Bobonong, an African Gehenna about seventy miles east. Getting there was a punishing three hour trip in a four-by-four vehicle and I had never seen so many rocks in one place. The heat at Bobonong was many degrees worse than anything we had yet experienced. Pippa was a stalwart nurse from England who had braved the elements of Botswana and had done the same for many years in Namibia, next door. She was from Yorkshire long and lanky, skin of leather and full of goodwill and a ready smile, she had managed to handle the heat and the locals with equanimity. She had labored long and hard in Africa, as so many dedicated British nurses did. In general, they were a selfless lot, and though late in coming,

---

[49] The title "Sister" is commonly used by the British to denote a registered nurse, and does not suggest any religious connotation.

Pippa would soon be acknowledged for her dedication to Africa. It is one of my favorite memories of dear Pippa Gaye, and it happened a few years after I was settled into the bishop's office. We received word she was to be given a royal cheer for her years of selfless service to Africa. She had been selected to receive an M.B.E. from Her Majesty and all were invited to the British High Commission for the presentation. I subsequently learned the M.B.E. is the lowest class of five in an order of chivalry, known collectively as the "Most Excellent Order of the British Empire" (tut tut). With a ring of a bygone era of conquest and Empire, the motto of this prestigious award was *"For God and Empire."* By now, the conquest was over, the Empire had all but collapsed, and God was somewhere in between. The presentation was typically low-key. After all the stiff-upper-lip hoopla of the occasion, Pippa, in her self-effacing manner, made the memorable comment (off camera) that "O.B.E. stood for *others* bloody efforts, but mine" she said, "mine stands for *my* bloody efforts!" The honor was all hers, for so it was!

Father Dan did his best to instruct me in Setswana. He wasn't much of a teacher, but he had a good heart and smiled his way through every lesson, then waved me off saying "Bishop will do just fine...." I didn't share his optimism. The guttural sounds were new to me, and nothing in the language resonated with Kwanyama. Although we were now only one country but several languages away from the African language I knew and loved, that dialect was useless in Botswana. Africa is an amazing continent of fifty five countries, untold ethnic groups, and a linguistic polyglot said to exceed 5,000. Some of them overlap but most do not. Hence, African countries have to rely on the European language left by colonial powers as the national language, usually English or French. In Botswana, the default language was English, but I couldn't rely on using it. Interpreters were around, but I disliked using them because it put me one person and an entire language away from the people I was trying to communicate with. (and many a funny tale can be told about using interpreters because often they didn't know English much better than I knew the local language).

During our sojourn at Mmadinare, I spent most of my time trying to learn vocabulary and greetings, sufficient to carry on a simple conversation. Grunts and smiles usually helped where language failed, for Africa was forgiving of learners. I tried to go beyond grunts and smiles but they were always a good back-up.

Mmadinare was miles from the rail line, situated in rocky bush that was new to me. Ovamboland was famous for not having a single rock, yet a mere thousand miles east, rocks were everywhere. Among those rocks, in a few short years and a few miles away there would be a geological find that would create an overnight city to be known as Selebi Phikwe (*"See-lee-be/Peek-way"*). It would be a shock for which Botswana would be ill-prepared. In record time, a deserted area of wild bush, rocks, and goats, would become a city of almost 50,000. There was nothing that could have revealed the secrets that only geologists knew, that beneath the deserted sands of two forlorn villages were huge reserves of copper and nickel and other extractable minerals. The area would become a major mining operation almost in the twinkling of an eye.

The sociological upheaval Selebi Phikwe would bring to the country would become one of my chief concerns. This instant city would be made up largely of Batswana men looking for work. They would be the farmers who had spent too many seasons waiting for rains that never came, too many years waiting for crops that never produced. This overnight city would become a huge magnet drawing people into it with faint promise of anything better; but alas, thousands would go in search of Camelot, which they would never find. For most of them, life would only get worse. It was the age-old tension between city and country, spelled out one way or another in practically every country in the world. Tragically, these farmers would leave families behind to fend for themselves and children to wonder where their fathers had gone. And all too soon, they would be followed by another work force from the village: young girls to ply that most ancient of trades, and young boys who no longer had a father to guide them into manhood. Unwittingly, Selebi Phikwe would become a sociological nightmare. Mining companies would not be totally oblivious to the problem, but it wasn't part of their profit incentive to do much about it. I had learned that corporate decisions were more often amoral rather than intentionally immoral, but the outcome was often the same.

This overnight city would produce shabeens, whorehouses and shacks built from whatever was available, erected by young boys straight from herding their father's cattle. And all of the ills of a slum city would quickly come to pass: neighbors who wouldn't know who lived next door, crime of every sort, people living in fear of invasion and robbery, slum neighborhoods and unsanitary living conditions, over-crowding with strangers living in one room and drinking and gambling hitherto unknown, sucking up in a moment the earnings of a week's hard work at the mine. And perhaps saddest of all, young people who would forget their way back home. Even when they knew better, they would become trapped in a lifestyle that was strange and harmful to everything they had known. It would be heartbreaking to see and it would happen on my watch. I had but a few years to get ready for it.

Our sojourn in Mmadinare couldn't come to an end soon enough for me. My mind was elsewhere and I wasn't learning that much of the language, the pull of moving to our new home and getting started overwhelmed everything else. Finally, our day of departure was at hand. We loaded everyone and everything we had into Father Daniel's old pick-up truck and headed for the train station in Francistown. Fatigue and frustration from the heat didn't help. We were still in that dreaded season before the rains when temperatures, humidity, and tempers rose almost in like amounts and patience was in short supply. It didn't make for a smooth boarding on the now-familiar Rhodesian Railway. But things improved once we got going. We would see occasional game in the *bushveldt* and the ubiquitous ant hills or occasional grotesque baobab tree, landmarks to remind us we were back in southern Africa.

The trip to Gaborone from Francistown was an overnight journey. Francistown was the second largest and northernmost town in the country, fifty miles from the Southern Rhodesian border. It was founded in 1897 as a gold mining settlement for the Monarch mine and named after an early English prospector, Daniel Francis, who had been prospecting the area for decades. When gold was found in 1869, it sparked the first gold rush in Africa, a full fifteen years before the South African motherlode was discovered on the Witwatersrand that would be the largest in Africa and the richest in the world. There isn't even gold dust remaining in Francistown, but the deep mines of Johannesburg are still being worked, hauling gold out for over a hundred years.

The old steam engine lumbered along, coal dust and breezes from the warm African *veldt* blowing upon us. It was quiet in our cabin as we each dealt with our own anxieties for what lay ahead, everything new again. Halfway there, we discovered old friends on the train who were coming from the United States to help us. It was the builder and his wife from Missouri who had given more than a year to help with construction in Ovamboland. They had spoken of the possibility of joining us in Botswana but no plans had been made. We were stunned to find them on the train, but by now being good friends, we were delighted and grateful they would travel halfway 'round the world to help us. He was the collector of bells and responsible for the one that sat atop Great St. Mary's Church at Odibo. Our gypsy caravan had suddenly increased to nine with bags now beyond counting.

We passed through Palapye, another sleepy town of a few buildings nestled along the rail line with nothing remarkable about it except its lonely situation, hundreds of miles from anything. In time, I would come to know a white shopkeeper who had lived there all his life, knew the language as his own as well as everybody in town, dead or alive— and was an encyclopedia of information. Within the next ten years, the largest coal deposit in the southern hemisphere would be found in this tiny dorp, a deposit so large they wouldn't even bother to develop it for years to come.

By now, we had at least learned how to pronounce the name of our new city, named after a chief of a bygone day and pronounced with a guttural "G", almost a harsh "H", thus: *"Gha-bore-row-knee"*. The British, with their penchant for mangling African languages, apparently also had an innate dislike of anything sounding remotely German [50]and were incapable of pronouncing the name correctly. They insisted on calling it "Gaborones", which became the mispronunciation of choice by most foreigners. I found it another expatriate embarrassment.

Though it was the new capital, Gaborone was still a small town of less than 30,000 when we arrived. At the time of independence, the Peace Corp were invited into the country and did much to help with town planning. They designed many of the government buildings and areas to be developed, most under a ten-year plan that was still a long way off. When we arrived, few of the roads were paved, there was one traffic signal, a small airport on the edge of town, and roundabouts everywhere, one of the few British ideas that survived into the new age.[51] Frugality was the order of the day for the young government: offices were strictly utilitarian, vehicles were modest even for ministers of State, and there was absolutely no extravagance. The President eschewed any display of excess and set a pattern of modesty for all government offices. It was a breath of fresh air. The limited foreign aid that was available in those early days was carefully guarded and used for the exact purpose for which it was given. Civil servants were civil, and the grassroots excitement of a new nation was everywhere apparent. Another great breath of fresh air. [52]

---

[50] Was this some sort of resentment that arose because of Queen Victoria's Consort, Prince Albert being German? Or could it have been the remains of World War II?

[51] When I returned for a visit thirty years later I got totally lost trying to drive from the new international airport into the city center. Paved roads, highways and freeways were everywhere, along with traffic lights and municipal names I had never heard and a number of impressive skyscrapers.

[52] Gaborone was the natural choice for the capital but for one thing: its close proximity to South Africa. The South African border was a mere twenty two miles away which made Gaborone vulnerable to illegal visits by the South African Police as well as a quick pass for refugees fleeing that country. The latter were welcome, the former were not.

No Welcoming Party...again!

Our arrival in Gaborone was the anticlimax of the year. In fact, it was a replay of another arrival eleven years earlier. The train had been delayed and we arrived around midnight. The station was another lonely building on a dusty road, miles out of town. Not that we expected it (actually I had!) but there was no sign of a welcoming party for the new bishop and family. Nor was there a station attendant, taxi, car, or signs to say which way into town. Neither was there a pay phone. It was hard to act like I was in charge of anything because clearly I wasn't. We didn't even know where the town was or how far away. Within about an hour, a taxi came ambling down the dirt road looking for work. It was a noisy old wreck that could barely roll, but it had four wheels, four doors, a front and a back seat, an engine, and a driver. I negotiated with the driver to take us into town in two loads, with luggage and bodies crammed into every space possible.

"Rra, where you go?" the driver asked me. I had no idea how to answer that. "Into town" would have sounded stupid, but what could appear more stupid than two white men with two women and five kids arriving at a deserted train station in the middle of the night and not knowing where they were going? He told us there were two hotels, proudly announcing the newest one "Holiday Inn with Casino".[53] That sounded enough like home for us. Any other time I would have shunned the glitz of a Holiday Inn with Casino in a young developing country, but we took the offer. Almost. It turned out that with nothing left of the night but a few early morning hours, the Holiday Inn with Casino wanted full payment. The Casino must have done poorly that night. While expressing my displeasure and trying to strike a bargain, several well-dressed gentlemen walked in and introduced themselves as our welcoming party. They would take us to our new home, which, they

---

[53] The new casino would become the subject of hot political debate for years to come. It would bring in money for the country but also become a quick way for poor laborers to lose their meagre wages. It would also become an easy spot for prostitution. But alas, after all the heated debate and opposition, Holiday Inn won out and the Casino remains to this day.

said, was only half a block away. Knowing African estimates of distance, I wondered how many miles a half a block would be. They had waited at the station for hours, but when an uncertain time of arrival was given, had returned home. Hearing the train whistle as it was departing, here they were. And that sure beat the arrival in Tsumeb!

Having made no progress in getting a reduced rate from the night clerk, we headed for the house with the welcoming party. It was now two in the morning. Our new home was on Phuti Crescent, and it actually was only a half a block away. [54] The house was quite new, with three bedrooms and beds but no bedding or furniture. Stripping curtains and towels for bedding, we salvaged a few hours of sleep before dawn. I spent most of that time wondering how we would accommodate four adults and five children for the long haul.

My circuits were on overload. Part of the anxiety was unpacking and settling into quarters that wouldn't fit our expanded number; another part included getting ready for the big service that would make me a bishop in a few weeks' time; but the principal worry was trying to figure out how to start a diocese, the reason for our being here at all. There was no instruction manual to go with the job, no suggestions, advice, prior experience anywhere around. To further unsettle things, if that was possible, there was no one to whom I could turn for advice: the Archbishop lived three countries away, and the closest bishop was five hundred miles away in Southern Rhodesia. I had always enjoyed challenges but I had now met my match. Starting a new diocese is not a course taught in any seminary in the world, nor does one learn it as a parish priest or for that matter, even as a bishop. These days, few bishops, even worldwide, have had to do it. None of my brother bishops in Central Africa had had that experience thrust upon them, not even the Archbishop. And here, it had landed on me, although I had tried to decline the offer once. And one more handicap to throw into the mix: I was the youngest bishop in the entire Anglican world at the time, with only eleven years' experience as a priest. It would be times like this when the mysterious way in which I had been elected would come to have

[54] The phuti is a little buck, not as small as the dik dik but similar in appearance.

meaning: this had definitely not been my idea! I was cheered on by a funny sign I once saw in a Jewish Temple which read, "Don't give up: Moses was once a basket case too." But his basket was floating down the Nile—I wasn't even sure mine was afloat.

The next few days would only add to it all. I would discover I had neither office, nor typewriter, nor desk, secretary, or telephone; no structures or committees to share my worries. Last but not least, I had no vehicle. I was expected to find these things on my own. I think there was an unspoken assumption that being connected to the United States meant I had a Golden Goose in my suitcase that had many eggs ready to hatch. How naive could they be. In all fairness, however, the local Anglicans had not been prepared as they should have been to anticipate what would be involved in this monumental venture.

Frivolously, I should add, I had no episcopal throne nor did I think I needed one but for the fact that that is technically what 'seats' a bishop and establishes a diocese; it is known as the 'cathedra,' for which cathedrals are named. Every bishop needs to have one, of one sort or another, with or without a formal cathedral. Botswana didn't have a cathedra, a cathedral, or even a church to use for the purpose. It was as close to not having a pot to pee in or a window to throw it out of that I had ever known. The coming months would be like sleep-walking.

But why a new diocese at all? Why was there a need for a Diocese of Botswana? There was good reason. Until our arrival, Botswana had been served by the Bishop of Matabeleland who lived five hundred miles away, in Bulawayo. That was in Southern Rhodesia, politically enemy territory so to speak, under the Ian Smith regime. It was both politically and psychologically impossible for the new Republic of Botswana to continue to be dependent on a diocese outside the country, especially one in the disputed white-ruled country of Southern Rhodesia. Moreover, it was not possible for the Bishop of Matabeleland to cover a country the size of Botswana in addition to his own. Botswana was over a quarter of a million square miles in size, took days to go from one corner to the other, and needed the undivided attention of its own bishop. That was more than ample compelling reason for a new Diocese of Botswana. In time I would learn even more of the politics behind it. Not surprisingly, the Batswana had grown resentful that they had to depend on a bishop not of their choosing, and from a neighboring country ruled by an avowed racist who denigrated Africans at every opportunity. The Batswana had plenty to be steamed up about, and in their frustration they demanded a diocese of their own, now! Little thought had been given to the details of how that would be done. They might as well have said, "Let's elect our own bishop and he will figure it out." What a welcome!

We learned some time in those early days that the creation of this diocese had been far from unanimously popular. That came as no surprise and pretty much as I expected: some of the local expatriate white community saw no need for Botswana to have its own diocese, saw no problem being tethered to a racist country, and thought it would be financially impossible to pull it off. But thoughts like these could not have been more out of step with virtually every African heart in the country. Such grumbling disfavor from the expatriate community would become a source of irritation and at times conflict in the years ahead.

Mondi and I moved into the garage to make space for our guests. We might as well have moved into a sweat lodge. The roof was corrugated iron without ceiling and by day too hot for human habitation. Nights were barely better. On the positive side, we were inundated with nice words by well-wishers and borrowed transportation was made available. Days before the consecration, a truckload of friends from Ovamboland arrived for the big event: two dozen Kwanyamas along with food and grain to make *omalodu,* my favorite African beverage. I haven't the vaguest remembrance where they all slept.

The day of the Service of Consecration came, New Year's Eve, 1972, ecclesiastically a strange date but perhaps a propitious way to end a year or start one. We had become friends with a young couple in the U.S.

Embassy who had a pool party for us the night before the big event. I have lasting memories of floating in that pool, looking at the night sky and wondering what the future held for us all. I figured it was one helluva way to sing Auld Lang Syne.

The Service was to take place in the Roman Catholic Cathedral, the largest venue available, which could seat around five hundred. I had gathered used items of episcopal haberdashery from deceased bishops to dress me like a bishop. I found it strangely humorous, knowing I was wearing dead men's stuff. With some things borrowed, some things used, that day began pretty much what would be a hand-to-mouth operation for the first year.

The Service filled the Cathedral and brought in the President and Lady Khama, countless governmental hoi paloy and bishops from all over central and southern Africa. That was not unusual. In the United States, there are frequently in excess of twenty bishops on such occasions. I had about half that number, which was a pretty fair showing for New Year's Eve in the middle of Africa. The Bishop of Mashonaland, acting as Dean of the Province, stood in for the Archbishop, who couldn't be present for some reason (which still puzzles me), and the Bishops of Northern Zambia, Lusaka, Lake Malawi and Matabeleland; and from South Africa, the Bishops of Swaziland, Zululand, Bloemfontein, George, Kimberly and Kuruman, and the Suffragan Bishop of Cape Town. No one came from the United States, but that wasn't expected. I was informed the moment I had been elected that my official connection with the Episcopal Church would cease, most notably my monthly paycheck, the princely sum of $450.00.[55]

The Service of Consecration that turns a priest into a bishop went without a hitch and was interminably long with not much comic relief. An old friend, Bishop Alpheus Zulu, of Zululand, preached the sermon; he was one of the ones who had inspired me to go to Africa. The choicest comment of the day came from the six-year old son of an African priest

---

[55] This action carried no judgment whatsoever. It was in keeping with the practice that no church entity could be responsible for the maintenance of a foreign bishop or diocese. Standard practice.

who was seated in the front row. There I was, kneeling and surrounded by a dozen bishops as they handed me my bishop's staff, and the little guy was heard by all to say, "Mama, what's that cane for? Have they made him a cripple?" Many times in the years ahead I thought that kid was a prophet.

Utterly exhausted from the four-hour Service of the morning, I was informed there would be another one that evening to install me as Bishop of the Diocese. I was soon corrected on the terminology. One British wag took me aside and said, "My Lord, you install horses, not bishops. You are being enthroned." I stood corrected but didn't much care for the sound of it, whether it had a stall or a throne. It took place in an erstwhile Anglican Church known as Trinity Church, which had become a bone of contention within the community and among Batswana Anglicans in particular. Trinity Church was a 'mashed-potatoes' church without any real identity because it was made up of a handful of expatriate Methodists, Presbyterians, Congregationalists, Anglicans, and, for a short time, Lutherans. The problem arose with the initial concept, which had been an expatriate idea, fashioned as a convenient way to provide one church for the small white membership of each denomination. No Batswana had been involved in the planning and few had agreed with it, which should have been a major signal to the expatriates, but it wasn't. Moreover, being a mashed-potatoes amalgamation of several non-liturgical traditions, this put-together lacked the rich liturgical tradition familiar to Anglicans in that part of Africa. Many a meeting to work things out had dissolved into arguments and walk-outs. The Anglicans were in a difficult position because they didn't have a church of their own in town, nor the means to build one; there was only a small parish on the edge of town, known as St. Francis. But there was no immediate solution to the problem, and they would have to hobble along with this awkward arrangement for several years.

Ecumenism is never easy when it involves compromise on things people believe are fundamental to their faith. I have no doubt the divisions between religions must be a huge disappointment to God, if he cares about the subject at all. However, the divisions among Christians ought to be of greater embarrassment to Christians because we all claim to profess "one Lord, one Faith, one Baptism, one God and Father of all." But we act as if it just isn't so. Still, union can never be forced, and pragmatic solutions like the Gaborone experiment are rarely a good idea. They may work well enough among Protestant denominations elsewhere in the world (notably India), but in Africa the record of successful ecumenical ventures is dismal, largely for the same reason it didn't work in Gaborone.

For better or worse, Anglicans throughout Central and Southern Africa have a strong sense of identity, often called "Anglo Catholic," expressed in liturgy, worship and general polity. In short, Anglo Catholics do not 'mix' well with other brands. Hence, the Trinity Church experiment was fated from the beginning, not only because it was presented as a *fait acompli* by enthusiastic expatriates who had decided a new nation should spawn a new church, but also because it totally under-estimated the strength of Anglican identity in the country. Most of the expatriate Anglicans in Gaborone came from an evangelical 'Low Church' background where identity was not important. I immediately sensed the problem Trinity Church presented and had to agree with the Batswana who wanted their own show and dreamed of their own cathedral. But that dream would have to wait until other pressing needs were addressed which would take most of the next five years. In the meantime, we continued to hold services at Trinity, attended mainly by the expatriate community. Little St. Francis Church relieved some of the tension and as more major services were held there, it served as a miniature cathedral for the early years.

Lady Ruth Khama was a strong advocate for an Anglican Cathedral and was stridently against the Trinity Church set-up. Lady Khama was regarded as the resident maven of many things and would let her thoughts be known at the drop of a hat, sometimes before. She became an active member of the Diocese, serving on major committees and casting her considerable influence hither and yon. Lady Ruth was an outspoken, dare I say "saucy" redhead, who brooked no nonsense or opposition from anyone, a good person to have around who could open a few doors here and there. Her influence would prove to be crucial in facilitating my travel through South Africa.

In the nineteenth century, the London Missionary Society (LMS) had come with great gusto into Bechuanaland with the arrival of David Livingstone and Robert Moffett. Their arrival was trumpeted in England as a monumental success, thought by some to signal the Coming of the Kingdom, of all things! Part of their strategy was to persuade the chieftains, by fair means or fowl, to convert to Christianity and many of them did. A related strategy was then to persuade these new Christian leaders to lead their people down the same path; so if it was good enough for the tribal leader, the people would feel it was good enough for them to follow suit. That path would eventually lead to a church which the chieftain would order the men of the tribe to build. These were usually large stone buildings, like the ones the missionaries left behind in Great Britain. They required a lot of labor and expense, all borne on the backs of the people. Thus, churches got built all over the place, and LMS missionaries looked upon this as a great success, with virtually no other denominations in the country. Their influence over the chieftains simply wouldn't allow other denominations in.

When independence came in 1965, there was a backlash. Batswana Christians had heard that St. Paul stressed that before Christ all were under the law, but with Christ all are free and 'saved by grace alone'. But they had been introduced to a religion that didn't feel free at all. Under that Christian religion they were conscripted to build and attend those churches under orders from the Chief. The locals were quick to see that with political independence also came freedom to worship (or not);

they now were freed from the power of a church[56] that had conscripted them. Coercing the people to become Christian and support the church ultimately became counter-productive, and as a result of that practice, I would find church growth more difficult in Botswana than in any other part of Africa.

Overwhelmed by the enormity of the task of this new diocese, God intervened in the strangest of ways: in my first month I contracted infectious hepatitis. Drained of energy, I was ordered to complete bed rest for at least six weeks. It was an illness that totally sapped my strength, and I had no choice but to lay in bed and think. Or sleep. I did a lot of both. My great treat was one egg a week, usually Sunday morning. Bored to distraction, I nevertheless had time to ponder what I needed to do with the impossible assignment ahead of me. And then came a harbinger I had no way of recognizing: I was visited by an old crone who had walked miles to come see me. Her face was wrinkled and baked from a lifetime in the sun, but with a sweet smile she made her presentation. It was a dead stick in a pot. "You water it and wait, Father" she said in broken English. Unimpressed, I did what she told me and in three days that dead stick burst into greenery and flower. I was told it was called the resurrection plant. If I was looking for a sign (and I was), that old stick coming alive suggested that, in time, I and the diocese would survive, resurrect, and maybe even flower.

Through a dreadfully slow recuperation I realized that before I did anything else, I needed to listen to as many people as I could from all over the country. To do that required visits to every part of the country to ask members what they thought the most important things were for the new diocese. That would take six months and dozens of meetings.

---

[56] It was the London Missionary Society (LMS), basically the Congregational Church of England, that Christianized the country and was associated with these practices. In effect, however, all churches suffered the backlash that came with national independence.

I traveled with an interpreter and the local priest, if there was one, and we did the usual bit of listing wants and needs on newsprint. At the end of those meetings, six priorities emerged in the following order: (1) more clergy; (2) training programs for everything; (3) women's work; (4) a Sunday School program; (5) buildings and transportation; and (6) a cathedral. It became our development plan for the first five to ten years.

We set about recruiting clergy from wherever we could find them. One came from Canada (Newfoundland, actually—we called him the goofy newfy), a couple from South Africa, and several from the United States. A training program was started to train Batswana for ordination. A social worker was hired to develop women's work and the wife of an archdeacon took on the Sunday School program.

One of the less obvious tasks in forming a new diocese is creating an identifying crest, a flag to fly from the mast, so to speak, otherwise known as a herald. Ecclesiastical heraldry originally was a way of identifying people, places, and things---like dioceses, I guess, in case they got lost. This one wasn't lost, but it was a far cry from founded with a stable and sure foundation.

Ecclesiastical heraldry got started in the eleventh century when heraldic signs and symbols were quite ornate. They would usually include crosses and, where a diocese was concerned, the bishop's 'hat', otherwise known as a 'mitre', and staff, otherwise known as a 'crozier' (that was the crutch the youngster in the front row had thought was handed to me during my consecration). Designing diocesan heraldry was another of the subjects never covered in any seminary course I had ever had, and I doubt if it's covered anywhere in the world—except perhaps in Rome where they love to delve into that sort of thing.

So, how to begin? The basic outline of the crest and mitre are standard boilerplate for every diocesan herald, so the task was to fill in the blanks. And thus I began the design of the heraldry of the Diocese of Botswana, which has since been registered in England at the place where such things are registered (see picture, elsewhere in the book). The black and white trim around the crest symbolizes the non-racial country of Botswana; the stalk of sorghum or corn symbolizes the agricultural economy; the water represents the country's dependence on it; and the bishop's crozier speaks for itself. I guess.

Heralds such as this never get changed; but if they did, this one should have a gear or something to represent the heavy industry that has become a strong part of the national economy

Passion for a cathedral was amazingly great throughout the country but especially in Gaborone. I found it interesting that people in tiny distant villages without a church of their own wanted a cathedral at the center of their diocese, hundreds of miles away. In time, we understood why this was: it was a symbol of identity for them, every bit as important as having a capital for a nation. Anglicans in Botswana had forever been without what they called a 'proper identity.' A 'proper cathedral' would remedy that. Many Batswana Anglicans had grown up in South Africa and knew of the fine Anglican cathedrals that existed there in virtually every diocese. For the Batswana, having a diocese would eventually require having a cathedral. All of this may have made sense theologically but not economically. We would have to raise every pula and thebe[57] of the cost, however much that turned out to be. The white expatriate objectors, ever with us, saw the cathedral as a *want* and not a real *need* and refused to understand the local thinking. Hence, there was continued resistance from that quarter. But sometimes wants can also be legitimate needs and this was one of those instances. Given the unsatisfactory existing worship situation and the inadequate little church of St. Francis on the edge of town, it was becoming a physical necessity to have a central church in Gaborone. Why not go for a cathedral? Fortunately, we had purchased three acres of land near the center of town for Diocesan offices, the Bishop's House and the eventual cathedral. By the time we focused on the cathedral project, the offices and residence were already built and in full use.

In the fifth year, action started on the cathedral, beginning with fundraising. Fred Snell, the Provincial Secretary, suggested an

---

[57] The pula is one hundred thebe. Exchange rates varying constantly, but the pula is roughly equivalent to US$1.50. In Setswana, "pula" means "rain" and "blessing." — no coincidence.

architectural firm in South Africa to do preliminary proposals.[58] Fred had served as Headmaster of Michael House in Natal for many years with enough experience of architects and building to know who was who. We formed a high-powered fundraising committee in Gaborone that included Lady Khama, the Chancellor, and other dignitaries and leaders of the congregation. The goal was to raise at least R500,000 initially, in today's economy roughly two million dollars. It would be a monumental task for Botswana.

One of the pivotal moments came early on when a good friend, Norman Hardie, arranged a meeting with Sir Harry Oppenheimer. Norman was Managing Director of Anglo American/De Beers Mining in Botswana, and Oppenheimer was Chairman of Anglo American/ De Beers in South Africa. This was a big deal by any measure, and a magnificent opportunity. Norman and I drove to Johannesburg and had our meeting with Mr. Oppenheimer, who was known to be a committed Anglican. We figured that would help a lot. He listened to the presentation of why the cathedral would be good for the young nation, what we would do with it, etc. At the end of the discussion, he simply gave a quiet assurance he would do something but left no indication what 'something' might be. When we returned to Botswana, he informed Norman that Anglo American would give R250,000 towards the cathedral, today the equivalent of about a million dollars. We were elated. It was a tremendous fillip for our efforts. Construction began shortly thereafter, engaging a local Italian construction company of good repute. Actual construction was projected to take approximately two years.

Then came the name: how do you name a cathedral? Another experience totally without precedent for me. Clergy are not taught how to start a diocese nor how to name cathedrals (nor how to drive bad spirits out of homes!). Naming new churches had become fairly routine for me—usually a saint's name was suggested to the congregation,

---

[58] Munnik & Visser, in Cape Town. Fred's daughter, Pippa Vincent, was a member of that Firm and would be one of the supervising architects on the job, visiting us frequently. My kids remember her as the one who went for a spin with me on my motorcycle…!

if they didn't have a favorite already. But a cathedral was a greater and more solemn matter, or so it seemed. I had a favorite in mind. I suggested we name it "The Cathedral of the Holy Cross," and for several reasons. In neighboring Ovamboland, Holy Cross Church was one of the first churches built and had produced many of that nation's leaders, both political and ecclesiastical. Holy Cross was also a great name that for some reason was rarely used, and I figured we ought to give it prominence. And there was no other church in all of Botswana with that name, only a few in South Africa, and no Cathedrals that I knew of. But finally, with perhaps more hubris than virtue, I wanted the holy cross on top of that cathedral to be the highest point in the capital. As I recall, no other names were proposed, and the name was accepted by the Cathedral Committee without a murmur.

It took two years to complete and the huge cross on top would be the highest spire in the capital for years to come. On the day of the dedication, the Cathedral was filled with over a thousand people from all over the country. Sir Seretse Khama, Lady Khama, and senior ministers of State were all there for the occasion. Attending church services was not the President's favorite activity, but I think he genuinely enjoyed that occasion when the dream his wife had nursed for years had finally become a reality. In years to come, Holy Cross Cathedral would have the distinction of serving as the National Cathedral, and Sir Seretse and his successors would eventually be comfortable there.

Holy Cross Cathedral was dedicated to the Glory of God on November 26, 1978, and in the same Service, three Batswana priests and six deacons were ordained. It was a weekend of frantic activity with visitors from out of the country, rehearsals for the Service, and dinner parties for visiting dignitaries including the entire architectural firm from South Africa. Following the Service, the President and Lady Khama had a small dinner party for us at State House. We were touched and honored as it turned out to be somewhat of a sentimental journey for us.

Three days later we would leave Botswana.

Seretse Khama was born July 1, 1921, into the royal Khama family. The name Seretse means "the clay that binds." It is said he was given that name to celebrate a reconciliation that had taken place between his father and grandfather. I have no knowledge of that; but those who take a longer view of history could say the name was prophetically given because Seretse would be the one who would bind the nation together at a time when political forces were seeking to do otherwise. Seretse Khama had the ability of a born statesman to bring people together to find a middle ground in disagreements, and to do it without rancor. He would be the clay that would bind a nation into one Republic. But before that, he would get his first challenge as a young man while studying in England.

Seretse spent much of his early youth in boarding schools and attending university, all in South Africa. It was a time when great future leaders were coincidentally thrown together at university and the winds of change were beginning to blow. Ironically, that university was in South Africa. Fort Hare University would be producing giants for the future, men like Nelson Mandela, Oliver Tambo, Mangosuthu Buthelezi, Robert Sobukwe, Desmond Tutu, Kenneth Kaunda, Julius Nyerere and Robert Mugabe.[59] Many of them were classmates of Seretse Khama. Fort Hare, like Makerere University in Uganda, was an environment that taught students to think and ask big questions. Having grown up in the royal family, Seretse was already in the habit of doing that. But in South Africa their sharp and inquiring minds would be headed for trouble, for they would challenge the racist system of *apartheid*. Mandela, Tambo and Sobukwe would lead that charge.

---

[59] Mandela would lead South Africa to freedom and become its first freely elected president; Oliver Tambo would become a driving force behind the ANC; Buthelezi would become Chief of the Zulu Nation; Sobukwe would found the Pan African Congress; Tutu would become an influential Archbishop who, with Mandela, would lead the country to a peaceful independence; and Mugabe, once a brilliant and inspired leader and first President of the Republic of Zimbabwe, has become an embarrassment to southern Africa because of his insistence on leading Zimbabwe even in senility and misjudgment.

Elsewhere, Kaunda, Nyerere, and Khama would form a close friendship that would sustain them in their later careers as heads of state.

The last and perhaps most famous skirmish the Bamangwato people (Seretse's tribal nation) had with outsiders was, ironically, with the British government, and it centered around Seretse, grandson of Khama the Great. Born into this powerful family, at the age of four, Seretse became King (Kgosi) of the Bamangwato under the guardianship of his uncle, who was Regent until Seretse came of age to rule. In 1950, while studying law at Oxford, young Seretse met and fell in love with an English woman named Ruth Williams. Their romance flourished and gathered an international whirlwind of gossip before it turned ugly. England's connection with South Africa was still strong but adversely affected by a recent election in South Africa. That was the election of 1948, when the Nationalist government came to power and immediately began passing *apartheid* laws, one of which made sexual relationships between different races illegal. Learning about the romance and impending marriage of Seretse and Ruth, South Africa urged the British government to stop the marriage. Accordingly, word was sent out from Westminster to every clergyman in Great Britain forbidding the marriage. It was a preposterous thing to do, but evidently even the Archbishop of Canterbury went along with it. Since all clergy in Britain were regarded as Marriage Officers of the Crown, this order effectively meant they could not be married in any church in all of Great Britain. Although there were no laws against interracial marriage in Great Britain, this government action was in effect saying *this* inter-racial union could not receive a Christian blessing anywhere in the Empire. So, on September 29, 1948, Seretse and Ruth had their marriage performed secretly by a Justice of the Peace.

Once again, a Khama had out-witted the powers that be, but now there were serious consequences both in England and South Africa. England could not afford to lose cheap South African gold and uranium, and South Africa could not afford to have an interracial couple ruling just across their northern border. South Africa again put pressure on the British government to ban Seretse and his wife from entering the Protectorate, which they did. In an effort to separate the couple, Seretse was enticed to England by an official invitation and then upon his return was refused re-entry to his own country by the British Administration. Things had gotten very ugly indeed. Seretse then returned to England and Ruth joined him, where they remained for the next six years. Astonishingly, Seretse Khama and his English wife were thus prohibited from entering the country where he was recognized as the rightful heir to the throne!

Widespread international protest followed, accusing Britain of racism; within Great Britain there were calls for the resignation of Lord Salisbury, the minister responsible for most of it. The British High Commission for the Protectorate then ordered the Bamangwato to replace Khama with another king and the people refused. Racism was rearing its ugly head in high places, and Ruth Williams Khama was the problem. The Khamas were informed that if the marriage was dissolved, all would be well. But Seretse was resolute in telling both his own people and the British government that he would not "put away" his wife for any government or tribal demands. His firm position was a measure of his integrity that, in time, would make him a great leader. Seretse then surprised everyone by renouncing the throne rather than renouncing his wife, and he and Ruth returned to Bechuanaland as private citizens. No one could out-fox a Khama!

Things were then at a stalemate until 1965, when internal self-government was introduced and Seretse took his rightful place as Chief of the Bamangwato and Prime Minister of the country. Independence followed in 1966, when the Bechuanaland Protectorate became the Republic of Botswana and Seretse Khama was unanimously elected President.

Then came the greatest irony of all. Upon gaining independence from Great Britain on September 30, 1966, Queen Elizabeth II appointed the new President of Botswana a Knight Commander of the Most Excellent Order of the British Empire. Seretse graciously accepted the K.B.E. with equanimity but probably also with tongue in cheek. Thereafter to be known as Sir Seretse Khama, he had indeed won in the struggle of principle over politics, which would become a trademark of his statesmanship. The olive branch offered by Great Britain was a dubious, if not disingenuous, honor and was probably received in that spirit.

By the time we met, Seretse's experience with organized religion was strained, to put it mildly. He knew of the bargaining and chicanery that had gone on with early missionaries to his country, and he had faced the politics and prejudice of the Church of England over his marriage to a white woman. He could have been justifiably suspicious of all Christian endeavors and tired of it all. But instead of bitterness and resentment, he described himself to me as a Christian beyond the Church and organized religion. Many times over the years, I have thought about what he said. His stated position wasn't too different from what German theologian Dietrich Bonhoeffer once described as "religionless Christianity," practiced by those who seek to live a Christ-like life without the burden and trappings of Church and ceremony. Seretse had been tempered by unchristian church politics, Bonhoeffer by Nazi Germany.

My direct experiences of Sir Seretse made lasting impressions. Whenever in his presence, by his demeanor it was apparent he was a born leader—always relaxed and jovial but fully in charge of every situation except his health. From an early age, he suffered various illnesses, eventually developing diabetes and dying at the early age of fifty-nine. The stress he endured over his marriage for almost two decades must have added to his health problems. Yet throughout those years he was resolute in maintaining his principles and his dignity.

For reasons best explained by British tradition, Anglican Bishops of Commonwealth countries are considered part of the Diplomatic Corps, which meant we received invitations to this and that diplomatic function, with the general expectation of attendance. My wife and I were introduced to this protocol with our first invitation to State House for some official but forgettable function. We went along as expected and were greeted by the various dignitaries including the President and First Lady. I didn't know it then but I would get to know her fairly well in the years to come. The initial event was rather boring but it was a fascinating study of who talked to whom, where the power circles were, and who to watch out for. When we thought we had been there long enough, in preparing to leave we thanked the First Lady for the evening, said how nice it had been, etc., and headed for the door. Whereupon she said, "Oh no, no, no—no one leaves until His Excellency leaves the room. Always!" Even in his own home! Everyone knew that but us. It was an embarrassment that wouldn't happen again.

Being informed I was a part of the Diplomatic Corps, I did my best to comply, but it wasn't always convenient. One type of command performance was whenever the President departed from or returned to the country. We would stand in a long line at the airport, in no particular order, obediently awaiting His Nib's plane. Fortunately, the airport was a five-minute drive from my office. I think Seretse took this formality with tongue in cheek most of the time, such as the time I arrived late, just as he was acknowledging his welcoming party. I slipped in at the end of the line and as he came to me, with a grin on his face he mumbled, "You're late!" I had the feeling he could have cared less.

We dined at State House with Sir Seretse and Lady Ruth on several occasions, none of which were that memorable. In our last year in Botswana, we had them to our home for dinner, which was memorable. This, of course, meant several cars arriving before and after the President with security aides, none of whom we had to entertain. The evening was as relaxed as was possible with the President of the country in our home, and the Khamas did their best to put us at ease. Seretse didn't drink but he was an inveterate smoker and my wife had been making her best effort to quit the habit. After dinner, as we settled into the lounge for casual conversation, in a playful and somewhat mischievous spirit, Sir Seretse offered her a cigarette and did his best to get her to take it. I cannot remember what she did, but we remember the moment. Saying no to a habit is hard enough. Saying no to the President of your country is probably harder.

The evening progressed. At the time we were well into our sixth year in Botswana and had announced we would be leaving at the end of that year. The conversation turned to that subject and he asked me why we were leaving Botswana "so soon." I didn't think it was so soon; unlike the Biblical seven years, mine hadn't been years of feast *or* famine, just a lot of hard work and I was tired. I answered something to the effect that my leaving was in keeping with his policy of the indigenization of as many jobs as possible. I truly believed it was time for a Motswana to take over as bishop. In response, we saw Seretse at his best: he leaned forward, raised a hand as if to wave off my answer and with a twinkle in his eye said, "Don't lecture me on my policies...!" He then went on to express a genuine regret that we would be leaving the country and that he had valued our presence and contribution to the country and the Church. The conversation made us sad to be leaving.

The evening went on with friendly banter, and then we got into a serious discussion of race relations in the United States. I was on shaky ground and had no idea how well read he was, but it became apparent he knew a lot more about this subject in my own country than I did. During the discussion, he quoted one great black leader in American history but couldn't remember his name, which frustrated him the remainder of the evening. As the evening ended, the Presidential party departed with a flurry of cars and noise; five minutes later the entire entourage returned, and one of his aides came to the door with a handwritten message from the President which read, "Remembered at the roundabout—the name was Marcus Garvey." I was touched he would send word back of the forgotten name, but also that he would prod his memory until he came up with it. Then I recalled the conversation about Garvey, most of which had been new to me. Seretse was up on his facts and had proceeded to tell us about him, except for his name.

The next morning I got out my books to learn about Marcus Garvey. He was born in Jamaica but lived in the United States and became a political leader, publisher, journalist, and orator of the early twentieth century—and a staunch proponent of Black Nationalism and Pan Africanist movements. Sir Seretse was particularly interested in a movement Garvey had started known as African Redemption, which sought to encourage those of African ancestry in North America to return to Africa to "redeem" the nations of Africa. The return of Afro-Americans to Africa didn't catch on and Garvey was ahead of his time in calling for decolonization. But listening to Seretse talk about Garvey helped me understand the depth of his thinking about race and culture, for he had lived in the cross hairs of that issue all of his adult life. Seretse's' vision of race relations was infinitely larger and more inspiring than Garvey's. He had become an integrationist, married a white woman and raised a family of four "mixed" children. By comparison, Garvey was a separatist who, in essence, believed in "separate development," the term that, years later, would become one of the official definitions of *apartheid* in South Africa.

The question could be raised, did Seretse Khama establish a non-racial nation because he was married to a white woman, or did he marry Ruth because he believed in non-racialism? Undoubtedly, it was the latter. But the fact that early in life Seretse Khama had come to believe in non-racialism went far beyond his tribal roots as King of the Bamangwato, and beyond the thinking of virtually all the white people he had known. The question arises, therefore, where did he get such radical ideas as inter-marriage and non-racialism when there were virtually *no* models or examples of either in his experience? Intermarriage was anathema to his tribal traditions and to the political powers at the time. Such ideas might have come from his early contacts with Christianity but for the fact that non-racialism was *neither taught nor practiced* by the Church, as it should have been. Even though St. Paul had once said, "there is neither Jew nor Greek, bond nor free, male nor female, all are one in Christ..." the Church had failed this teaching in a shameful international display of bigotry years before. Seretse and Ruth had lived through the humiliation of having every Anglican priest and bishop in England, including the Archbishop of Canterbury, turn their backs on them because they were black and white. That had been, as previously noted, by order of the Crown, the titular head of the Anglican Church in Great Britain.[60] Nor was it likely that non-racialism would have been taught in any secular school or university anywhere on earth at the time. Non-racialism was a noble idea but ahead of its time in the teaching of the Church or institutions of higher learning Seretse had been exposed to, including Fort Hare and Oxford. The fact that he

---

[60] Despite all this bitter background, I often marveled at Ruth's continued allegiance to her Anglican roots in later life, when she so ardently pressed for the new Anglican diocese and cathedral. She did enjoy teasing me about the "Red Dean" in England, but I had no idea which one it was!

had believed in non-racialism years before he was called to lead a nation in that direction is one of those astonishing qualities that made him a natural statesman and leader. Some great leaders are just born that way. Seretse Khama was one of them.

After a rather rough beginning in Botswana, we settled into a routine rather quickly, given the number of uncertainties we faced. Meanwhile, my old nemesis was not far away. I was still considered a Prohibited Immigrant in neighboring South Africa which meant I could not enter that country for any reason. What I didn't yet know was that I wouldn't even be allowed to travel *in transit* through the international airport in Johannesburg. Johannesburg served all of Southern Africa for international flights. I was land-locked in Botswana, and the only way out would be by rail or road through Southern Rhodesia. The Anglican Province of Central Africa consisting of the four countries of Malawi, Zambia, Zimbabwe and Botswana meant I would not be able to move about without great difficulty.

Fortunately, we were not without friends in high places and it was Lady Khama's moment to shine. Unbeknown to me, she got on the phone to some well-placed officials in South Africa. She wouldn't reveal the exact conversation, but used some choice words in telling them they had better address my situation. "This is no way to treat a Bishop of the Church and you'd better straighten things out" was the polite version I was given. Fearful of no one, she had a way of getting things to happen, having been tempered in the fires of bitter politics in her younger years. But since Botswana didn't have normal diplomatic relations with the South African government, it was a moot point whether or not they would respond favorably, even to the First Lady.

The South African government did respond. Because of her intervention, the South African authorities agreed to allow me to transit through Jan Smuts Airport in Johannesburg—but only under very strict conditions.[61] That meant whenever I traveled through Johannesburg on an international flight, the South African government would incarcerate me in a room for the duration of the wait between flights. The room was situated above the Immigration Hall and had a wall of glass so I could be seen at all times. It was a fishbowl by design, with few comforts of home—a bed, a chair, and a very spartan bathroom. It was obviously for people the government didn't much like.

The arrangement worked fairly well the first few times I used it. The friendly skies of United didn't fly there so I didn't have their smiling welcome, but neither did I get any warmth of human kindness from the South African authorities. I didn't really expect that. Unless they were tourists, whites who traveled to black African countries from South Africa were generally looked upon with suspicion and disfavor. After all, why would a white person want to travel to a black African country? As for living there…well! With a few grumbles and annoyed looks, I would be escorted to my place of incarceration above the Immigration Hall. Trouble came unexpectedly one day when my onward flight got cancelled and my ticket was no longer valid. No one had anticipated this. There I was in a secured 'holding room' as they called it, without a ticket. "Meneer, hoekom is jy nog hier?" they barked at me. "Please speak English, gentlemen"I replied, not trying to rile them and knowing their English wasn't that good. I explained what had happened with my flight but that hardly phased them. "Verstan jy, dat jy geen reg het om in Suid Africa te wees in?" ("You understand you do not have permission to be in South Africa?") Yes yes, of course I know that" I replied. Finally they spoke English, "Then why are you here?" Going over it all once again I said, "Because my flight to London got cancelled and I cannot go downstairs to negotiate another flight" to which they replied with a *non sequitur* that made no sense whatsoever, "Well, that's your problem, meneer!" Then they continued with the same banter, "Why you want to go to London?" I didn't think that was any of their business but

---

[61] General Smuts was an early Boer politician and Prime Minister. After independence, the name of the airport was changed to honor Oliver Tambo, who was Mandela's first law partner and imprisoned with him on Robben Island. Tambo was the brother of one of our closest friends in Gaborone, Euphemia Thlapane.

didn't say so. "Business" was all I muttered. "Business! We know you a troublemaker and you business is probably to make trouble." "You prohibited from being in South Africa, you know that?" I wanted to say, *"Of course I know that, stupid!"* but didn't. And the interrogation went on and on, getting nowhere. Finally, a senior immigration official came into the room and whispered something in Afrikaans, and everyone left. I sat alone for another hour, not knowing what would come next. I couldn't contact the U.S. Embassy because they didn't have one, nor did Botswana have diplomatic ties or personnel in South Africa. It was unnerving and annoying, in like amounts.

At last, the senior official returned and informed me that this screw-up must not happen again, again suggesting it was my fault the flight had been cancelled. And, filled with his own importance, he droned the obvious, "Bishop, you must be more careful in the future," as if I had carelessly gotten myself into South Africa on some wild fling. Acting magnanimous in conclusion he said, "We will make a special exception just this one time and arrange for your return to Botswana. But this must not happen again! Do you understand?" And then, as he left, he barked at me like a school boy, "Wait here until someone comes to escort you to your plane!" I don't know where he thought I would go. It was two more hours before I was led away from my incarceration—the only thing missing was a collar and a leash. I was rattled by the episode and fumed for the entire flight back to Botswana, all fifty minutes of it.

When Lady Khama got wind of it, she was mad as hell. That was a good thing because it meant something would get done about it. I never learned what got done, but I never missed a flight again and my incarceration went without a hitch thereafter. It was a miserable way to travel; fortunately, I didn't have to go that way often.

Botswana was a safe haven for political refugees and a major operation for the United Nations High Commissioner for Refugees

(UNHCR). Those in the so-called free world typically know little about the United Nations, but the UNHCR is one of those agencies of the United Nations that does great good around the world, and has won two Nobel Peace Prizes for it. It started in 1947 as the International Refugee Organization in an effort to deal with the millions of people displaced as a result of World War II, mainly Jews. From the beginning, member states of the young United Nations were in disagreement over whether such an organization was necessary at all, and if so how long it should exist. I find it puzzling why nations balk at doing good together. The young UN gave a conservative response that the organization would be authorized for three years only, with a mandate "to provide, on a non-political and humanitarian basis, international protection to refugees and to seek durable solutions for them."

In 1950, the UNHCR was officially established as an organization of the United Nations. Soon after that it became clear that refugees were not restricted to Europe: decolonization in Africa in the sixties would create a massive challenge that would transform the UNHCR. Unlike the refugee crisis in Europe, there were no "durable solutions" in Africa, as refugees fled from one country to the next. In the eighties, there were new challenges, with many states unwilling to resettle refugees, due to the sharp rise in numbers. This would become a problem for Botswana, yet that government never refused to accept refugees. Currently, the number of refugees in Africa alone exceeds seven million.

The safe haven the UNHCR provided in Botswana wasn't all that safe. The South African Police, only a few miles over the border, made illegal nightly raids into Botswana, usually coming in search of escapees from their political system. South Africa wouldn't acknowledge they were legitimate refugees. Such raids were in violation of international law, and each time Botswana would make official protest, but the behavior never stopped. The authorities in South Africa had many fears. One of them was the assumption that anyone who sought asylum outside their *apartheid* state would be joining other forces to overthrow their government. That was only true for those who were active members of the African National Congress (ANC) in South Africa. The truth is that most simply wanted a better place to live, without racial persecution. Yet someone once said, refugees are like autumn leaves: they get blown about, this way and that, and for many it may be their last season. Great numbers of South Africans, especially the Colored population, left South Africa during those years, sometimes referred to as the "brain drain", for many were highly educated professionals and academics.

Another fear was that refugees would be bad publicity for South Africa. That was certainly true. A refugee's simple story of what life was like in South Africa was condemnation enough. But fueling their paranoia was a deep-seated hatred of any African who raised a hand or a voice in protest against their system, a hatred for any 'cheeky' *kaffir* who dared speak out. "Those blacks simply had to be dealt with," the standard line I must have heard a thousand times. Botswana was better than that by light years: it wasn't merely a multi-racial country, it was a *non*-racial nation, and enshrined that principle in their constitution.

There were a fair number of South Africans living and working in Botswana who were not refugees, but they were different. They were the ones who opposed *apartheid* and supported the principles of a non-racial society. Some were in business for themselves, a few were farmers, some owned or ran tourist camps, but most South Africans in Gaborone worked for the government in some capacity. I was continually impressed by the openness of the Batswana to accept any white person who had the right attitude: there was no apparent residual bitterness over the way the world of the white man had treated them in bygone days.[62] It was that greatness of spirit which Desmond Tutu and Nelson Mandela demonstrated years later with the formation of the Truth and Reconciliation Commission in South Africa. That Commission undoubtedly prevented a bloodbath. But from the beginning, Botswana was truly different, which made us proud to live there. Although it was surrounded by racist governments, wars, and fighting, it held true to

---

[62] Our children attended a superior private school. There one daughter regularly complained of what she called "reverse racism" which was the terror of her existence. (It could have been exacerbated by Winnie Mandela's niece who was a classmate from South Africa, where *apartheid* was still in full swing).

its course not to get involved and to be a non-racial state, thanks to the leadership of Sir Seretse Khama.

Botswana is a vast country. We had moved from a small equatorial country of rain forests to an enormous country of dry and arid savannah. As the big game was being depleted in East Africa for one reason or another, there was a noticeable shift of game into Botswana, and it was rapidly becoming the latest tourist attraction. The Chobe Game Park and the Okavango Delta became the destinations of choice for photo tourism. Unfortunately, much of the tourist trade flew directly from Johannesburg to the game parks, never setting foot in Gaborone, which meant they didn't see the real Botswana. This bothered me. My annoyance was because for years we had seen tourists that were more interested in the wild game and souvenirs of Africa than they were in the people and the culture. They were out to collect things and pictures, not to meet their neighbors in another part of the world. More's the pity! There were those who avoided the packaged tours, but they were the exception. Consequently, the majority of these visitors to Botswana knew little or nothing about its capital or government, little or nothing about its economy, culture or politics, and nothing of its great history and the fact that it is one of Africa's strongest democracies and economies.

The Anglican Church had a presence and a priest in Maun, the main town in the Okavango Delta, where every tourist flight landed, almost a thousand miles from Gaborone. Getting there for me required a lot of time and effort. Direct flight was, of course, the fastest but also the most expensive. Other modes included taking the train to Francistown and driving from there, which would take two full days, one way. Driving all the way was the other means but required a hard two- to three-day trip, one way. Roads were unpaved, which made the journey harder and dangerous. South West Africa had taught me how to navigate those roads but the dangerous moment was always in passing another vehicle: so much dust would be churned up that a head-on collision was likely if a second vehicle was passing. To overtake a vehicle could be death-defying for the same reason. I had only one experience of this, in South West Africa, so terrifying I cannot remember the details of coming within inches of a head-on collision at great speed. Botswana offered more of the same. Paving of roads was not among the top priorities of the new nation because only a small percentage of the people had vehicles.

One of the principle attractions of the Okavango region was the Delta, which was a huge brute. Covering up to 7,000 square miles in the northwest Kalahari, in 2013 it was named one of the Seven Natural Wonders of Africa. It is widely believed it is the world's largest inland delta but it isn't, it just looks bigger. One in South Sudan and one in Mali are actually larger. The Okavango Delta is formed by the Okavango River, which collects from the Angola highlands and flows eastward along the northern border of Namibia, eventually to collect in the northwest Kalahari, the only river in Africa flowing inland. The lush greenery of the delta is not the result of tropical climate but an oasis in an arid country. Much of this water is used by plant life in the swamp delta, about a third goes to evaporation, and only two percent percolates into an underground aquifer, believed to feed water sources in Botswana and Namibia. Wildlife in the Okavango Delta provides a happy hunting ground for tourists with an amazing variety of game that includes elephant, giraffe, crocodile, lion, cheetah, leopard, hyena, springbok, sable antelope, black and white rhino, and zebra.

I have fond memories of the "Okavango gang," erstwhile Anglicans who lived in Maun and served the tourist trade. On my final visit, they presented me with an elephant's foot, previously discussed, nicely finished with zebra hide for the seat. I received it with mixed pleasure, and it sat in our living room, also with mixed pleasure. Someone had probably chopped that foot off of an elephant with an ax, and that thought made me sick. But there it was, presented in good faith and with good hearts, and I received it in that spirit.

How could I ever forget the folks in Maun? Big on hospitality, they weren't so big on church, so I didn't make it a habit of subjecting them to it too often. That was partly because I didn't want them to resent my visits but also because of the ordeal of getting there. On those occasions when I did make the trip, I had to improvise a lot, like putting together an altar from whatever was available—usually finding bread and wine left over from the night before, the bread hard, the wine going sour. There was nothing as daunting as singing hymns, when I usually ended up singing a solo, so we stopped that. It was usually a collection of hunters, lodge people, and a few tourists, and sometimes I wondered why I came. But this was the Church in Maun, for better or worse, and they had gathered for the Sacrament, however they understood it. Who was I to question that?

The other equally arduous place to get to was the Kalahari Desert, almost a thousand miles away at the other end of the country. We had a fledgling church at Tsabong, a remote village in the far southwest corner of the Kalahari. Peter was the catechist and the congregation was largely what we used to call Bushmen, now known as the San people. Driving to Tsabong required going through South Africa, always a potential problem we tried to avoid. The few times I traveled that way, we fortunately found sleepy immigration officers who were not aware of my prohibited status. To go from Gaborone to Tsabong was a distance of about six hundred miles, all on dirt or gravel roads, which meant Tsabong didn't get visited all that often.

While visiting the States I met a young priest in Dallas who agreed to come and work in Botswana. A man of many talents, Joe Harte became my pilot, the diocesan photographer, and the first rector of the new church in Selepi Phikwe. Our first flight to Tsabong was a white-knuckler. The Kalahari is a huge desert and had nothing that resembled a signal beacon or runway. We had to rely on visuals over country we had never seen before from the air. Joe would sweep low whenever we saw signs of civilization but that scared the game and the people, so we tried to limit that approach. Finally, we saw a man waving a huge white sheet—it was Peter the catechist. We had sent word by the regional radio, and since no airplanes ever flew there, he was certain of his prey.

Landing was the next problem. The ground was so littered with rocks that finding enough ground without sand or rocks took a dozen passes, rolling from side to side. Despite all that, in approximately three hours we had made a trip that would have taken three days by road.

Because distances in Africa are often so great and difficult to cross, in my early days I had dreamed of acquiring a plane. Preparing for that, I had taken flight training the summer before our departure. At St. Mary's Mission, still nurturing the dream, we found enough hard ground for a landing strip and had it cleared and packed. Truth is, I hadn't really done my homework and quickly learned that the expense of having a plane would have been completely beyond our means. It would have required a minimum of flying a hundred hours a year to make it viable, not to mention the expense of maintenance and servicing. I had been inspired by the Australian Bush Brotherhood, a group of flying priests who cover the outback, but theirs is a huge operation with a lot of financing and years of experience. My other inspiration had been Bill Gordon, then Bishop of Alaska, who for years flew himself all over that vast area in a plane he called the Blue Box. But alas, my dream crashed before any plane did. Having Joe winging me around brought back some of the dream, at least for a while.

The Kalahari Desert is probably one of the best known features of Botswana, although often badly represented. One travel book speaks of "a flat sea of sand in a dry and featureless world," then compounding their error by stating many explorers have died there trying to find lost cities and treasure. Hardly. Lost cities there have never been, and they would be hard pressed to find a flat sea of sand or a featureless world. One of the modern glories of the area is the Orapa Diamond Mine that was discovered soon after independence. Squarely in the Kalahari Desert, it is the largest rough diamond mine in the southern hemisphere, if not the world. I didn't know it then, but my friendship with the Managing Director responsible for the Orapa mine would span the next forty years.

The size of the Kalahari is immense, roughly the size of all New England, covering much of Botswana and parts of Namibia and South Africa. It is the last domain of the nomadic San (Bushmen) people, who now reside mainly in a few small villages. One of the major headaches the young government of Botswana faced early on was whether the San should be integrated into the life of the nation or left to wander in the nomadic life they have known for 20,000 years as hunter-gatherers. It was a classic conflict between anthropologists and nation-builders. Eventually, compromise was reached by settling the San in villages in their native Kalahari, which seems to have worked.

The name *Kalahari* means "waterless place" and is derived from the Setswana word *gala*, meaning "the great thirst." However, the Kalahari is far from being waterless, and many areas have dense ground cover and huge subterranean water reserves, possibly the residue of ancient lakes. Moreover, with an average altitude between 2,000 and 3,500 feet, it has a cooler climate than the Sahara Desert, many thousands of miles to the north. Winter frost is common from June to August. Vegetation is mainly savannah, interspersed with trees such as the camel thorn (*Tortilis*), Rhodesian teak, and several species of acacia. Because it is considered a semi-desert, the Kalahari has excellent grazing. The national cattle herd in the early seventies was estimated at one million, co-existing with a wide variety of wild game. It is said that the biggest threats to wildlife are the fences erected to manage herds and the cattle ranchers who hunt or poison predators. A cheetah rescue project, now known internationally, has been one effort to curb this problem. I have memories of the Kalahari in springtime when amazing flushes of wildflowers could be seen everywhere.

The final humiliation for the British came only a few years after independence. Under the earlier British administration, it would be an understatement to say the Bechuanaland Protectorate had suffered from benign neglect. There was such little interest in the territory that much of it was administered from the town of Mafeking, seventy-five miles across the border in South Africa. Bechuanaland was treated pretty much as a lost cause, regarded as a huge wasteland of sand with a few scattered inhabitants, the Kalahari Desert, a lot of cattle and little else. Or so they thought. The Batswana knew differently. They might not have discerned there were diamonds in the area, but there was plenty of common sense wisdom in the ancients—people we Westerners have since named "primitives." To our chagrin, we are now realizing there has been "indigenous technology" in ancient civilizations that knew about things long before Western science arrived to teach them. The Batswana knew their land was rich.

One of the first things Seretse Khama did following independence was to invite Anglo American geologists into Botswana to begin mining exploration. Within one year, the discovery of the Orapa diamond mine in the northern Kalahari put Botswana on the map. Soon thereafter the coal fields at Palapye followed, and then the rich deposits at Selebi Phikwe that blossomed overnight into a city. All of this beneath an assumed wasteland of sand to which the British cocked a snoot for almost a century.

At the time of independence, Botswana was among the poorest countries in the world, poorer than most other African countries. Sir Seretse Khama set out on a vigorous economic program intended to transform the young Republic into an export-based economy built around beef, copper, and diamonds, and between 1966 and 1980 Botswana became the fastest growing economy in the world. Much of the resulting wealth was reinvested into national infrastructure such as health, education, and development. The economy has since extended into light and heavy manufacturing and investments. Today, every citizen receives free education and medical care, thanks to Sir Serete's vision and formative leadership.

On the foreign policy front, one week after independence Khama announced his government's policy that Botswana would not become a base of operations for attacking any neighbor. It was the right policy but a costly one for Botswana in terms of refugees who would pour in from all sides. The *apartheid* situation in South Africa and neighboring South West Africa was past the boiling point; together with the ongoing struggle of a dying white regime in Southern Rhodesia to the north, great numbers of refugees poured into the country seeking political asylum. As is so often the case, the concentration of refugees would become a major sociological problem. Yet despite these pressures, Sir Seretse upheld both liberal democracy and non-racialism in the midst of a region embroiled in civil war, racial enmity and corruption.

Seretse simply did not have the capacity to hate. Even though the forces against him had been so great and cruel, he forgave them without recrimination. He never spoke against those who had mistreated him and never allowed others to speak evil of them. He could have been soured by his years of persecution by the British Government but he was not. In a speech on a visit to Malawi in 1967 he said "Bitterness does not pay. Certain things have happened to all of us in the past and it is for us to forget those and to look to the future. It is not for our own benefit. but for the benefit of our children and children's children that we ourselves should put this world right." Surely, words to live by.

Sir Seretse Khama was indeed one of Africa's great statesmen whose leadership provided a beacon of hope for the rest of Africa. At last we had found the African country we had sought for twelve years. Botswana was non-racial, a liberal democracy, and had one of the most enlightened constitutions in the world. It was the country we had sought since leaving South Africa.

Seretse Khama died at State House, Gaborone, on Sunday July 13th, 1980 with Ruth Khama holding him. Forty thousand people filed through the building of the National Assembly where his body lay in state in a closed coffin. The casket was taken to rest overnight in the Anglican Cathedral, eventually to be buried next to his ancestors in the royal family graveyard high on a hill in his home town of Serowe. His grave bears a simple inscription, a favorite quotation he once spoke in our home:

The world is my church.
Lefatshe ke kereke yame.
To do good my religion.
Go dira milemo tumelo yame.

Chapter Ten

Africa's Last Bite

We left Gaborone on November 29, 1978. We left Africa ten days later, not knowing if any of us would ever see the beloved continent again. (As it turned out, I would see it more than a half dozen times in the next thirty five years in varying contexts). We decided how we wanted to make our final exit from the continent. It would be difficult, so we tried to make it pleasant. Each of the five kids had grown up there, it was home to them and they were filled with early memories. One place that had touched us all was the island of Mombasa on the Kenya coast. We had spent Christmas there years before, when we were living in Uganda. We decided that would be the place where we would spend our last days in Africa. Amazingly, we were able to find the same primitive cottages at Kanamai, which was situated in a coconut grove on Nyali Beach. There we would spend our last week in a simple thatched cottage with wide open windows, palm frond ceilings, and gentle breezes from the Indian Ocean wafting through day and night. Our cottage was surrounded by a coconut grove where the locals harvested coconuts every morning. We would awake to the sounds of a loud *whack whack*, followed by a heavy thud as the nuts fell from their towering perch. Young boys shinnied to the top of these trees with only a machete, carried in their mouth, and an eye on the spoils. It was fascinating watching them. We had to wonder if these young boys ever fell out of those tall trees. Did they ever miss and the machete fall? Did the coconuts ever hit the houses? The answer was yes to some of those. With a white man's naivete, I was reminded of a similar situation years before in Ovamboland, when we were watching the old *memes (*women) holding nuts between their toes and whacking them open with an ax, then to pick out the meat. We asked them if they ever missed. They thought that a very funny question and countered with one of their own: "Do you ever fall when you walk?" And then they would laugh and laugh at our naive question.

Mombasa is Kenya's second largest city and had a population of around a million at that time. We didn't spend much time in the city, just enough to get the flavor of an ancient Muslim town. What remained of Fort Jesus stood at the water's edge, a crumbling reminder of battles long lost. Only a few hundred miles north was the "Horn of Africa", a huge area of three quarters of a million square miles, extending like a rhino's horn into the Arabian Sea. "The Horn" actually denotes that region of Africa that contains parts of the four countries of Eritrea, Djibouti, Ethiopia, and Somalia, the tip of the horn comprising the Somalia Peninsula which has become a hotbed for pirates in recent years. Just north of Mombasa and not far off the coast lay the ancient Arab Island of Lamu, surrounded by dhows and traders. Lamu is Kenya's oldest city, believed to have been founded around 1370 and one of the original Swahili settlements on the east coast of Africa. In recent years, it has been declared a UNESCO World Heritage Site. It was one of the places I wanted to visit and never did. It still has ancient lanes and streets, richly draped with the Arab culture of centuries past where automobiles are forbidden. Lamu and the Horn give East Africa a lot of its Arab flavor. That got mixed with Chinese culture in the nineteenth century, when laborers from China were imported to build the railway from Mombasa to Nairobi and on to Kampala in Uganda. Entire families never returned to China but became citizens of East Africa. Their great grandchildren would be some of the Ugandan citizens Idi Amin drove out of their homeland a hundred years later.

We enjoyed lazy days on Nyali Beach, wading in the shallows of the warm Indian Ocean, collecting exotic shells and negotiating the coral reef. The water was azure blue, shells were everywhere, and there were no crowds. We were far enough away to avoid tourists and had the beach to ourselves. We had fun collecting our memories, like the last time we had been in this place. That was Christmas of 1971, and we had come by road from Kampala. For a Christmas tree, we had used a large palm frond, fixed to the wall and snipped into the shape of a Christmas tree. We had been surprised how quickly that palm frond became a Christmas tree we would never forget. And from that memory, we turned to other African holidays for a lazy trip down memory lane...

All of us had happy memories of a family vacation in Rustenburg, a campground in the Northern Transvaal[63] of South Africa. The place was a simple setup with a cottage, a picnic table, a community swimming pool, lawns for games, and an ample supply of books for a family that devoured them. Evenings were mellow, usually with a *braaivleis* (South African BBQ) and the usual mix of meats—*boervors* (Afrikaner sausage), mutton chops and steak. Calling it 'mutton' instead of lamb was one of those nomenclature divides that separated Americans from the British and South Africans.

As observed before, sunrise in Africa was always breathtaking. First the rooster and rustle of little creatures in the bush, then a chorus of exotic birds, followed perhaps by the beat of a drum and morning has broken. In South Africa, it might include the chanting of a native rhythm as workers made their long way to the white man's employ. Sunrises came with a huge sky, trimmed with puffs of gold or pink clouds, the fresh aroma of the *veldt*, perhaps wet from a night rain, and the smell of smoke from African fires. I think the magic of sunrise over Africa must live on in the memory of anyone having seen it.

And then there was the memory of driving to the Eastern Cape from Ovamboland, a distance of almost two thousand miles. At the end of that drive, we spent a few weeks in the Drakensberg Mountains at a place as close as we ever got to heaven. It was named 'Innesfree'. There we laughed and played in a family home that had been given to the Church as a place for weary workers. It was a stone mansion set on

---

[63] In those days, South Africa had four Provinces: Cape Province, the Transvaal, Natal and the Orange Free State. Today there are nine.

a hillside, with sweeping lawns, a brook running through them, willow trees weeping everywhere, and ponds and pools, nooks and crannies waiting to be found by excited children. The kids thought they were in heaven, or at least in a great fantasy land, where native azaleas, arum lilies and lily pads grew in great abundance. Decades later, they still have memories of rolling carefree down those lawns, laughing and giggling and being the wonderful children they were. The eldest (now in her fifties and living in Israel) has a rose garden she named Innesfree.

In the evenings, Innesfree was a bit on the cool side which gave us an excuse to build a fire, even in summer. Occasionally, a mist or fog would settle 'round the place, adding another layer of enchantment. There were times when the girls were certain they had seen an elf or a gnome.

And thus we played as others labored. The African staff at Innesfree were an ever-present reminder not to be so carefree as to forget entirely where we were and those whose labor made it possible. We had such loving African people to help us with things like firewood, tending the kitchen stove, and cleaning the house that we were constantly reminded how much life had been blessed by the sweat of others' brow.

Whenever we traveled in beautiful South Africa, we were constantly aware that race relations were far from beautiful, and not being able to mix with our black neighbors was first evidence of that. This was especially noticeable for our children whose playmates in Ovamboland had all been African. That was the anomaly of living at St. Mary's, outside the Police Zone. Although the authorities disapproved of our mixing with the Africans even in their homeland, there was little they could do about it. In our final years in Botswana we regained that experience of living in a truly non-racial society. But those years in Ovamboland had also given us the experience blacks have all the time in America, of being a racial minority.

We traveled several times to the Cape, where we spent happy days at Onrust, a coastal village about one hundred and twenty miles east of Cape Town, near the seaside town of Hermanus. Our place overlooked a beach and a lagoon formed at the mouth of the Onrust River, with great places to play or lie in the sun. Again, nights usually meant a *braaivleis* on the deck and an evening spent playing games or reading. Twice we vacationed and stayed in another cottage in Hermanus, right on the coast. That one looked like something out of the English countryside, with thatched roof, thick stone walls, dark wood rafters, and nooks everywhere. The kids thought it had been built by an English elf.

Further around the coast, north of the city of Port Elizabeth, were memories from another seaside cottage. I remember reading many books there and putting my kids through confirmation class, to which they submitted at the time but I have since learned it was essentially an ordeal. My apologies, kids, and if you've forgotten it all, that's payback enough. We were far enough away from the surf to have a grassy lawn in front of our cottage but sand immediately beyond that, where the hunt for shells and relics was always beckoning.

Motoring along the Garden Route took us along some of the most beautiful parts of the Indian Ocean on the southern coast of South Africa. Those included Plettenberg Bay, reputed to have some of the finest surfing in the world, and the Tsitsikama Forest, famous for its beauty and mystery.

And then there was the memory of the Sudan. Ah, the Sudan... that oven! That happened when we lived in Uganda and spent a week in Khartoum. It brought back the amusing memories of what it was like living for a week in a poor Arab home, men on one side and women on the other. The men took their ease, waited on by the women of the household but our girls figured the women had more fun. They huddled together over their fires, preparing a great variety of tasty things, all of which they had amply sampled before the men stuffed themselves.

And the never-to-be-forgotten holiday at Victoria Falls on the Zambezi River...the one when I was the sole chaperone for five kids and my parents—for a week. My father was seventy eight at the time, my mother was seventy three, and the five kids ranged from seven to sixteen. In hindsight, it was probably a cruel ordeal for my parents, but the kids thought it was a lark. It began with a day-and-a-half train trip from Gaborone to Bulawayo, then transferring to land transport for a very long and dusty ride to the Falls. By the time we arrived, my mother was a basketcase and dad wasn't speaking much. The chase on the Bulawayo train platform had taken the starch out of mom and set the tone for the rest of the day. Bedraggled, with everyone running low on patience, when we arrived at the Falls we checked into a luxurious English style hotel. It was five stars with an international reputation, and that helped soothe things a bit. From the days that followed came glorious memories of dashing through the mist of the Falls, dinners in the huge lodge with a roaring fire in the Dickensian fireplace, listening to Zimbabwean marimba bands and lunching on the patio; and at the end of the day, bedding down in luxurious sheets and duvets that puffed up around you. Multigenerational vacations are a challenge in the best of times, without adding the strain of another continent and culture. But that's what we did.

What was euphemistically called 'home leaves' or 'furloughs' hardly qualified as vacations, for we were usually traveling and raising funds for the work in Africa. It's no longer possible to imagine how we traveled the world with five kids and untold pieces of luggage, stopping in Europe, Great Britain, Canada, New York City and elsewhere en route. Two of those trips began on shipboard when we sailed up the east coast of Africa on the Lloyd Tristino Line. One of those sailings took us from Cape Town to Trieste on the "Africa", the other from Durban to Venice on the "Asia". They were excellent ships, spotlessly clean with a due amount of activity to keep our brood engaged. Part of that was a swimming pool on deck. I have one memory of that pool I would just as soon forget. It was fetching a young Indian girl out of it who thought she could walk right over the water, and down she went. Now, what would you think if you had never seen a swimming pool or people swimming? Swimming and floating must have looked so easy…

Our first visit to Venice was a perplexity. We were surrounded by art and history and the Italian culture and to complete the twentieth century scene, I ordered a pizza from a street vendor. He popped something into an oven and in a minute I had my pizza! What a disappointment, in this place where I thought it had been invented. The gondolas were everywhere, operating more as motor taxis than romantic barques. The canal was a disappointing murky green, but there were plenty of historic prompters to help fill in the scene of bygone ages before motorboats and mopeds and frozen pizzas.

The most extraordinary home leave we ever had was in 1972, when we had what we thought was our final home leave: the plan was to return home for good later that year. That was when I was ruminating over the idea of remaining in Africa as a new bishop. Having received a bucketful of advice supporting our wish to return to the United States, we left our two eldest children with their grandparents, and returned to Africa with the understanding that we would be returning within months. When it didn't turn out that way, it meant having our two daughters, ages ten and twelve, take an international flight on their own, halfway around the world, to meet us. The destination was Blantyre, Malawi, which might as well have read Timbuktu for the average American. That was in the days when they all but wrapped children in packages with labels and handed them on. And thus we received our two daughters, wearing labels around their necks and handed lovingly along their world flight by 'stewardesses' who took them under a maternal wing and looked after them. It was the airlines at their best.

Those were our days down memory lane…

On our final trip home, after our halcyon days in Mombasa, we planned a number of stops en route. The first was Jerusalem, where we met our eldest, who had gone before us and fallen madly in love with a young Israeli. Her father (yours truly) did not think it a good idea they should get married, but they were determined. And thus, we had what I have come to call "The Jerusalem Summit," a meeting of just the two of us, my daughter and me. I lost. [64]

It was wintertime in Jerusalem, and I was cold. It felt like I had a touch of a cold or the 'flu, but nothing to keep me from my morning run. I figured it would do me good and fancied running around the wall of the Old City. That was a bad idea. Half way around, I discovered the wall doesn't go all the way around and ended up getting lost and doubling my distance. It was a run I would remember not to do again. I felt no better after it.

---

[64] They eventually did get married in our home in Carmel Valley, with me happily giving the blessing, and returned to live in Israel to raise a wonderful family, I had been very wrong on that one!

On to Paris for a few days, still feeling aches and pains but blaming it on the winter cold. Paris had a dusting of snow, which made the morning jog beautiful if challenging. Running by Notre Dame and down the deserted Champs d'Elisee in the early morning hours was fun. That run didn't make me feel any better either, just tired. I thought it must be the damp cold of Paris.

On to London, more damp cold, more aches and pains. I was still determined to run it off by sheer will, which proved not to be a smart decision and I didn't run anything off. Barely surviving a miserable flight from London, we to stopped in New York City for several days for debriefing and a routine medical examination. The former was little more than an informal chat, the latter was equally perfunctory. I remember the doctor exhorting me to take care of the cold but gave me nothing to help it. By then, Tylenol had become my best friend.

Days later we arrived at Los Angeles International Airport and were met by my in-laws, who took us to their home where we settled for an undetermined length of time. By now my situation was definitely acting like influenza. I was exhausted, annoyed, and grouchy that our return home should be marred by this. More Tylenol and bed rest, while the kids played in the pool and sucked up sunshine as only southern California can produce in December. At least they were happy. I definitely was not, and my condition was weighing on my wife.

Finally, we sought the advice of a doctor, who thought I should be hospitalized for tests and 'observation.' I remember the next part well: we arrived at Valley Presbyterian with me sick as a dog and sitting in a wheelchair. There, at what should have been the welcome desk, the Admitting Department made their case with the finesse of a collection agency: one thousand bucks up front or my wheelchair doesn't roll through the door. How sick I was or how miserable I felt had nothing to do with it. We couldn't believe what we were hearing. "Is this the way you treat your sick here?" "Sorry, hospital policy!" was the short conversation on that subject. We had been away from the U.S. so long, plying my trade all over Africa, and not once had had to ante up like this for medical treatment. It was a tense moment. They weren't going to budge, and nothing would move the admitting clerk who was unimpressed by our situation. They had probably heard so many hard luck stories that they had lost all human compassion, or indefinitely suspended it. Either way, without the bucks I could die in the street, as I guess some did. Miraculously, my wife came to the rescue. I had forgotten we had been given going-away gifts of cash, and like the good manager she was, she had put it in Traveler's Checks and tucked it safely away. Up she stepped to the desk and slapped down one thousand simoleons in Travelers Checks. Saving the day and me, she was rightfully proud, and I melted a little further into my wheelchair. Feeling like the plague had passed through me, this was a performance we did not need. All I wanted was to lie down and be put out of my misery.

No such luck. Having settled my worth at one thousand dollars, they rolled me into an examining room and ran batteries of tests, some of which I thought were completely irrelevant to my situation. No bed yet. Scientific tests seem to get doctors all excited, sometimes forgetting that the patient feels like hell and the symptoms need attention. But alas, when they got around to that, they had no magic pill to make me feel better, just more Tylenol, now the one thousand dollar kind. Headache, aches and pains in joints and muscles, fatigue, a bit of a fever and they concluded it was probably a bad case of influenza picked up somewhere between Africa, Europe and air travel. I could have told them that and saved a thousand bucks.

So they shipped me off to a ward for further 'observation.' Several days went by and things didn't improve. Actually, they got worse—the symptoms progressed to include chills, sweats, occasional nausea and vomiting. I was more miserable than any 'flu I could remember, and irritated that the medics couldn't figure out what was wrong with me. A few more days went by, and the fever became the problem— shaking chills and temperature rising, now well above 103, with profuse sweating. After a week of this, they were sticking me for blood every hour and finally figured out my influenza-like illness was malaria. That made sense to me, having been through it twice before, but I was chagrined it hadn't occurred to me. So at least they had a diagnosis. It also made sense why it took them so long to arrive at it: in those days they simply didn't have enough cases of malaria in the United States to recognize the symptoms or the pathology. [65]

Knowing the diagnosis now brought little comfort. The question then was what could they do about it? I remembered suffering from this stuff in Ovamboland and there had been virtually nothing they could do to 'cure' malaria, just ameliorate the symptoms. Naively, I thought a modern American hospital would be smarter. Now into the second week with no signs of improvement, everyone was beginning to worry. They were giving me massive doses of chloroquine and quinine sulfate. They also tried mefloquine. None of these seemed to make any difference. The fever continued to rise, peaking at times over 106, and the sweating and shaking chills intensified; this was surely worse than any malaria I had ever known. Were they so unfamiliar with it that they really didn't know what to do?

Christmas was just days away and I was looking forward to being together for our first Christmas in America. There would be grandparents, aunts, uncles and cousins around, some of whom our kids had never met. But I wasn't going anywhere. I felt like something the plague had left behind. More tests. More blood draws. I wasn't eating. Everything hurt and the sweats, chills and dry heaves had me utterly exhausted.

Finally, they narrowed the diagnosis. It was not only malaria, it was *Plasmodium Falciparum* malaria, the kind that goes to the brain and kills, sometimes called cerebral malaria. And now we were all very worried. *Falciparum* is the strain found most commonly in Southeast Asia but some in Africa as well. But where could I have contracted it? We zeroed it down to Mombasa. We had spent a vacation there years ago, when the area had been free of malaria due to intensive local health efforts; but it had returned in the ensuing years, and we did not know it and were not told. The incubation period for *Falciparum* is nine to forty days, which explained the lengthy case of what acted like influenza

---

[65] Unfortunately, it is now a fairly common occurrence in the United States with constant air travel to and from those parts of the world that are heavily infected. Also, parts of the U.S. now have infected mosquitoes, making malaria common to those parts.

as we crossed Europe and the United States. As it was explained to me, this type of malaria attacks the central nervous system and the red blood cells burst, sometimes causing damage to other organs as well; swelling of the brain is the primary target, and the death rate is high. The symptomatology is confusing, for many of the symptoms are 'flu like: fever, fatigue, headache, muscle aches, shaking chills, profuse sweating, nausea and vomiting. I had all of them. Mercifully I didn't know then that over ninety percent of those who suffer from *Falciparum* malaria die.

I was semi-conscious and had no idea that Christmas had come and gone. Over two weeks now with no signs of improvement. My wife, Mondi, kept a faithful vigil day in and day out, almost hour by hour. The children would make cameo appearances, but this was a hard visit for them, seeing me so sick. One old friend was a regular visitor, Father Evan Williams, one of my Examining Chaplains when I was ordained eighteen years ago, now the Rector of St. Nicholas' Church in Encino. Over the ensuing years, we had become good friends, and I had preached and taken Services in his Church on several occasions.

By now, my temperature was over 105, and they decided to pack me in an ice bed. I remember Evan making some wisecrack about my body pack; when I was conscious enough to feel, it felt good, except then I would get chills from the cold. Basically, nothing was working. Evan made regular visits, but I wasn't improving—and prayer wasn't working either.

New Year's Day had come and gone. Now packed in ice to hold the fever in check, it had been a full three weeks, and I was worn out and didn't have the strength to go on. That night, Evan came 'round and in great distress (he told me later) administered Last Rites. I barely knew he was there. Was this the way I was going to leave Africa? Dead? Evan told me later he was brokenhearted. Everyone was. The next day, he told my Mondi he always had a premonition when people were going to die and he'd had that ghostly feeling that night, when he gave me Last Rites.

And then something happened, as mysteriously I was one more time snatched from the jaws of death. That night, the fever broke and by morning the chills and shakes were dissipating, the aches a little relieved. Last Rites are meant to be last, but not in this case. Somehow I had made it through. Africa had almost had the last word…but not quite.

Friends ask if I would do it all over again, and I would in a heartbeat. With certain modifications.

Epilogue

arly in 2002, my late wife and I returned to Southern Africa after
twenty five years away. We were stunned to see what had taken
place in Namibia since our departure: light and heavy industry had
developed, roads, highways and freeways were everywhere, schools,
colleges, a national university, and a bustling capital city. I struggled to
find landmarks from a distant past.

Ovamboland was a different story. Our visit to St. Mary's was
heartbreaking. Great St. Mary's Church still stood but looked tired
and beaten. The seminary, high school, library, hostel residences, and
maintenance shops had been destroyed. The hospital was reduced in
size, and the only part remaining of the beloved home of our years there
was the foundation. That house where three of our children had been
born was reduced to rubble. St. Mary's had been through a war. Bombs,
mortars, shells, and grenades had reduced fifty years of dedicated labor
to dust and ashes. Nor had the Church escaped unscathed: windows
had been shot out, the interior abused, and the magnificent Italian
Stations of the Cross all but destroyed. Even the bell had been pulled
down and destroyed, lest it be used to signal the insurgents—so said the
South African forces, as they excused their deed to the people.

It was all the handiwork of the South African government. The
repeated attacks on Odibo had been the result of decades of pent-up
hatred coming to a boil. War had come to Ovamboland, and the
Anglican headquarters had been one perceived enemy. The other was
SWAPO and all those fighting for their independence in "the Struggle".

We walked silently through the rubble, the spirit gone out of us. The spirit had long since gone out of those whose home it had been, where they had discovered their dignity and purpose in life. We were walking through a ghost town. The once-happy paths through the Mission were overgrown with weeds and the blight of war and destruction was everywhere. It was the low point of our return visit to a now-independent Namibia. I felt like throwing up.

One thing that hadn't changed was the indomitable spirit of the Ovambo people. Back in Windhoek, several dozen old students from St. Mary's threw a reception for us. Many were now senior members of government, including the current Ambassador to Washington, who happened to be in town. Kwanyama food and fellowship brought back the very best of memories. I stuttered broken phrases from a language I hadn't spoken in forty years, my wife communicated with her wonderful language of the heart.

Had I been twenty years younger, I would have exchanged my return ticket for tools and stayed to help rebuild the Mission. But I was sixty six, and neither of us had the fresh energy that a new Namibia required. Realizing that, at the end of the evening I said to my wife, half in jest, "What would you think if we came back and gave a year to help rebuild the Mission?" And almost without taking a breath she replied, "I think it would be a blast!" "What?" "A blast?" "Are you kidding?" She wasn't, and thus began another experience of a lifetime...with one more near-death experience. Africa would have another chance at that!

Returning to the State, we spent all of the next year raising as much of a war chest as we could. Having spent countless hours while in Africa trying to raise funds, I thought I knew the task well but this year would be an eye opener. I trundled off to the local library in search of information and found all I needed in a door stopper volume entitled "Grant Making Organizations in the U.S." All of them were non-governmental organizations, commonly known as NGOs. The big book told all: size and source of endowment, what they supported, size of grants, who to write to, etc. It was a treasure trove, or so I thought.

Dutifully, I sat days without end, mining the trove for fine gold. "Africa/southern/educational/higher education/development..." all good signs. In a volume of approximately ten thousand listings, I ferreted out roughly one hundred and fifty, to whom I sent a personal letter describing our project. I signed each one and sent it winging off with a prayer and lots of hope. And then we waited. And waited. It seemed like weeks of waiting without anything to show for it. After over a month of expectant hope, we had received just three replies. All of *three*! That was a two percent return on my effort to sell our project. I had forgotten how hard it is to raise money for good causes. Despite the miserable showing, I was touched that one of the three was from the wealthiest couple in the world, Bill and Melinda Gates, to say the Gates Foundation had recently moved away from education in southern Africa but to wish us well. The richest couple in the world had taken the time and care to respond and wish us well!

We struggled for the remainder of that year to raise money, speaking to whoever would listen, writing to whoever would read, traveling to grovel before groups that would throw us a coin. Many widows' mites went into the coffers, along with a few sizable gifts. Dear friends in Missouri contributed greatly with the with the help of a 401c3, created for the purpose of helping work in Southern Africa. By the time of our departure, we had collected nearly $100,000. We would eventually spend more than twice that amount.

I called it the "year of hard labor," known to everyone else as 2004. We arrived in February and departed ten months later, leaving a bit early because of a near-fatal accident. The shape of things upon arrival was depressing. The people were depressed, and so were we when we surveyed what needed to be done. We needed a bulldozer, a dump truck, a few jack hammers, a fork lift, and an experienced crew of maybe twenty five. What we had was a few tools I had brought with me, and a four-wheel drive pickup which we had named Big Blue for obvious reasons. Eventually, I would have a work crew of about twenty five young men who knew nothing about building but for two of them: Festus and Titus knew a little about bricklaying but not much—no bulldozer, dump truck, forklift or jack hammers. To face this challenge, I would be going back to long gone years of experience in Ovamboland, and to the years of my youth when my father and I built a mountain cabin at Lake Arrowhead. This *would* be a year of hard labor!

A few ghost buildings still stood, some of them reminding me of when they were built, forty years earlier. Mortars and grenades had leveled the rest. A partial end of the library stood like a wall of Coventry Cathedral in 1944, a jagged cross carved into it by bullets and mortars. Trusses without roofs dangled like mangled scarecrows, windows and doors torn from their moorings made open house for grazing goats. Everywhere we looked were shattered memories of happier days when those buildings had held eager learners and laughter had filled the space.

It took nearly two months just to get rid of the rubble. For anyone eager as we were to begin, it felt more like an ending. Clearing away the destruction was like trying to erase a horrible nightmare that kept sticking to the eraser. It made us feel like we were fighting a losing battle even before we began. Even the partial walls left standing had to be leveled to start over; of the foundations that had survived, only portions of a few could be salvaged.

With the working crew of young men and boys we made a start. Barking orders was difficult in a language I had for the most part forgotten. Miraculously, perforce my faded memory of Kwanyama got dusted off daily and by the end of the first month I was able to communicate both pleasure and displeasure at the way things were or were not going. One evening a Jack-o-lantern moon appeared on the horizon, and out of the blue, like a child learning to name things, I pointed to it and said "ohani." I hadn't uttered that word in forty years.

We worked ten-hour days six days a week for the first months. Figuring the weekly payroll was usually a nuisance I did not need; counting it out was a task that would eventually signal my undoing. Keeping building materials on hand was a constant challenge, since none of it was close by. Frequently, it required a drive to Oshakati seventy miles away, or worse yet to Windhoek six hundred miles distant. Bricks were made locally, and we devoured them by the thousands. Everything we purchased with cash, which required the constant attention of our friends in Missouri through whose organization money was transferred.

Our year of hard labor eventually produced a teachers' residence, a library/conference building, and two high school buildings with twelve classrooms, it restored one primary school building and rebuilt the boys hostel building and the central dining hall. The latter nearly became my Waterloo. Late one afternoon, I climbed a scaffold to check on some brick work at the dining hall. All was well up top but not coming down. On my descent, I missed a step and fell twelve feet, with scaffold planks following me down. Unconscious, they carried me to our room which was only fifty yards away, and I quickly came to with only a headache, or so I thought. Just to make sure, I was driven to a neighboring mission hospital for x-rays. They found no broken bones which thrilled me, and I was back on the job the next day. But thus began six unbelievable weeks.

That first morning I awoke with a severe pain in my groin. Assuming it was just a badly pulled muscle, I improvised a crutch to hobble to the job and I made my way around that day with my funny crutch. The next few days were a little worse, so we returned for more x-rays, which again showed nothing. I concluded the pulled muscles would take a while longer and continued working. Five weeks later my mentation went screwy: I couldn't do the simple counting of the payroll, and my emails looked like the scrambled verbiage when an email doesn't go through. Everyone concluded something was seriously wrong; even the x-ray doc got alarmed and ordered me flown to the capital immediately, at a flying altitude of no more than a thousand feet because they were afraid of pressure on the brain.

My memory tapes of the next ten days have been erased and others have filled in the details. I was flown to the State Hospital in Windhoek and put in a general ward until they could figure me out. This took an overnight, during which time I was moved out of a general ward into a pre-surgical ward. The brain specialist concluded I had a *double* hematoma, one on either side of the brain, and they would have to do a craniotomy. And here began an unbelievable miracle. Two years earlier, a noted German neurosurgeon had moved to Namibia in order to help the country which he knew and loved decades prior. As it happened, he was the *only* neurosurgeon in the entire country who could perform the operation needed. Without him, there were no Namibian neurosurgeons in existence, and they would have had to airlift me to Cape Town or begin folding my tent. Dr. Fred Gartner[66] was heaven-sent to help Namibians, and guys who fall off scaffolds. He was a master surgeon who saved my life. Three holes were drilled in my head, positioned sort of like the holes in a bowling ball, the pressure was relieved, my brain was flushed out and the rest would be up to me. (Fred told me later that during that same week an international conference of neurosurgeons was being held in Cape Town and he was able to consult with colleagues about my situation: a free consultation from among the world's best!).

For five days, I lay unconscious in an intensive care hospital, not remembering anything except some terrible hallucinations. I was not responding, and there was serious doubt I would survive. Then suddenly one morning I awoke and asked for breakfast…! Five more days and I was discharged. There was amazement and joy everywhere, especially among the nursing staff. It would be a hard journey, but I insisted we return to Odibo so the people could see I was still alive. Rumors had circulated to the contrary.

My late wife and I had dinner with Dr. Gartner the night before we flew home, and we talked about the whole episode. Good doctor that he was, he reluctantly admitted there may have been a miracle in there someplace for me to have continued working for five weeks with a double hematoma, getting to Windhoek with an emergency flight, and then experiencing the long coma and rapid recovery. I eventually got up the courage to ask him about the usual outcome for someone 68 years old going through this. Enjoying the fine Windhoek Lager we were sharing, he shook his head and paused. "In my experience," he replied, "almost always there will be physical or mental impairment." I had neither.

---

[66] Dr. Gartner had served as a doctor at the refugee camp at Cassinga forty years earlier, during the Struggle, where he met and became good friends with the current President of Namibia and most of the senior members of Parliament when they were all political refugees fighting for their lives.

Several times, Africa tried in vain to take me…or was it to test me… or maybe just keep me from leaving. She need not worry. I shall not leave her…she is now a part of my soul.

Deo Gratias!

Postscript

I n 1961, while at Rhodes University, I conducted a social-anthropology survey to determine how much Christianity had been assimilated by the Ovambo people. After four decades of exposure to High Church Anglicanism, I wondered if it had really changed the deepest traditional values of the people. The results of the study were eventually written up in a dissertation in partial fulfillment of a Master's Degree from Rhodes University. The following is excerpted from the published dissertation.

In much of Africa today, Christianity has become an institution so taken for granted that little is said about it. The Conference on African History and Archaeology held in 1961 included 123 scholarly presentations, and only one touched even briefly on the Christian Church.[67] Similarly, the First International Congress of Africanists, held in Accra the following year, ignored entirely the subject of Christianity and its influence in Africa today. That the Church's former position of influence and unquestioned authority in Africa exists no longer is everywhere apparent. National governments have assumed responsibility for social services once provided by Christian missions. In quite another way, the spiritual teaching and authority of Christianity is being challenged and ignored: challenged by the forces of nationalism and chauvinism which have given a new dignity and respectability to African culture, and ignored by a growing number who believe the outdated teachings and moral codes of earlier missionaries have

---

[67] Even this reference had nothing to do with present day Christianity, but referred to the ninth century, when Christianity had largely failed to root itself in Africa.

nothing to say to modern Africa. In short, Christianity in Africa is at a crossroads. Stripped of its former power and glory by secular advances, and with the rightness of many traditional teachings being questioned, the Church urgently needs a critical review of its role in present-day Africa.[68]

As missionaries taught their converts to sing the *Magnificat*, a revolutionary canticle in any society,[69] and proclaimed the infinite value of each individual in the sight of God, it was inevitable that a social revolution should follow. But many of the earlier missionaries were blind to the implications of their teachings. Indeed, "part of the tragedy of our day is that Christians have rejected the revolution they created, and others stepped in to claim it who have had no part in creating it"[70] and whose systems now often stand diametrically opposed to the Christian ideal and philosophy of life. Many have suggested that the process of emancipation from religious constraint, often referred to as 'secularization', is itself the product of Western Christian civilization.

Anthropologists have maintained it is easier for a society to embrace a new culture in its entirety, than to attempt to piece together two cultures. Christian missionaries in Africa have generally operated on this principle. H. Richard Niebuhr has described five classical patterns of interaction between Christianity and culture, in which two are most clearly represented in Africa[71]. Missionaries from the west have tended to accept the 'Christ *against* culture' attitude towards African culture. This is clearly the characteristic tendency in the history of the Anglican

---

[68] While such 'critical reviews' may have been made on a local basis, I am not aware of any major reviews or studies having been made by the institutional church, nor serious efforts made to engage the critical thinking of scholars of African Traditional Religion in making needed changes.

[69] Sometimes known as the Song of Mary, the *Magnificat* speaks of the lowliness of people being lifted up, of the humble being exalted, the proud being scattered, the mighty being put down from their seat, and the hungry being filled with good things, the rich being sent away empty. Revolutionary sentiments, to be sure!

[70] All Africa Consultation of Churches, 1965, p. 38

[71] See H.R.Niebuhr, "Christ and Culture", New York, Harper, 1951. The five types developed by Niebuhr are Christ *in* Culture, Christ *against* Culture, Christ *of* Culture, Christ *above* Culture, and Christ *transforming* Culture.

Mission in Ovamboland. Missionary efforts to civilize and Christianize were inextricably bound up together, and on occasion this accounted for the condemnation of traditional practices that could not be condemned purely on Christian principles alone.

It was inevitable that early missionaries in Ovamboland should make numerous assumptions in their approaches; yet whenever their superiority was assumed, the life of the mission church was jeopardized. "It is the gravest possible mistake for Europeans to suppose, because of the technological success of modern Western civilization, that other cultures can offer no desirable alternative...the white man must at least respect the African's right to be different, even if he is too slow to realize how much the world needs the African vision."[72]

Although tribal society depended upon the mutual support and interdependence of every member, the mission church failed to exercise these relationships in a meaningful way. The unquestioned authority of the missionaries introduced a rift, and clericalism, once entrenched, made it complete. A significant opportunity to build upon an existing essential social principle was thus lost to the young mission church: "the essence of native social values is a readiness to give mutual help, a feeling of interdependence which is really in service. If this is not present in an African Church, it has lost the best of its national heritage".[73] There was little sense of mutual responsibility with the people for the life and maintenance of the church, as these were largely clerical concerns. Thus, the people were separated from the very life and heartbeat of the Church and became spectators at a pageant that was meant to involve them in every way.

While missionaries frequently saw the need for making Christian worship more relevant to the Ovambo culture, the issue was never examined on a sufficiently fundamental level to achieve anything. The Church as a whole has been reluctant to study this issue deeply, partly because of traditional assumptions that Anglicanism cannot survive too far removed from Prayer Book terminology and plainsong

---

[72] "Christianity and Politics in Africa", J.V. Taylor, 1957, p. 102
[73] "Africa and Christianity", D. Westerman, 1937, p. 173.

settings. Instead, attempts to relate local culture to obviously foreign forms of worship have been confined to periodic minor compromises. The essential problem is not the adaptation of African ceremonial by foreign hands, but to make clear that *Christian worship is a responsive act performed by many different cultures*, and that the authenticity and spontaneity of the response depends essentially upon a meaningful expression of the culture.

In attempting to introduce scientific medicine into a primitive society, two approaches are possible. One may regard traditional beliefs about sickness as nonsense and try to disprove them by scientific argument and evidence. Or one may employ the approach used by Jesus in dealing with a bewitched person: he maintained that no power of magic is omnipotent and that God's healing power is sufficient to overcome all power and devices of man. The wisdom of the second approach does not deny the reality of the individual's conviction that he was bewitched, but can still make full use of scientific medicine. But it is equally certain that attempts to deny, argue, cajole, or ridicule the sick and the bewitched into submission have succeeded in doing little. Witchcraft is still a force to be reckoned with and the witchdoctors likely have as many customers as ever. Little has been achieved by condemnation, especially as this has generally occurred without real understanding.

Although missionaries in Ovamboland were aware of the cultural characteristics of the society, insufficient cognizance was taken of the psychological and mental characteristics of the people in teaching the Christian faith. Essentially, one catechism has been used throughout the worldwide Anglican Communion, and missionaries have used it virtually unaltered in dealing with widely differing cultures. Whereas in Indian, China, and Japan, early attempts were taken to adapt Christian missions to the indigenous religions, "in Africa a distinguishing mark of missions has been their almost unanimous refusal to incorporate element of the local traditional cults in any shape or form within the Christian system of religious thought and practice."[74]

---

[74] "Christianity in Tropical Africa", C.G.Baeta, 1968, p. 6.

A dilemma was created by the introduction of Western education into the mission schools, in which experienced-based learning was clearly not possible. Teaching in the schools was understandably more concerned with content than with method; but the same approach was used in teaching the elements of Christianity, and extensive use of memorization and recitation become indispensable aids to 'learning.' Thus in dealing with the task of educating the African for 'intelligent' participation, the solution often adopted by missionaries was to try to transform the minds of native children into European minds; this was a solution in appearance only. Much of what was taught about religion to the indigenous people was, in fact, quite unintelligible.

Unfortunately, as the Church encountered primitive societies it invariably emphasized a religion of law rather than grace, and frequently the laws were ready-made.

The effect of imposing a legalistic moral code upon a primitive society is strikingly apparent in the mission church's dealing with sin. Previous analysis has shown a common lack of any sense of personal responsibility for sin. Hence, in presenting Christian morality to a society formerly guided by corporate social pressure and mutual responsibility to the tribe, the individual was taught that he was personally responsible to God for his own actions, and the Church was the arbiter of that. But stressing Christian morality by means of injunctions and prohibitions imposed by an outside authority (the Church) generally did two things. First, it relieved the individual from being *answerable to society for misconduct;* and secondly, for many it *denied any sense of personal responsibility to God for sin and misconduct.* Had teaching on sin and forgiveness been more evangelical in nature, stressing judgement before God, understanding might have been different; however, "judgment" was invariably seen as a function of the Church, imposed by the clergy with varying degrees of discipline on sinners, the logic of which was by no means obvious to anyone.

In conclusion, one can suggest at least two weaknesses in the approach to presenting Christian morality to Africa. First, ideals as they have developed in the West, tend to be individualistic, wherein the place of the individual is more important than that of society;

personal acquisition, competition, and excellence have become desirable standards for individual conduct. The conscience of the individual plays an important role in that one is held personally responsible for success or failure, right conduct or wrong, within the limits of the standards. African society, on the other hand is based psychologically and emotionally on tribal man as the personification of a number of forces. He "exists" *because* of his society, not in competition *with* it, and morality and conformity are the result of social pressure rather than individual responsibility. But Christian missionaries from the West have taken little account of these fundamental differences in attempting to teach personal moral responsibility. This has liberated the individual from the restraint of social forces, and at the same time made him answerable to an external code of conduct laid down by the mission church to which he feels only limited commitment. One African therefore has concluded, "What is distressing is that the fear of the consequences of immorality which once existed with superstition… has been dispelled by Christianity and education, resulting in a lack of any moral restraint for most."[75]

Secondly, as a result of this individualistic emphasis in the mission church, there has been nothing comparable to replace the tribal community which within the primitive standards of its day were mutually supportive and corrective. The mission church probably could have become an effective substitute for the old society, but the laity were not given sufficient responsibility or authority for this to develop. Smith warned of this happening half a century earlier: "The invasion of Africa by Europeans means the inoculation of the Africans with the germs of individualism…which is carrying everything before it with a rush: taxes are levied and paid by individuals; wages are paid to individuals; when a crime is committed it is the single person and not the clan that expiates it; the missionary seeks the conversion of individuals and teaches that every man and woman is personally responsible to God."[76]

---

[75] "Witchcraft in Ghana, H. Debrunner, 1958, p. 69
[76] "The Golden Stool", E. Smith, 1926, p. 214

Suggested Reading

"Africa"(Third Edition), Edited by P.M. Martin &. O'Meara (Indiana Univ. Press, 1995)

"The Scramble for Africa", Thomas Pakenham (Avon Books, NY, 1991)

"Ya Toivo Gave Me Namibia", (The Namibian Newspaper, Toivo's 90th Birthday, p. 10)

"Never Follow the Wolf", H. Shityuwete, London, 1990

"Namibia Under South African Rule", (Out of Africa Press, Windhoek, 1998)

"Blood River", Barbara Villet (Everest House, NY, 1982)

"Broederbond: The Most Powerful Secret Society in the World", Wilkins & Strydom, 1979

"Nelson Mandela: Conversations with Myself", Mandela, (Farrar, Strauss, Giroux, NY 2010)

"Long Walk to Freedom", Mandela, (Little, Brown & Co., NY. 1995)

"Robben Island", Charlene Smith (Mayibuye History & Literature, Series No. 76, 1997)

"The Troublemaker: Michael Scott & His Lonely Struggle Against Injustice,"_Anne Yates & Lewis Chester, (Arum Press, London, 2006)

"Sudan Odyssey: Through a State from Ruin to Hope," (Joseph Lagu Memoirs, 2006)

"Out of Uganda in 90 Days", Urmila Patel (U. Patel, 2014)

"Colour Bar: The Triumph of Seretse Khama & His Nation", (Susan Williams, 2007)

"A Marriage of Convenience", Michael Dutfield, 1990

"We Shall Not Fail: Values in the National Leadership of Seretse Khama, Nelson Mandela and Julius Nyerere", Dickson A. Mungazi, 2005

"Seretse Khama", Thomas Tlou & Neil Parsons, 1995

"Laying the Foundations of Nationhood", Speech by Sir Seretse Khama, 1982

"A People's Progress", Speech by His Excellency the President, Sir Seretse Khama, at the opening of Parliament, 1971.

"Biblical Revelation and African Beliefs", Dickson & Ellingworth (Lutterworth Press, London, 1969)

"Understanding Contemporary Africa", Gordon & Gordon, (Lynn Rienner, London, 2001)

"South West Africa", Ruth First (Penguin African Library, London, 1963)

"African Religions & Philosophy", John S. Mbiti (Heinemann, 1969)

"Concepts of God in Africa", John S. Mbiti (SPCK, London, 1970)

"Bible and Theology in African Christianity", John S. Mbiti (Oxford Univ. Press, 1987)

"The Gifts of the Jews", Thomas Cahill, Doubleday, 1998

—

Printed in the United States
By Bookmasters